W9-BWR-328

Evocative Strategies in Child and Adolescent Psychotherapy

Evocative Strategies in Child and Adolescent Psychotherapy

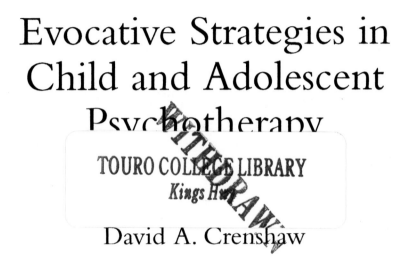

David A. Crenshaw

JASON ARONSON

Lanham • Boulder • New York • Toronto • Oxford

KH

Published in the United States of America
by Jason Aronson
An imprint of Rowman & Littlefield Publishers, Inc.

A wholly owned subsidiary of
The Rowman & Littlefield Publishing Group, Inc.
4501 Forbes Boulevard, Suite 200, Lanham, Maryland 20706
www.rowmanlittlefield.com

PO Box 317
Oxford
OX2 9RU, UK

British Library Cataloguing in Publication Information Available

Library of Congress Cataloging-in-Publication Data

Crenshaw, David A.
  Evocative strategies in child and adolescent psychotherapy / David Crenshaw.
    p. cm.
  Includes bibliographical references and index.
  ISBN-13: 978-0-7657-0414-6 (cloth : alk. paper)
  ISBN-10: 0-7657-0414-5 (cloth : alk. paper)
  1. Child psychotherapy. 2. Adolescent psychotherapy. I. Title.

RJ504.C74 2006
618.92'8914—dc22   2006005308

Printed in the United States of America

♾™ The paper used in this publication meets the minimum requirements of
American National Standard for Information Sciences—Permanence of Paper
for Printed Library Materials, ANSI/NISO Z39.48-1992.

1/28/08

This book is dedicated to Kenneth V. Hardy, Ph.D., director of the Eikenberg Institute for Relationships in New York City, a valued friend, and colleague, who is both the kind of clinician and human being I aspire to be. Dr. Hardy is a professor in the department of Marriage and Family Therapy at Syracuse University. Dr. Hardy is internationally known for his work in the area of family therapy and diversity. He is the author of numerous publications devoted to working effectively with diverse and oppressed families. His passionate advocacy for children and families who have been marginalized by societal forms of discrimination and oppression has inspired me and moved me deeply. His courage, dedication, and commitment are beyond belief, and I am proud to be able to call him my friend.

Contents

Foreword

*T*herapists use evocative techniques to elicit vivid memories, recollections, or associations. The word "evoke" suggests depth and "summoning forth." Because images are more powerful than words, images associated with unpleasant experiences usually cause more suffering than words. An alcoholic parent's foul breath, hostile glare, shaking fists, and rigid body posture usually accompany their biting words. These images may be as troubling, if not more troubling, than their words and when others display any of these behaviors, but with different intentions, a child can experience an anxiety attack that has no readily observable cause. Victims of trauma and loss make every effort to repress troubling images, but their exposure to reminders brings the images to consciousness, as flashbacks, nightmares or panic attacks, and cause constant anxiety or pain until they can, once again, be repressed. But if the images can be called forth when the client is in a safe place where the vividness of the images can be controlled, the client can profit from image recall and the surplus meanings associated with the images, such as shame or guilt, can be corrected. The client, now freed from the anxiety associated with the images, and the words related to them, can direct the energy once needed for repression to self-fulfilling activities.

Over the years, I have tried many techniques suggested by other play therapists, such as Gardiner's "Mutual Story Telling Technique" or Donald Winnicott's "Swiggle Lines," but most were less useful than their originators claimed or were at odds with my understanding of what needed to take place to effect meaningful change. Therapy, especially therapy of traumatized children, is directed at re-working trauma related experiences and correcting cognitive distortions about them, but it must take place in a manner that contains the strong emotions associated with them. Therapy is also directed at changing action-oriented trauma re-enactments, many of which get the client into trouble with others, into symbolic reenactments.

In many cases, early work involves creating, or shoring up, defenses, an approach Dr. Crenshaw calls "The Coping Approach," so the child can begin to tackle painful experiences. For a brief period, I studied with behavior therapist Dr. Joseph Wolpe and treated clients with phobias using systematic exposure to anxiety arousing stimuli, graded on intensity and paired with deep muscle relaxation. While doing so it became abundantly clear that even relatively well-functioning adults tolerate only small amounts of anxiety. Treating children, whose egos are not yet fully developed, is similar to treating adults with weak egos. Neither can tolerate the strong emotions aroused by direct efforts to recall painful experiences. Both need gentle, non-obtrusive exploration of the topic, often in symbolic rather than in direct ways.

Dr. Crenshaw expands upon earlier work presented in his guidebook, *Engaging Resistant Children in Therapy*, and presents structured activities, often metaphoric, that evoke specific emotions in relatively non-threatening ways. They are also "playful techniques" as well as play-therapy techniques. When therapy includes not only play but also "play-full" experiences, the better will children respond to it. Many of the activities described by Dr. Crenshaw are enjoyable, as well as humorous, both feeling states that minimize disruptive anxiety. In addition, the activities can be modified to minimize anxiety.

For many years, I used only traditional playroom materials, such as collapsible theaters and hand puppets, dollhouses and miniature people, and magic markers and drawing paper. Because children's play often arouses more anxiety than the children can bear, or because therapy can be an emotionally draining experience, I accepted the fact that treatment would include some "downtime." Productive sessions were often followed by sessions where the child wouldn't play imaginatively, and, as a result, the child and I did something together that had no foreseeable outcome, other than mutual enjoyment of a pleasing task.

In the meantime, Dr. Crenshaw, along with his staff and the doctoral level psychology interns he supervised, were developing structured activities that helped children convert impulsive actions into symbolic ones, as well as helping them to express feelings and master conflicts in enjoyable ways. In fact, the structured activities became the primary treatment tools for some children instead of activities to use only when the child showed no interest in playing symbolically with the traditional playroom toys. The techniques, if used judiciously, can actually jump-start therapy, enabling and empowering troubled children to discover feelings and to share them more easily with trusted adults.

Evocative strategies engage the minds of clients, but, more importantly, they engage their hearts. When therapy becomes sterile, dry, and cerebral, it fails to reach the inner recesses where clients actually live. Evocative techniques can make therapeutic interactions moving and memorable. A guiding principle of Dr. Crenshaw's work is that meaningful changes occur when therapy touches the hearts and souls of clients rather than just their minds. Severe abuse has been called "Soul Murder" and the victim's soul needs "touching" to overcome it. The evocative techniques described in this book are designed to facilitate "heart-to-heart" exchange within therapy. All children, but especially those who are frightened, inhibited, guarded, or even uncooperative find evocative techniques a face-saving way to meaningfully participate in therapy.

Dr. Crenshaw also includes a list of questions to ask children after they have completed an evocative activity. Originally trained in Client-Centered Therapy by C. H. Paterson, a colleague of Carl Rogers, I avoided asking clients direct questions for a number of years. Under Patterson's close tutelage at the University of Illinois, I learned that many therapists "regressed" to asking direct questions when they couldn't adequately reflect the client's feelings. In supervision, they would receive a "slap on the wrist" and told to say nothing if they couldn't reflect a feeling. Over the years, however, I realized that children actively avoid anxiety-arousing topics and that I often needed to ask them direct questions about their experiences before they would even engage in play related to them. The questions elicited just enough anxiety that the children were stimulated to play in an effort to manage the anxiety and the scenes they played were usually associated with the unpleasant images my questions had aroused. Other children needed to be asked questions about the images they compulsively repeated in their play. I learned to ask them in an "ignorant interrogator" fashion through a puppet I called "Nosey." If a child didn't answer Nosey's questions, a second puppet, "Mr. Wizard," would answer the questions for them. Sometimes, "Mr. Wizard," because of information in the child's clinical record, knew the answers, but when he didn't, he used Theodore Reik's technique of "sharing his own fantasies." In Dr. Crenshaw's approach, the questions naturally follow the evocative activities and the children may experience them as "game related" and, therefore, less intrusive.

Adlerian therapists ask lots of questions. Instead of punishing a misbehaving child, Adlerian Rudolf Dreikurs, in an effort to understand the child's actions, asked sensitively put questions until he found the one that revealed the child's motives and then he addressed the motives rather than the misbehaviors. In fact, some Adlerians believe that the best questioners are the best therapists. Dr. Crenshaw's list of suggested questions after each structured activity helps us to become more successful questioners.

The projective drawing and storytelling strategies Dr. Crenshaw describes are based on common themes in children's play observed by he and his colleagues over a thirty-year period of providing intensive psychotherapy to young children in a residential treatment center, as well as to adolescents and families in his private practice. Most of the children in the residential center were placed following severe sociocultural and relational traumas, including multiple incidents of physical and/or sexual abuse.

Many of the evocative strategies Dr. Crenshaw describes are also useful in group therapy, provided that each group member experiences the group as a "safe place." Art therapists will also find many of the strategies useful adjuncts to their treatment methods. While Dr. Crenshaw's evocative techniques were developed within a psychodynamic/attachment theory framework, they will be useful to therapist's practicing within a variety of theoretical frameworks, such as cognitive-behavioral, gestalt, family systems, emotion-focused, solution-focused, as well as Ericksonian hypnotherapy. The evocative strategies help achieve a crucial goal, one shared by most practitioners—to create and expand meaningful therapeutic dialogue.

Dr. Crenshaw demonstrates the use of the evocative techniques through case-vignettes of children suffering from a variety of disorders. Throughout the book, the reader is introduced to a number of troubled children who respond favorably to the evocative strategies and to the therapist-child dialogs that follow. The conversations between Dr. Crenshaw and the children serve as a model for others to follow. The rationale for the use of particular techniques with particular children is also presented. To illustrate the use of the techniques in combination, each of the last three chapters is devoted to an in-depth presentation of one child's treatment. Chapter 15 presents Roy, a severely depressed, eleven-year-old who suffers from self-loathing, as well as from symptoms of post-traumatic stress disorder, following a long period of sexual abuse by his piano teacher and from complications following its discovery. Chapter 16 presents Max, a twelve-year-old who became defiant and oppositional after suffering from several tragic losses. Chapter 17 presents Jeremy, a ten-year-old bully who himself was bullied by his alcoholic father who regularly demeaned and insulted his wife in front of his children. In each case, the reader follows the dialog between therapist and child after the introduction of evocative techniques and then witnesses the changes in the child over time.

In summary, the evocative techniques presented by Dr. Crenshaw are useful aids, not only in child therapy, but also in family therapy and especially in the simultaneous therapy of parent and child. Adults, as well as children, respond best to techniques that place emotional distance between themselves and their painful problems. Whenever therapy can become a playful enterprise, everyone profits, including the therapist!

John B. Mordock, Ph.D., ABPP
Poughkeepsie, New York

Acknowledgments

$\mathcal{I}$ owe so much to so many for their wisdom, teaching, writing, inspiration, and encouragement and support of my work, it would not be possible to mention them all by name but I gratefully acknowledge all who have enriched my knowledge and understanding of children. I especially am indebted to the two masterful clinicians and human beings, the late Walter Bonime, M.D., and Kenneth V. Hardy, Ph.D. I am deeply grateful to my long-time colleague and friend, Christine Foreacre, for her careful reading of the entire manuscript and for her helpful suggestions. I am appreciative beyond words to Dr. Jason Aronson, whose support, expert input, and encouragement of my writing has enriched this book and the previous ones that Jason Aronson has published. I am grateful to Dr. Ross Miller and Dr. Art Pomponio, the previous and current psychotherapy editors at Rowman & Littlefield. Sonya Kolba, Alla Corey, Karolina Zarychta, and Terry Fischer at Rowman & Littlefield have been patient and helpful with endless details.

I would like to thank my graduate school cohort and friend Dr. Edward Zneimer, who gave me my first job in a children's residential treatment center, and the children, families, and staff of the Rhinebeck Country School will always be special to me. I would like to thank my friend and colleague Dr. John B. Mordock, for giving me the opportunity to work at the Astor Home for Children.

I am thankful to the present and former executive directors, Sister Rose Logan and Dr. James McGuirk, for the opportunity to continue my affiliation with Astor by nominating me to be a member of the Board of Directors. I am proud to count Dr. James McGuirk as one of many former outstanding interns at the Astor Home for Children who are making meaningful contributions to the field and who have enriched my career. Working closely with this highly capable group of young psychologists through the years was one of the high-lights and greatest joys of my career. The dedicated staff of Astor, including my talented clinical colleagues, the courageous children, and their families will always occupy a special place in my heart.

Intellectually I have been enriched enormously by the writings of Beverly James, Charles Schaefer, Garry Landreth, Kevin O'Connor, Alan Kazdin, Dan Siegel, John Weisz, Violet Oaklander, Jon Allen, Greg Furth, Cathy Malchiodi, Allan Schore, and many others. I have been privileged to get to know some of the leading teachers and practitioners in the field from whom I have learned a great deal and value deeply their friendship including James Garbarino, Joyce Mills, Eliana Gil, Lois Carey, Nancy Boyd Webb, and Athena Drewes.

I wish to give special mention to my graduate school mentor Dr. Ray A. Craddick, who, along with his lovely wife Noreen, continues to be a source of warm support and encouragement. Finally, I wish to recognize my long-time colleague and friend Dr. John B. Mordock, a coauthor of two of my previous books, for the inspiration and encouragement he provides both personally and by example of his own prolific writing.

Evocative Strategies in the Therapeutic Engagement of Children and Adolescents

> Many of us have made our world so familiar that we do not see it anymore.
>
> John O'Donohue, Irish Poet and Philosopher,
> *Anam Cara* (2004a, p. 61)

INTRODUCTION

*S*tephen Appelbaum (2000) writes eloquently about evocativeness in psychotherapy. He explains, "Just as certain works of art move us and others do not, the same is true with regard to psychotherapeutic sessions. In some sessions, feelings and ideas are so powerfully communicated and experienced that not only does the patient cry or exults, but so (usually inwardly) does the therapist. In other sessions, both therapist and patient may find themselves privately ruminating over where to go for lunch" (p. 9). Appelbaum goes on to explain that some therapists have the ability to inspire, create, and evoke, while others leave the listener cold, uninvolved, and bored. Children and adolescents get bored quickly and easily, so this issue is of even greater concern in child therapy. Even when I have done my best to create a spark, stimulation, and interest in the child through the use of a wide range of strategies, sometimes children will still complain, "This is boring." At that point I am thinking: What can I do? Sing, dance, play video games? Only the latter would have any appeal to the children, and all three are unacceptable to me, since I have no intention of turning my office into a video arcade. The children bombarded with action-oriented electronic stimuli and media images, rely on adults to razzle and dazzle them in order to capture and hold their attention.

"Our ace in the hole," as Appelbaum, delineates, is called *evocativeness.* The dictionary definition most relevant to psychotherapy, Appelbaum states, is "tending to inspire or evoke vivid memories, recollection, or associations" (p. 10). In writing about supervision in psychotherapy, Appelbaum (1966) explained that an overlooked factor that affects the supervisory relationship and the relationship between supervisee and patient is evocativeness. In that paper, he defined evocativeness as the characteristic that makes interactions moving and memorable. He stressed the importance of evocativeness in both the psychotherapy and supervisory relationship.

A deeper level of exploration is implied by evocativeness in therapy.

> The very word "evoke" suggests depth, having its linguistic inception in the image of summoning forth, "as from seclusion or the grave." So long as one subscribes to the fundamental idea of images coming before words—the preverbal life—one is committed to remembering as far back (as deeply) as possible, and taking seriously the communication in dreams (as well as art) that is dependent upon buried imagery. (Appelbaum, 2000, p. 19)

Appelbaum's work strikes a responsive chord as it pertains to my clinical work with children and adolescents. It has always been a guiding principle of my work that in order to foment change in therapy we must touch and engage the hearts of children and not just their minds. The new projective drawing and storytelling strategies and other evocative techniques described in this book are designed to facilitate heart-to-heart exchange within therapy. Throughout this volume the word "children" is used to refer to both children and adolescents.

A TRANS-THEORETICAL FRAMEWORK

The evocative techniques offered in this volume are informed by an integration of psychoanalytic and attachment theory and can be integrated into a variety of therapy methods including evidenced-based cognitive-behavioral, social learning, family systems, emotion-focused, Ericksonian solution–focused approaches, gestalt, psychodynamic, narrative approaches, play therapy, and creative arts therapies such as art, music, and drama.

The evocative strategies have been developed for the purpose of engaging children in an emotional meaningful process. If therapy is sterile, dry, or too cerebral, it will not reach the inner place where children in their essence live. It will not reach the inner recesses of their hearts and souls that are collectively the home of what James Garbarino (1999) calls "the divine spark." To engage children in a meaningful way, to create moments of transformation and change in the therapy process, we have to learn the language of the heart.

Therapy with children needs to be child responsive (Benedict, 2004, 2005), developmentally sensitive (Shelby, 2000), and culturally competent (Gil and Drewes, 2005). In other words, therapy needs to be titrated to what an individual child needs at a specific point in time and delivered in a culturally sensitive manner in keeping with the developmental capacities of the child.

THE CRUCIAL ROLE OF THERAPEUTIC ALLIANCE IN PSYCHOTHERAPY OUTCOME RESEARCH

Evidenced-Based Role of the Therapeutic Relationship

Since more than two thousand studies (Kazdin, 2005a) point to the crucial role of the therapeutic alliance in psychotherapy outcome research, these strategies offer a potentially valuable tool to strengthen the therapeutic alliance. It should be noted that Kazdin (2005b) clarified in a personal communication that in the two-thousand-plus adult studies and twenty-three-plus child studies the therapeutic relationship has not been shown to play a causal role in symptom/problem improvement. Nevertheless, the importance of this ingredient in the therapeutic equation is underlined by Kazdin's statement that the vast number of research studies "have shown that alliance or relationship processes early in treatment 'predicts' (statistically) treatment outcome among adults [Kazdin cites the work of Horvath and Bedi, 2002], the better the alliance/relationship, the greater the change" (Kazdin, 2005a, p. 185). Since the strategies are designed to facilitate the child's sharing of their private and often guarded internal life, it can enhance the working alliance between the child and therapist. The heartfelt exchanges facilitated by these techniques serve to enhance the bond between child and therapist as a result of the child's sharing of emotionally significant events in his life with a therapist whom he or she gradually learns to trust.

An Integrative Approach

The nonspecific factors accounting for change in psychotherapy—including client resources and assets, quality of the therapeutic relationship, empathy, and clients' expectations of change—can potentially all be enhanced by the use of these strategies. This is not a stand-alone or all-encompassing approach to therapy but a compilation of clinical strategies that can be included in a wide variety of treatment approaches and protocols to address specific issues and facilitate progress toward defined goals. The cutting-edge researchers in the behavioral sciences regard development as the result of complex interwoven factors, including biological, genetic, psychological, social, contextual, and cultural; no one discipline can supply a complete picture or understanding of the developmental outcome of a specific individual. Eric Kandel, the first American psychiatrist to win the Nobel Prize, lays the groundwork in a recent book (2005), *Psychiatry, Psychoanalysis, and the New Biology of Mind,* for integration of cognitive and behavioral psychology, neuroscience, and molecular biology. A recent book edited by David M. Stoff and Elizabeth J. Susman (2005), *Developmental Psychobiology of Aggression,* was the product of a memorial conference to honor the extraordinary contributions of Robert B. Cairns, an internationally acclaimed interdisciplinary developmental scientist. The book focuses on three integrative themes that were central to Cairn's work: neural and developmental plasticity, brain-behavior bidirectionality, and gene-environment interactions. In that book Susman and Stoff state, "Importantly, new theoretical orientations point out the continuous and dynamic interactions among biological, psychological, and contextual processes (Cairns, 1979; Gottlieb, 1998; Hinde, 1987; Lerner, 2002; Magnusson, 1999; Magnusson and Stattin, 1998; Susman, Dorn, and Schiefelbein, 2003; Susman and Rogol, 2004 [as cited by Stoff and Susman, 2005]). Finally, biological processes require an environment in which to be expressed, with the most obvious example of genes requiring a specific environment in which to be translated into proteins" (Stoff and Susman, 2005, p. 284).

In addition to the integration of various conceptual and therapeutic approaches dictated by the needs of a specific child, it is important to respect the place of such modalities of treatment as individual, group, family, and expressive-arts therapies in the application of these strategies. I was trained extensively in both the psychodynamic and family-systems approaches and have a preference when working with children for seeing them in family therapy. Typically, I find that family therapy offers greater leverage for change and that the therapy process tends to move quicker. It is not always possible, however, for many practical as well as therapeutic reasons, to assemble the whole family for therapy.

Overwhelmed and heavily burdened single parents at times simply can't focus on the child's issues, because their own needs are so pressing. In these cases the therapist may be able to accomplish more by having individual sessions with the mother or father to offer support and to assist with parenting issues while meeting with the children separately. Some children need time to forge a strong relationship with the therapist before entering what they perceive as the treacherous waters of family sessions. This is particularly true for children who have been coerced into coming to therapy and view it as a punishment. Indeed, in spite of the family therapist's best efforts to frame problems as systemic and relational, the child may feel as if he or she were in the principal's office, particularly if the family is quite angry and blaming toward the child. In these situations, as well as in separated, divorced families, I find it can be helpful to create a safe and protected place for the child to do therapeutic work, offering separate times to the parents to work on their issues.

Many of these strategies can be used in group work, provided an adequate level of cohesion, trust, and support has been established in the group for members to feel they are in a "safe place." Otherwise, the evocative strategies that are designed to activate strong emotion and powerful themes may leave the group members too exposed and vulnerable. Many of the methods lend themselves well to use by the expressive-arts therapist, who as a matter of practice does not rely on strictly verbal means of communication but rather routinely utilizes creative methods of expression.

EVOCATIVE STRATEGIES TO FACILITATE THERAPEUTIC COMMUNICATION

Children's Drawings and Stories

This book expands a project that has evolved over many years, work that includes a book (Crenshaw, 2001, 2004) describing ten major projective drawing and storytelling strategies that contribute to dialogue between children and therapists.

The theme-centered approach that guided the development of the projective drawing and storytelling strategies is based on both empirical findings deriving from research at Baylor University (Benedict, 2004, 2005) on common themes in children's play and from clinical observation by the author over a thirty-year period of the play themes in psychotherapy with children, ages five to twelve, in a residential treatment center. These children were being treated for the effects of severe sociocultural trauma or relational trauma, often the impact of extreme deprivation, and frequently the consequences of multiple incidents of physical and/or sexual abuse. In addition themes were derived from a review of an extensive body of child development and developmental psychopathology research.

Building on a Rich Tradition

These techniques build on a rich tradition in child and family therapy of the clinical use of drawings and storytelling (Allan, 1988; Berger and Gehart-Brooks, 2000; Burns, 2005; Cattanach, 1997, 2002; Chang, 1999; Eth and Pynoos, 1985;

Freeman, Epston, and Lobovits, 1997; Furth, 2002; Gabel, 1984; Gardner, 1971; Hanney, 2002; Johnson, 1987; Kozlowska and Hanney, 2001; Lankton and Lankton, 1989; Larner, 1995; Malchiodi, 1997; 2003; Mills and Crowley, 1986; Moore, 1994a, 1994b; Nagel, 2004; Newman, 1976; Oaklander, 1988; O'Toole, 1995; Schavarian, 1992; Smith and Nylund, 1997; Stacey and Lopston, 1995; Steele, 1998; Stronach-Buschel, 1990; Udwin, 1993; Waller, 1993; Webb, 2002; Winnicott, 1971).

The evocative strategies were developed to achieve a modest but crucial goal that is shared by a wide variety of theoretical and therapy approaches, that of creating and expanding meaningful therapeutic dialogue. They offer the additional important advantage of being appealing to many children and adolescents.

EVOCATIVE TECHNIQUES THAT ELICIT THE EMOTIONAL LIFE OF THE CHILD

Feeling is where the heart lives.

John O'Donohue (*Beauty: The Invisible Embrace,* 2004b, p. 61)

The Empirically Supported Emotion-Focused Model

This volume includes a wide range of evocative strategies designed not simply to engage the child's cognitive capacities but to tap the rich integrative functions of the child's emotional life. The work of Daniel Siegel (2005) has highlighted the role emotion plays in neural integration of the brain. The research of Leslie Greenburg (Elliott, Watson, Goldman, and Greenberg, 2004; Greenburg, 2002; Greenburg and Pavio, 1997; Greenberg and Safran, 1987; Kennedy-Moore and Watson, 1999) on Emotion-Focused Therapy points to the importance of evocative techniques that bring into awareness and expression the emotional life of the child and family. The emotion-focused therapy approach as developed by Greenberg derives from the humanistic tradition and entails the integration of client-centered, gestalt, existential approaches, and systemic perspectives.

The strategies in this volume range from the highly evocative reprocessing tasks that directly address difficult or traumatic experiences (Elliott et al., 2004) to less evocative interventions that rely on metaphor or symbolization especially appropriate for children early in treatment and for anxious or overwhelmed children who are struggling with formidable life events. These strategies are especially essential for helping children acquire key emotional abilities, such as developing access to immediate experience and systematically examining and reflecting on their internal experience (Elliott et al., 2004).

Reprocessing problematic experiences according to the Emotion-Focused Therapy model involves three tasks: systematic evocative unfolding, trauma retelling, and meaning creation (Elliott et al., 2004). This work takes place in the Invitational track of therapy, to be described in chapter 2. Children are encouraged to process, re-experience, or re-examine inexplicable, onerous, harrowing, or critical life events. These tasks are singularly helpful for children who have faced sudden, unexpected life events or dramatic personal reactions, such as post-traumatic stress responses, panic and phobic reactions or borderline personality processes (Elliott et al., 2004). In the emotion-focused therapeutic framework, systematic evocative unfolding and trauma retelling are evocative or emotionally arousing and are helpful when children are relatively distanced from their emotions, whereas meaning creation is used, in part, to help children contain powerful painful feelings. Emotion-focused therapists are very careful to provide significant interpersonal support and empathic acceptance when children or adults enter states of emotional vulnerability (Elliott et al., 2004).

Empathic evocation is described by Greenberg and Elliott (1997):

> The therapist brings the client's experience to life through the use of metaphor, expressive language, evocative imagery, or speaking as the client. The therapist's communication is from within the client's frame of reference. The intention is to elicit, arouse, or evoke experience so that it is re-experienced in the moment. There is no new information added by the therapist, but evocation enhances the possibility of accessing new information from the client's own experience. The therapist selectively attends to poignant information that seems suitable to evoke. (p. 176)

IMPLICATION OF NEUROBIOLOGY RESEARCH FOR EMOTIONALLY EVOCATIVE TECHNIQUES

Recent studies in neurobiology have found that emotionally evocative stimuli are better remembered than neutral stimuli, an effect called "emotional enhancement" (Leigland, Schulz, and Janowsky, 2004). In addition, studies in cognitive neuroscience indicate that the neural mechanisms underlying social and emotional information processing may be interconnected (Norris, Chen, Zhu, Small, and Cacioppo, 2004). These investigators found that the amygdala and part of the visual cortex is more active to emotionally evocative pictures than to neutral pictures and that the superior temporal sulcus is more reactive to social than to nonsocial pictures. In addition they found evidence of interactive effects that occur in the stream of processing, suggesting that social and emotional information garner greater attentional resources and that the combination of social and emotional cues result in synergistic early processing. It appears that our neurobiological systems are especially attuned and responsive to socially and emotionally relevant information. Emotion to a large extent regulates attention, as revealed in experiments that found faster and more accurate detection of threatening than of friendly faces, even when only one facial feature conveyed the emotion (Lundqvist and Ohman, 2005).

The work of Daniel Siegel (2005) at UCLA in interpersonal neurobiology has led to the view that emotion plays a crucial integrative role in the psychotherapy process. In addition Siegel (1999) cites the studies of Dawson, who found (1994) that infants of clinically depressed mothers have a markedly reduced capacity to experience joy and excitement, particularly if the maternal depression lasts beyond the first year. The implications of these findings are that the experience of sharing positive emotional states may be missing in depressed dyads, making it hard for these children to tolerate or enjoy intense positive emotional states. Siegel (1999) explains, "Feeling comfortable with intense arousal and engagement with others may have its origins in both constitutional and experiential features of the individual" (p. 247).

Relevant to evocative strategies in therapy is the degree of sensitivity to emotional activation. Siegel (1999) states, "Repeated patterns of intense emotional experiences may engrain chronic alterations in the degree of sensitivity. For example, overwhelming terror, especially early in life, may permanently alter the sensitivity of an individual to a particular stimulus related to the trauma" (p. 248). A traumatized combat veteran might not, for example, be able to tolerate fireworks, a car backfiring, or a door slamming without diving to the floor.

Also relevant to the use of evocative techniques is Siegel's (1999) description of "windows of tolerance." He explains, "Each of us has a 'window of tolerance' in which various intensities of emotional arousal can be processed without disrupting the functioning of the system. For some people, high degrees of intensity feel comfortable and allow them to think, behave, and feel with balance and effectiveness. For others, certain emotions (such as anger or sadness), or all emotions, may be quite disruptive to functioning if they are active in even mild degrees" (p. 253).

TWENTY SPECIFIC KINDS OF EVOCATIVE STRATEGIES

This book goes beyond the projective drawing and storytelling techniques introduced in previous writing (Crenshaw and Mordock, 2005a, 2005b; Crenshaw and Hardy, 2005; Crenshaw, 2001, 2004, 2005) to include evocative strategies in the following categories:

1. Evocative Narrative Stems
2. Evocative Stories
3. Evocative Drawings
4. Evocative Projective Drawing and Storytelling
5. Evocative Scenarios
6. Evocative Proverbs, Ancient Parables
7. Evocative Quotations and Sayings
8. Evocative Imagery and Fantasy Techniques
9. Evocative Role Playing Techniques
10. Evocative Writing Assignments
11. Evocative Child-Centered Symbolic Play
12. Evocative Directive Symbolic Play Interventions
13. Evocative "Child-Friendly" Cognitive Behavioral Techniques (CBT) Interventions
14. Evocative Dramatic Skits
15. Evocative Rituals
16. Evocative Use of Symbols
17. Evocative Use of Dream Symbols as Metaphors
18. Evocative Use of the Self of the Therapist
19. Evocative Child Statements and Empathic Translations
20. Evocative Positive Memories.

While all of these strategies are illustrated in this book, there is an emphasis on evocative storytelling and drawing techniques; however, most of the methods can be modified and tailored to the kind of evocative approach most appealing and useful to a given child. An expanding body of empirical research demonstrates that, particularly with adolescents, providing some degree of choice with respect to their participation in therapy may enhance the potential for therapeutic engagement (Church, 1994; Hanna and Hunt, 1999; Liddle, 1995; Loar, 2001; Oetzel and Scherer, 2003; Rubenstein, 1996). Thus the diverse range of evocative techniques delineated above offer a number of options or choices for therapeutic engagement in a given session.

Proverbs, ancient tales, riddles, and similar metaphorical structures, such as parables, along with cultural sayings, are potentially clinically useful tools (Boesky, 1976; Cottino, 1995; Dundes, 2002; Heffner, Greco, and Eifert, 2003; Honeck, 1997; Gandara, 2004; Kahn, 1983; McAdoo and McWright, 1994; Tracy, Greco, Felix, and Kilburg, 2002–2003; and Whaley, 1993). Whaley (1993) studied the rhetorical characteristics of proverbs in relation to their potential for promoting behavioral change and concluded many linguistic facets inherent in proverbs have been successful in the therapeutic context. Kahn (1983) in a psychoanalytic review states that direct and indirect declarations, proverbs, and maxims serve the purpose of imparting understanding to others before their impending experiences, derived after similar experiences. Kahn viewed proverbs, analogies, and parables as falling somewhere between the fully unconscious, egocentric, affective experiences of a child and the fully conscious, logical level of thought. She viewed proverbs and similar metaphorical structures as well suited to addressing the preconscious.

Proverbs can assist in the transmission of values from one generation to another, such as grandparents to grandchildren (McAdoo and McWright, 1994), or in transmission of cultural norms and beliefs (Cottino, 1995). Proverbs may have special evocative potential because of their illocutionary force in argumentation (Gandara, 2004). Dundes (2002) studied myths, legends, customs, tales, songs, proverbs, jokes, curses, charms, games, superstitions, and rituals from psychoanalytical and anthropological perspectives. He referred to these various forms of folklore as "folkloristics." He viewed these various forms of metaphor as rich in the understanding and transmission of culture. Honeck (1997) undertook a comprehensive study of proverbial wit and wisdom, examining proverbs in terms of how they are used, the thought processes involved, and how they are remembered from a range of theoretical positions of interest to cognitive scientists and those concerned with figurative language.

Boesky (1976) saw, from a psychoanalytic perspective, proverbs as clinically useful and analogous to typical dreams and as enjoying close affinity to riddles as well as dreams. Boesky viewed proverbs stemming from the same common matrix as dreams, myths, symptoms, and folklore. The inclusion of symptoms is interesting and consistent with clinical experience that symptoms often have metaphorical significance.

One explanation of the evocative potential of proverbs and similar figurative language for conveying wisdom is that they help people to reframe life's predicaments (Tracy et al., 2002–2003). Van Lancker (1990) studied the neurology of proverbs and concluded that the right hemisphere plays an important role in the processing of nonliteral language. The evocative strategies listed above take various metaphorical forms, including famous quotations, ancient sayings, proverbs, and rituals. The use of these forms of figurative language and metaphorical techniques is particularly recommended for pre-teens and adolescents, although the age at which children are able to comprehend proverbs has been a subject of some dispute among researchers.

In one study of six-to-nine-year-olds, these children demonstrated the capability of abstracting the base meaning of proverbs, contradicting Piaget's position that age of onset is later (Pasamanick, 1983). Another study indicated that fourth graders performed well on a proverb-comprehension task involving contextual information and a written multiple-choice format (Nippold, Martin, and Erskine, 1988). It was also found that performance consistently improved at least through eighth grade. Another study found the majority of third graders were able to translate metaphors and dual-function words into figurative language successfully (Douglas and Peel, 1979). This study, however, concluded that the ability to translate proverbs requires a level of comprehension that does not appear in most children until seventh grade, consistent with Piaget's observations.

In a comprehensive review of the literature, Gibbs and Beitel (1995) rejected the widely held idea that failure to provide a figurative interpretation of a proverb necessarily reflects a deficit in abstract thinking. Conversely, they stated, the ability to explain correctly what a proverb means does not necessarily imply that an individual can think abstractly. They provide empirical evidence suggesting that the ability to understand many proverbs reveals the presence of metaphorical schemes that are ubiquitous in everyday thought.

Consistent with this position is a study of proverb understanding with groups of typically achieving children and adolescents, aged nine, eleven, and fourteen years. The researchers concluded that the children's early-emerging ability to think metaphorically is consistent with the view that figurative language is in keeping with the direct, automatic and natural mode of the way people think, reason, and imagine (Power, Taylor, and Nippold, 2001). Nevertheless, reading ability does play a role, as revealed in a study that found proficient readers outperform less proficient readers on comprehension of proverbs (Nippold, Allen, and Kirsch, 2001). In view of these conflicting findings, it seems safe to conclude that pre-adolescents and teens will make the best use of proverbs and other similar metaphorical evocative techniques but that younger children, especially those with highly developed language ability and advanced reading levels, may make productive use of them as well.

The evocative power of symbol enjoys a long and rich tradition in psychotherapy, especially in sand-play therapy and in Jungian (1960) analysis. Eliana Gil (2004, 2005) has combined the evocative power of symbol with one of family therapy's time-honored tools, the family genogram, to create the individual and family-play genogram. Instead of placing names in the diagram of the family's history, the child or family selects a symbol from a group of miniatures to represent each family member. Rubin and Gil (2005) employ symbols as powerful tools in working with countertransference issues in child and family therapy.

Kenney-Noziska (2005a) calls on the evocative power of symbols in her work with sexually traumatized children. One of her strategies is "My Support Pyramid" (Kenney-Noziska, 2005a). She has the child draw a pyramid with the "capstone" at the top—which, she explains, is the most expensive stone but requires the support of all those below. She then uses symbols such as smiling erasers to represent the people who have been supportive to the child, and, interestingly, she asks the child to leave those who have not been supportive to the child outside the pyramid. This creative use of symbol work facilitates the child's capacity to convey feelings about a sensitive issue that in many cases she/he would not be able to verbalize directly.

Another strategy developed by Kenney-Noziska (2005a) is her technique "Paving the Way to My Future." She uses this strategy with children from ages nine to seventeen. The materials required are a map, star stickers, transportation beads, and a glue stick or glue gun. She educates the sexually traumatized child about five "potholes" on the journey through life that are likely to resurface or re-trigger the sexual trauma. The pothole metaphor, Kenney-Noziska explains, is based on the work of Hindman (1999), who named the potholes "First Sexual Step," "Arousal Reality," "Sanctioned Sex," "And Baby Makes Three," and "Age at Onset Crisis." Kenney-Noziska (2005b) renamed the potholes to be more developmentally sensitive, since the above phrases do not resonate with most pre-adolescents and adolescents. The first pothole she renamed "Puberty," when children physiologically come of age sexually. The second pothole Kenney-Noziska calls "Sexual Activity," which occurs during the teen's early sexual experimentation. The third pothole she renamed "Marriage/Commitment," which includes sex in the intimate context of marriage and/or a committed relationship. The fourth pothole Kenney-Noziska calls "Baby," when they may become anxious and vigilant about protecting their baby from the abuse/trauma they experienced. The fifth and final pothole, which she renamed "Same Age," occurs when their child reaches the same age as when the onset of abuse occurred in the mother's life. This imaginative strategy is an example of creative use of symbols and metaphors in a psychoeducational approach that provides anticipatory guidance to sexual-trauma survivors. Kenney-Noziska asks the girls to draw a winding road through the map to represent their futures. Then the five potholes are placed on the map marked by the stars. The transportation beads are placed over the pothole to symbolize what the survivor would do to cope with the trouble that the pothole may present. Thus, the strategy identifies, highlights, and reinforces coping skills helping to build competence, confidence, and hope.

Preston-Dillon (2005a) has developed the *Way of the Little Box,* which she describes as a psychotherapeutic window for viewing alternative "ways of Being," wherein the client and clinician co-construct healing journeys. Her approach is based on a combination of Narrative therapy and Jungian perspectives within a Zen framework. Part of the protocol for this process includes the use of fairy tales. Preston-Dillon (2005b) explains that playful engagement with fairy tales bridges creativity with emotional healing. She states,

> Fairy tales are a portal through which we can dialogue with characters, explore alternative plots, identify skills to solve problems and increase insights. Clinicians who combine fairy tales with Narrative Therapy draw on a variety of projective techniques. For example, therapist and client can exchange fairy tales and discuss the associations the child makes to the story. Together they co-construct and re-author characters and plots empowering the client with alternatives for his or her life-world. The *Way of the Little Box* provides a safe space for these rich journeys of imagination. (Preston-Dillon, 2005b)

Some of the strategies have been developed in response to Shelby's (2004) characterization of CBT techniques as not "child-friendly." Yet, because of the solid research basis supporting the efficacy of CBT with certain clinical conditions—panic disorder and phobias, for example—it is vital to develop child-friendly formats for delivery of these techniques. A number of the evocative strategies in this book were designed with this purpose in mind, to embed CBT strategies in a playful, engaging, and child-responsive approach.

The healing power of rituals has been recognized since ancient times. Evan Imber-Black (2004) observes that people have called on the power of rituals to mark transitions, create community, and focus our emotions. Imber-Black (2004) has demonstrated how therapists can draw on the evocative potential of ritual to create contexts for new behavior that can promote healing. Among the rituals illustrated in this book are rituals to assist in the healing of loss and facilitate forgiveness and reconciliation. Rituals can also be used to celebrate life and special accomplishments.

The intent of this book is to add to the repertoire of existing techniques for working with children and adolescents. I will therefore largely avoid any description of previously established techniques. Obviously, there are other kinds of evocative methods that can be used especially with adolescents, such as evocative video clips, poetry, songs, and even rap songs (see specific descriptions in Hardy and Laszloffy, 2005). Lawrence, Condon, and Nicholson (2005) use interactive storytelling card sets well suited to narrative therapy in individual and group settings (information about the card sets are available through Shared Vision, Inc., 1200 Harger Road, Suite 505, Oak Brook, IL 60523; e-mail: sharedvsn@msn.com). The card sets comprise watercolor images painted by artists around the world. These evocative art images facilitate imaginative storytelling that helps individuals re-construct their personal narratives. Using the cards in a group setting creates a bond between participants and foments the integration of emotions, thoughts, and feelings of the individuals.

Each therapist will need to tailor these approaches not only to what the child or adolescent or family needs but also to his or her own comfort level with any particular modality. Even though I did not make music a separate approach, adolescents have brought into sessions music that evokes a feeling that they need to talk about; others have written songs and poetry that were deeply moving and expressive of heartfelt emotions that they would not have been able to express in other ways. Some may bring in paintings and other artwork that expresses what they are unable to say in words. Obviously, in the case of the child or adolescent who spontaneously picks an evocative mode of expression the therapist needs not be directive but simply follows the lead of his or her creatively expressive child client. In this case, the therapist need not structure or direct anything unless the child starts to flounder and looks to the therapist for direction. Although, purist child-centered therapists will disagree with my approach, there are times in the course of child-centered play when I believe it is important to intervene; one example is when the child is engaged in post-traumatic play, and another is when the child is "stuck" in identification with the aggressor, which is explained in chapter 5.

THEME-CENTERED ORGANIZATION OF THE STRATEGIES

Organization of the stories, drawings, and other evocative techniques according to major themes will enable therapists to select more easily and quickly stories and other strategies that are relevant for a particular child at a specific point in the therapy. In the material that follows the rationale for choosing the selected themes will be discussed.

Research on Children's Play-Therapy Themes

Helen Benedict (2003, 2004, 2005; Benedict and Hastings, 2002; Benedict and Mongoven, 1997) and associates at Baylor University have been engaged in a multiyear project studying the play themes of young children (ages two to eight) in a clinical population. Benedict (Benedict and Mongoven, 1997) has developed a thematic play-therapy model to treat attachment disorders in young children. This model is based on attachment theory, the work of John Bowlby, and the contributions of Fairbairn, Winnicott, and Mahler on object-relation theory. The therapy method places emphasis on the therapeutic relationship with focused interventions around themes presented in the child's play. The goal of this approach is to enable the child to change his inner model of relationships and engage in healthy attachment relationships more easily.

In the Baylor research on play themes, the boys in the study population outnumbered girls two to one, and many of the children suffered from attachment disorders. The age range selected by the Baylor research team was based on the prevalence of pretend play during this stage of development. After age eight, pretend play decreases dramatically and the children are more likely to be drawn to board games and competitive games of all kinds. In one study of gender differences in children's play-therapy themes, both gender and trauma histories of the children were found to impact both the frequency and types of themes that children play out in therapy (Holmberg, Benedict, and Hynan, 1998).

Clinical Observation and Experience

In addition, the themes chosen were based on consistent observation of children's symbolic play in a weekly child psychotherapy seminar led by the author in a residential treatment center from 1981 to 2001. In residential treatment populations, however, the upper age range for therapeutic use of symbolic play is extended considerably, since the prevalence of severe sociocultural and relational trauma in these children leads to developmental arrests at earlier ages, often coinciding with the time of the initial exposure to trauma. Thus, a child who was beaten for the first time at age three but endured physical assaults from care-taking adults until removed from the home at age five may exhibit emotional and social functioning more typical of a three-to-five-year-old child. Even if this child is chronologically age ten, he or she may be drawn to pretend play to unburden and tell his story in the natural language (symbolic play) of a three-or-four-year-old child.

I once worked with a fourteen-year-old boy who had been so severely traumatized by physical and sexual abuse that he sat on the floor and played with a dollhouse and enacted with the dollhouse family extreme scenes of violence and violation. He continued this practice well into the second year of therapy, before he was ready to move on and for the first time became interested in age-appropriate board games. When his father was shortly to be released from prison and the boy was ordered to have a court-ordered visit with him, he returned to the floor and temporarily resumed, at age fifteen, play with the dollhouse family. In that play the children in the family hid in terror waiting for the father to return. While the severity of the relational trauma in this instance was extreme and the return to pretend dollhouse play at age fifteen is quite rare, it is not unusual that the themes identified by the research team at Baylor continue to exert a powerful influence in the lives of children when they no longer engage in pretend play. It is for this reason that I developed the three-step projective drawing and storytelling strategy and the other evocative strategies to provide a creative and age appropriate vehicle of symbolic expression for older children, ages seven to seventeen, strategies that enable them to work with these organizing and sometimes defining themes in their emotional lives.

The evocative techniques to be described beginning in chapter 4 are designed for children in the seven-to-twelve age range, with the exception of those indicated for pre-teens and adolescents, which are intended for use only with children in the eleven-to-seventeen-year age range. In addition the Bramley Story Series, introduced in chapter 4, is designed for use with pre-school children through age eight. This series of five stories can be used with children as young as three; it was developed because of the frequent confusion among parents and even therapists about how to create dialogue with pre-school and early school-age bereaved children. Due to the impact of developmental arrests related to trauma, therapists may decide that some adolescents may be able to benefit from strategies designed for the younger children; conversely, some younger children may be precocious, and their therapists may deem that some of the strategies designed for teens may be useful for a particular child.

Themes Derived from Developmental Research

The selection of themes to organize the strategies of this book is also based on review of an extensive developmental research literature. The body of research is so extensive that even a summary of this literature is beyond the scope of this book. Readers are referred to the following recent texts for a summary of the developmental psychopathology research: Achenbach (2004); Atkinson and Goldberg (2004); Mills (2005); Phares (2003); Sroufe, Egeland, Carlson, and Collins (2005); and Wieder and Greenspan (2005).

CHILDREN FOR WHOM THESE STRATEGIES ARE CONTRAINDICATED

Some children need little in the way of direction, structuring, or facilitating by the therapist. Spontaneous drawings are therapeutic tools that allow therapists to gather data and formulate tentative hypotheses about children's inner lives, thoughts, conflicts, emotions, dreams, and hopes (Crenshaw and Mordock, 2005a). Cathy Malchiodi (1998) states, "Some children have well-developed ideas about what they want to express and seem to have an intuitive sense about art making and their images. They need little or no direction from the therapist, are happy to create spontaneous images, and are content to have the therapist present as a catalyst, witness, and support for their work" (1998, p. 57).

Eliana Gil (1996) made a similar observation regarding children in therapeutic play. She noted that some children know what they want to do in symbolic play; the therapist just needs to get out of their way and follow their lead. For these children there will be little need to use the evocative strategies in this book, because they take the initiative and know where they need to go. Even these self-directed children, however, at times lose their focus and look to the therapist to be more directive. At those times these directive interventions may be helpful.

In addition these techniques except for some of the strengths-based and coping skills strategies are intended only for children in the "Invitational Track" of therapy, which will be explained in detail in chapter 3. Therapists are encouraged to titrate and modify the strategies according to the needs and requirements of the children, based on their knowledge of the individual needs and sensitivities of the children. Questions offered in the follow-up to the strategies are samples of meaningful questions to ask, but they can be modified or discarded in favor of more useful questions for a particular youngster. Some children will not be receptive to the drawing strategies but be drawn to story-telling, or vice versa. Some of the stories will be too long for certain children. The therapist, noticing signs of restlessness, can skip to the drawing task and then summarize the remainder of the story prior to child creating his/her own story. Some kids may enjoy evocative proverbs or ancient tales, while others will prefer to work with evocative symbols or writing. It is important to make the therapy intervention responsive to the individual needs, styles, and natural modes of expression of our child and adolescent clients. A set of twenty different evocative means of therapeutic communication offers a wide range of tools from which to match the specific natural mode of expression for any given child. I do not suggest that this is an exhaustive or complete list of such potential tools. Flexibility and the ability to modify, titrate, pace, and time these strategies are skills that only the therapist can bring to the therapeutic table, and they are crucial to success. In the long run, no variable will be more crucial than the quality of the bond and the level of trust that is developed in the therapeutic relationship with the child or teen. That is by far our greatest and most influential strategy for change.

2

Exploring the Meaning of
Metaphors and Symbols

The human mind is in itself a world with huge mountains, deep
valleys and forests of the unknown. Given the private depths, deep
strangeness and wonders of our interior life, it is amazing that we
can reach out toward the world and to each other with such intimacy and understanding.

John O' Donohue (*Beauty: The Invisible Embrace,* 2004b, p. 50)

UNDERSTANDING CHILDREN'S DRAWINGS:
PRACTICAL GUIDELINES

*E*vocative strategies are tools used to engage children in a productive therapeutic exchange rather than a diagnostic purpose. The questions regarding the
meaning of a drawing or story serve as means for therapists to gain additional
insight about the child and family. Nevertheless, a background in understanding the meaning of drawings and stories assists in developing tentative hypotheses, which can be discarded or confirmed as the therapy evolves. In some
cases the therapist can explore this with the child in a collaborative manner.

The Work of Greg Furth

Greg Furth's (2002) book *The Secret World of Drawings: A Jungian Approach to
Healing through Art,* 2nd edition, is a useful guide in the analysis of client drawings. Furth cautions against early attempts to interpret a client's drawings, especially if based on a single drawing rather than on a series of drawings that reflect unfolding events in the child's life over time. With single drawings only

tentative hypotheses can be made. Far more data can be integrated after studying a series of drawings. Therapists often discard their early hypotheses in favor of new ones supported by the child's unfolding story as communicated through his/her artwork.

Similarly, John Allan, a Jungian therapist who utilizes serial drawings in his analytic work with children, defines serial drawing as drawings done consecutively over time in the presence of the therapist (Allan, 1988). Both Furth and Allan have been influenced by Jung (1960), who emphasized the importance of analyzing drawings over time. In spite of his work on universal symbols, Jung avoided making "wild" interpretations from a few drawings made at single points in time. Readers interested in using drawings for diagnostic rather than therapeutic purposes are urged to study the detailed guidelines offered in Furth's (2002) chapter 4, "Focal Points to Understanding Drawings: Diagnostic and Therapeutic Aids" (pp. 32–100) and chapter 5, "Advice and Precautions" (pp. 101–12).

Cathy Malchiodi's Work

Another approach to understanding children's drawings is delineated by Malchiodi (1998, p. 55). She follows up the drawings with questions that are both process related and product related. Process-related questions would include: How does the child respond to directions? Is the child focused or distracted? Is the child calm or agitated? What changes are observed during the session related to shifts in the art activity? Does the child rely on direction or work independently? Is the child confident or anxious? Does the child have difficulty with transitions, such as ending the session or a particular activity?

Product-related questions suggested by Malchiodi (1998, p. 55) include the following: Does the child take pride in the artwork or does she/he devalue it? How original or creative is the artwork as compared to conventional or stereotypical images? Is the child responsive or not to questions about the artwork? Does the child identify the symbols in the artwork as associated with self or not? How difficult is it for the child to discuss the drawing either metaphorically or in relationship with self? Is the drawing age appropriate? See Malchiodi's (1998) chapter 4, pp. 64–108, for detailed developmental expectations.

Along with Furth, Allan, Jung, and Bonime (with respect to analysis of dreams), Malchiodi (1998) urges therapists to be open to the wide range of meanings that children's drawings may have. Malchiodi's approach is similar to the one adopted in this book as revealed in her statement, "When looking at a child's finished drawing I usually ask myself, 'What seems unusual, emphasized, or important in the drawing?' and may use it as a point of conversation with the child. Such features or subjects can provide significant information about the child" (1998, p. 56). Thus, Malchiodi also uses the drawings as a springboard to therapeutic dialogue.

A Collaborative Rather than Cookbook Approach

The approach that my colleague, John Mordock, and I (Crenshaw, 2004; Crenshaw and Mordock, 2005a, 2005b) take in understanding and interpreting drawings is consistent with the guidelines proposed by Klorer (2000) as well as Malchiodi (1998) for understanding spontaneous artwork, and by Bonime (1962, 1989) for understanding dreams. We adhere to a collaborative approach, with the assumption that the meaning of a specific symbol should be explored with each child. We reject a cookbook approach or the assumption that universal meanings for symbols apply to individual children (Crenshaw and Mordock, 2005a).

UNDERSTANDING CHILDREN'S STORIES: PRACTICAL GUIDELINES

Eliana Gil (1991), noting that therapeutic stories are effective tools in child therapy, emphasized that "because children's imagination and ability to identify is so powerful, they can easily enter a story, making unconscious connections to heroes, conflicts, and resolutions" (p. 65). Similarly, Beverly James (1989) asserts, "Stories capture the child's imagination and are easily remembered; since they do not obviously and directly relate to the child's issues, the youngster does not actively defend against the presented ideas" (p. 212). As is the case when analyzing drawings, humility when analyzing stories is a therapeutic virtue.

My mentor, the late Walter Bonime, M.D., a senior training psychoanalyst, was well known for his book *Clinical Use of Dreams* (1962). Bonime, like Greg Furth in his approach to interpreting drawings, rejected a simplistic approach to understanding symbols in dreams. He made hypotheses and checked their value in dialogues with the patient, either confirming or discarding them as therapy progressed. Bonime's approach is recommended in this book, modified by the expectation that children are less capable than adults of collaboration. Nevertheless, therapists should never underestimate the ability of children to offer their own hypotheses about the meaning of symbols, whether in their artwork or play; some children display an amazing ability to associate to facets of stories that yield insights into their hidden inner life. Most of the time, however, the hunches of the therapist will need to be tested against the reality of the child's story as it unfolds over time.

The Meaning of Story Symbols Is Idiosyncratic

Both Furth and Bonime considered story content to be important and symbols to have unique meanings. As is the case in dreams and in drawings, the meaning of each story, as well as the symbols embedded within it, is idiosyncratic rather than universal and needs exploration in each case. I do not devalue the study of the cultural meaning of symbols or the exploration of symbols used in art, literature, or mythology; however, one should not assume a traditional, cultural, or mythological meaning for a symbol but rather pursue the meaning by utilizing other sources of data, including the child's own associative responses.

Collaboration Is Essential

In England, Ann Cattanach (1997, 2002) has used stories in play therapy as a way of understanding the common themes and metaphors that emerge and also as a way of furthering the communication between the child and therapist. Cattanach states, "In play therapy children tell stories as containers for their experiences, constructed into the fictional narration of a story. There is a playfulness in the communication, whatever the horror of the story, and an equality in the relationship" (1997, p. 3). Cattanach's approach and philosophy of treatment resonates with my approach in another way. We both place emphasis on the collaborative nature of the therapeutic relationship. Cattanach explains, "There has to be a spark of recognition between storyteller and listener as the story unfolds. This is not a therapeutic intervention when the 'wise one' listens and interprets to the child, but an equal relationship between narrator and listener to facilitate the unfolding of the story. Together they share the drama of the story as the meaning unfolds" (1997, p. 3).

Healing through Symbolization and Metaphor

In addition to the emphasis on collaborative therapeutic activity that can contribute to healing (Bonime, 1989), another point of emphasis of my work shared with Cattanach's work is the therapeutic healing possible through symbolization and metaphor, whether through play, drama, art, sand play, or storytelling. Cattanach describes the healing potential within stories: "One of the most important functions of a story or folk tale is the sense of hope and consolation it can bring" (1997, p. 166). She cites Tolkien's (1996) delineation of four factors that give potency to folk and fairy stories: fantasy, recovery, escape, and consolation. Cattanach explains, "He considered that by moving to another world the fairy tale enables the reader to regain a clear view of their situations. The placing of objects from our everyday world in a luminous, estranged setting compels us to perceive and cherish them in a new way, to see new connections between past and present" (Cattanach, 1997, p. 167).

APPROACHES TO THERAPEUTIC STORYTELLING

Mutual Storytelling Technique

Richard Gardner's (1971) "Mutual Storytelling Technique" was a major contribution in the use of storytelling techniques to engage resistant children in therapy. The child is invited to tell a story that he makes up, not one based on TV or a movie. The therapist then listens to the central conflicts in the child's story and tells in response to the child's story a new story that offers a more adaptive way of resolving the issue. Gardner (1971) developed other techniques to engage the resistant child including his popular child therapy board game, "The Talking, Doing, and Feeling Game."

Draw a Story Game

Gabel (1984) introduced the "Draw a Story Game" as another tool to engage children in therapy. Both the child and the therapist would draw pictures and then tell stories about their pictures. The objective was to establish rapport with children who were unable or unwilling to participate in more direct verbal exchange with the therapist, and also to gain access indirectly about the child's psychological functioning and cogent emotional issues.

The Narrative Approach

Michael White and David Epston (1990) in their groundbreaking work in Australia on a narrative approach, view therapy as a process of storying or re-storying the lives and experiences of people. Karl Tomm explains in the preface to their book,

> Not only do we, as humans, give meaning to our experience by "storying" our lives, but we are also empowered to "perform" our stories through our knowledge of them. Stories can, of course, be liabilities as well as assets. For instance, most of us have a multiplicity of stories available to us about ourselves, about others and our relationships. Some of these stories promote competence and wellness. Others serve to constrain, trivialize, disqualify, or otherwise pathologize ourselves, others and our relationships. Still other stories can be reassuring, uplifting, liberating, revitalizing, or healing. The particular story that prevails or dominates in giving meaning to the events

of our lives determines, to a large extent, the nature of our lived experience and our patterns of action. When a problem-saturated story predominates, we are repeatedly invited into disappointment and misery. (p. x, preface)

In the strategies outlined in this book, the child is invited to tell his or her own story through the artistic metaphors of drawing, storytelling, imagery, writing, or other evocative strategies. By listening intently the therapist can come to appreciate the child's own dominant story. In the language of narrative therapy (White and Epston, 1990) stories can be problem saturated, predominantly pathologizing, or liberating and healing stories that reflect their embracing of new and more complex narratives reflecting assets and strengths, not just pathology.

Fairy Tales

Bettelheim (1977) in his well-known book *The Use of Enchantment* explored the use and value of fairy tales. Bettelheim maintained that children could learn more about inner conflicts and their adaptive solutions from fairy tales than from any other story they could understand. Barker (1985) notes that there is an important difference between the use of fairy tales in families in the normal course of children growing up and the therapeutic use of fairy tales or stories. Barker explains, "Fairy tales, like many proverbs and biblical parables, usually make rather specific points and aim to teach specific lessons; therapeutic metaphors, on the other hand, offer new choices, especially new ways of looking at things, and can tap a variety of experiences, beliefs, and ideas that have been dormant in the listener's mind" (1985, p. 13).

Therapeutic Storytelling in Family Therapy

Illustrated storybooks created within family therapy sessions are another way therapeutic storytelling has been used with traumatized children (Hanney, 2002). Kozlowska and Hanney (2001) have created the "illustrated storybook" tool for working with children with a complex history of trauma. The storybooks are created collaboratively by the family and in turn stimulate dialogue and discussion within the family context that can contribute to healing. The authors recommend that the storybook should begin with the non-traumatic period of the child's life to minimize the anxiety and to enjoy the collaborative family art project prior to exploring the trauma-related events. Detailed instructions for this intervention can be found in Kozlowska and Hanney (2001).

Stories That Speak Directly to the Unconscious: The Ericksonian Approach

Another contributor to the creative roots of therapeutic storytelling is Nancy Davis (1985, 1996). Her first book was devoted to stories to heal abused children; her second book focused on stories that heal and teach children with a wide range of symptoms and disorders. Davis suggests that her therapeutic stories could be used in individual, group, or family therapy. Davis states that parents, guardians, and other caregivers can also use the stories. She emphasizes that the therapeutic stories are designed, through metaphor and symbols, to speak to the right brain and that they are not to be interpreted when the stories are told. Davis, like Milton Erickson and his followers, believes that the metaphors and symbols speak directly to the unconscious. The unconscious, in contrast to the rather ominous view held by classical Freudians, is viewed by Erickson as the depository of healthy forces for healing and growth.

The approach of Davis contrasts with Richard Gardner's technique of *Mutual Storytelling* (1971), in which the therapist tells a story that provides a more adaptive resolution to the conflict embedded in the child's story. It should be noted, however, that Gardner made use of stories for therapeutic purposes including the retelling of popular fairy tales with adaptive resolutions, such as *Dorothy and the Lizard of Oz* (1980) and a book called *Dr. Gardner's Stories about the Real World* (1972)—stories about children facing common problems such as dealing with bullying, telling a lie, fearfulness, and denial.

Joyce Mills's and and Richard Crowley's (1986) approach to storytelling is also based on an Ericksonian approach. Joyce Mills coined the phrase "Ericksonian Play Therapy" (Mills, 1974, 2001) and her ground breaking work in applying Ericksonian principles to play therapy inspired and profoundly the development of the stories and strategies in this book. I use Joyce Mills's story "The Three Legged Dog" when treating children and families who have suffered loss. Again, in contrast to Richard Gardner's *Mutual Storytelling Technique* (1971), the Ericksonian approach assumes that the power of the story speaks for itself. The story itself activates the healing resources of the unconscious, a chief tenet of Ericksonian theory, which postulates that no interpretation or direct work with the story is needed. I have found support for this view when using the story of the three-legged dog (Mills and Crowley, 1986, p. 76).

In working with grieving children and families, I sometimes open a session by reading "The Three Legged Dog." I will simply say, "I would like to read you a story—if that is okay?" No one has ever objected. I then read "The Three Legged Dog," and when finished, I pause briefly and then say, "I just wanted to share that story with you." I continue with the issue presented by the family and direct no further attention to the story. The power of this story to create hope and activate healthy resources is validated by the frequent requests I receive from families at the beginning of later sessions: "Could you please read us again the story of 'The Three Legged Dog?'" Another example of Joyce Mills's creative work is her story "A Work of Art," told to an eleven-year-old girl caught in the middle of a custody battle. Mills told the little girl about a beautiful work of art, a real masterpiece that was put up for auction. The masterpiece was described in great detail in terms of its uniqueness and beauty. The bidding activity was introduced as a metaphor for the custody and visitation battle the child was witnessing. To emphasize the reality of the love each parent had for the girl, even as they fought over her, the child was told, "Even though each person upped the bid in order to own this work of art, they each loved this masterpiece and felt they had a right to have it in their home" (Mills and Crowley, 1986, p. 80).

An Australian clinical psychologist, George Burns, director of the Milton H. Erickson Institute of Western Australia, has developed healing stories for kids and teens (Burns, 2005), stories based on the Ericksonian model and offers suggestions for use of storytelling and metaphors in a variety of clinical settings.

PROJECTIVE DRAWING AND STORYTELLING TECHNIQUES

In *Engaging Resistant Children in Therapy* (Crenshaw, 2004), I introduced a three-step projective drawing and storytelling strategy. The techniques consist of brief original stories that the therapist reads or tells to the child, laying the groundwork for the child to express thoughts or feelings, first through a drawing about the story then by a story the child tells on his or her own. The children's drawings and stories help therapists to gain access to the internal world of children, building a bridge by giving children tools to share their internal world.

Step One: The Story

The purpose of Step One is to encourage the child to produce a drawing by providing structure, stimulating interest, and motivating the child. The story also lays the foundation for the child's own story in Step Three. The stories focus on a central theme that captures common psychodynamic or social conflicts and struggles that children face.

Step Two: The Child's Drawing

The drawing serves to initiate dialogue between therapist and child. Suggested follow-up questions and considerations for the therapist to keep in mind are offered after the child has completed a drawing. While some child therapists may use drawings produced for other purposes, such as generating psychodynamic hypotheses or as diagnostic clues, the primary purpose of the drawing in a therapeutic context is to further therapist-child dialogue in meaningful ways. When the therapist asks the child, "What title would you give your picture?" or "Does your picture remind you of anyone?" he or she is looking for an exchange that can be a springboard to further discussion, as well as an opportunity to get to know the child in ways that are not possible when playing board games. Children will often prefer board games because they wish to evade verbal therapeutic exploration, due to the anxiety it creates.

Step Three: The Child's Storytelling

The third step of this therapeutic strategy requires each child to tell his or her own story. Each story read or told to the child sets a specific stage upon which the child must act. Some require the child to focus on finding missing pieces for the proper understanding of the central character (e.g., "The Misunderstood Mouse," "The Animal That Nobody Wants to Hug," "The Bee That Couldn't Stop Stinging"—Crenshaw, 2004). Others require the child to involve the central character in a critical decision making process (e.g., "The Pig That Didn't Fit," "Blow-Up Bernie"—Crenshaw, 2004). Still others involve retelling a projective story that is open-ended and ambiguous (e.g., "The Tree on Top of the Hill"—Crenshaw, 2004). "The Ballistic Stallion" (Crenshaw, 2004) requires children to create a story about a time when they prevailed against the odds and showed the same fighting spirit as the story characters Sally and the stallion. "Behind the Closed Door" (Crenshaw, 2004) requires children to look at the redeeming qualities of a child who is often in trouble and to tell a story based on this theme. Perhaps the most important intervention a therapist can make is to change the adversarial orientation of the child toward the therapist to a collaborative one; these techniques can facilitate that goal.

CREATING A RICHER, MORE COMPLEX VIEW OF SELF AND OTHERS

White and Epston (1990) observe, "A case has been made for the notions that persons are rich in lived experience, that only a fraction of this experience can be storied and expressed at any one time, and that a great deal of lived experience inevitably falls outside the dominant stories about the lives and relationships of persons. Those aspects of lived experience that fall outside of the dominant story provide a rich and fertile source for the generation, or re-generation, of alternative stories" (p. 15). The evocative strategies detailed in this work are intended to expand the dialogue and help the child and family create a richer and more complex view of the problem, as well as self and others.

The wide range of human motives, feelings, thoughts, and experiences that at any given time reside outside of awareness for an individual child or family becomes the fodder that the therapist can use to help the child or family create a new story that offers new possibilities for growth and healing, when their rigidly held problem-saturated story has left them stuck, frustrated, and feeling helpless, if not hopeless.

3

The Use of Evocative Strategies in Child and Adolescent Therapy

The central therapeutic issue is not how to eliminate the symptom but what will happen if it is eliminated; the therapeutic argument is shifted from the problem, who has it, what caused it, and how to get rid of it, to how the family will function without it, what price will have to be paid for its removal, who will pay it, and whether it is worth it.

Peggy Papp (1983, p. 13)

THE DUBIOUS CONCEPT OF "RESISTANCE"

During the course of treating children and of supervising others to do so, I have learned that many children, in contrast to the kids who engage in spontaneous symbolic play or artistic expression with little or no therapeutic direction, need structure if they are to make constructive use of therapy sessions. Often what therapists consider as "resistance" is actually the therapist's failure to provide the proper structure, within an appropriate context, to facilitate therapeutic communication.

Malchiodi (1998) explains, "I rarely find that children are resistant to drawing. I think that extensive experience in both art therapy and clinical counseling helps me to make the art process interesting and appealing to children. One intuitively knows what is exciting about art making, and children will get caught up in the therapist's enthusiasm" (1998, p. 57). Conversely, Malchiodi points out that if the therapist is uncomfortable with art, never enjoyed drawing or painting, or lacks ability or interest in creative expression, this lack of enthusiasm will invariably be communicated to the child, and the child may be reluctant to undertake art expression.

29

Strategies to Negate "Resistance"

Malchiodi offers a number of helpful suggestions to overcome "resistance" to drawing in children (1998). She will sometimes begin drawing herself and ask the child for input, directions, and feedback. Although Malchiodi is a skilled artist, "sometimes," she states, "it actually is helpful not to be skilled artistically. A bit of fumbling can induce the child to want to get involved and to correct the therapist's inaccuracies or lack of skill. One can even draw primitive stick figures and suddenly find that a child is adding details or 'improving' upon the drawing" (1998, p. 58).

It is interesting that I find the same to be true when exploring the meaning of a child's art activity. It sometimes pays to be wrong, because children tend to love to correct adults and may then tell them the real meaning behind their drawings. It also shows the child that the therapist is willing to take a risk. We ask children to risk exposing their inner lives of thought, feeling, and fantasies; why should we not expose our sometimes rather inadequate skill of drawing certain figures or offer in a tentative way a hypothesis about what the art work of a child might mean? We may be off the mark, but doing so shows that we are willing to take that risk; it establishes a more level playing field, as we encourage the child to take risks, and it underlines the therapeutic value of collaboration.

Another strategy that Malchiodi (1998) uses to set the stage for reluctant children to draw is to play a cartoon game. She becomes the cartoonist and takes direction from the child about what to draw. Malchiodi often starts with a familiar cartoon figure, like Garfield, and then asks the child to tell her what the cartoon figure is doing. Often children become so interested in developing the story they will take the process over, including the drawing of the cartoon figures. In other words, with proper stimulus, many children who need facilitation and structuring of therapeutic activity will be able to participate in a productive way. When we view children as "resistant," perhaps the first question we should ask is whether the resistance resides in the child or the therapist. Is the child truly resistant, or is she or he simply anxious, inhibited, or intimidated by the demands and expectations of the therapist?

The more ways we are willing to structure the therapeutic context and to adjust our demands based on sensitivity to the needs of a particular child at a specific time, the more the therapy will be developmentally and culturally sensitive as well as child responsive, and the less "resistance" will be seen. Resistance in therapy is too often the result of the therapist attempting to impose his or her agenda, his or her own pace or tempo, on the child, or to demonstrate progress, rather than being responsive to the child's or family's need.

The child's lack of confidence, insecurity, anxiety, or uncertainty about how to get started can masquerade as "resistance" (Malchiodi, 1998). Malchiodi suggests that a good way to ease such a reluctant child into art expression is ask the child to name one feature of what he or she was intending to draw. If the child was going to draw a baseball diamond, he or she could be asked to draw only home plate. Once under way, the task may not seem so intimidating or overwhelming for the anxious, insecure child.

The technique developed by Steele (1997, as cited by Malchiodi, 1998) is another way to encourage reluctant children to draw. Steele asks the child to make a thumbprint on a small index card and then to add details to create a special friend or companion. With such a running start, children may amplify and build a rich scene around the created figure that was originally a thumbprint.

Another suggestion offered by Malchiodi (1998) in overcoming reluctance in children to engage in creative art expression is showing the children the drawings and images of other children. She also suggests that Silver's "Drawing Test" (1996) may be useful to children who are blocking on ideas of things to draw. The Silver Drawing Test consists of simple line drawings of people, animals, and objects. In one interesting variation of her work, Silver offered children the opportunity to draw from imagination by choosing from a series of pictures and combining them in a drawing. She would then ask them to give the drawing a title and tell a story. The projective drawing and storytelling strategies in this book provide detailed directions and structure for children to undertake their drawings and their stories, but at the same time they leave plenty of room for children to project their own unique thoughts, feelings, and fantasies in their drawings or stories. These strategies were developed with the rationale that there are many children in the seven-to-seventeen age range who find direct verbalization with a therapist intimidating or inhibiting and do not easily engage in spontaneous artistic activities but do respond to specific structure and directives that give them a running start to express a story they need to tell.

A final important cautionary note on the issue of resistance is wisely expressed by Malchiodi (1998):

> It is important to note that there are some children who will comply with the therapist's requests to draw even when drawing may not be the most productive means of expression for them. Some may be more suited to a different form of art expression, such as collage or clay work, and others may be more expressive through media such as puppets, drama, play, or movement. While most children will engage in drawing, the therapist has to be sensitive to what modality, whether art, movement, play, or storytelling, is most conducive to engaging them in therapy and getting children to express themselves freely. (1998, p. 59)

A CLINICAL ILLUSTRATION OF NEGATING RESISTANCE

A clinical example illustrates how these tools can be used to overcome even extreme resistance and build a therapeutic alliance. A fourteen-year-old girl was brought to the therapist's office under protest. She had been angry and defiant at home with her parents and involved in frequent conflicts with her friends. She refused to participate except in the most minimal way in the first session. The therapist considered it a major achievement when she agreed reluctantly to return for a second session two weeks later. It was suspected that heavy bribes on the part of the parents were instrumental in this decision. The therapist considered it fortunate that his schedule at that time didn't allow for a weekly appointment, since he felt a more gradual induction into therapy might work better for this adolescent. At the second visit, it became clear within a few minutes that direct talk was going to be futile. She offered nothing spontaneously and responded to questions with brief mumbling.

What was most striking to the therapist was the degree to which this teen felt uncomfortable in the therapy context. Beverly James (1993) comments that adolescents believe therapists can see right through them, as if they have no skin. It was clear that if the therapist did not do something to make her more comfortable, attempting to engage her in a productive way in therapy was going to be a losing battle. The therapist therefore asked, "Do you like to draw?" She said, "Kind of." The therapist asked, "Do you prefer to pick something you would like to draw, or would you like me to tell you a brief story and then you could draw something in relation to the story?" She agreed to the story. The therapist then offered her some choices of stories that might interest an adolescent and told her a little about each of the stories.

She chose "Behind the Closed Door" (Crenshaw, 2004). The story that she picked is about a boy who is always in trouble. After the therapist told the story, he asked her to picture Jerome in the story in whatever way she wished and then to draw him as best she could. After she made her drawing, she was willing to answer questions about it, and although her responses were not elaborate they were more forthcoming than any of previous attempts to engage her had been. Then the therapist asked her to create a story based on the directives of this particular strategy.

She took the task seriously and was able to create a story that was revealing in terms of the loneliness and alienation that Jerome in the story was suffering. No attempt was made to connect Jerome's experience to her own at this early point, since staying in the metaphor was deemed essential to give her a face-saving way to participate in therapy. After that session, she no longer protested to her parents about coming, and two weeks after the session she asked the therapist if she could come weekly instead of every other week. Even

more cogent is the fact that subsequent sessions were marked by active participation of this pre-adolescent in therapy by her identification with the story
characters and her ability to express in a face-saving way her own anguish and
internal distress through artistic and storytelling metaphors.

Aggressive and anxious children, often distrustful of others, are usually reluctant to share their private thoughts, feelings, and fantasies, but just as often
they lack the communication and/or cognitive skills to identify and then label
the sometimes-frightening inhabitants of their inner worlds. In addition, they
often feel their inner worlds are too scary to share with another, even a trusted
person. Other children may be in touch with the thoughts and feelings that
trouble them but unable to find the words to express them to others.

PACING AND TIMING CRUCIAL

John Allan (1988) emphasized that children's drawings, like the themes revealed
in spontaneous fantasy play, have direct relevance to inner struggles. But Allan
also urged therapists to respect the pace set by the child, as one that the child
can safely sustain. In spite of managed care's emphasis on brief treatment, successful treatment of troubled and especially traumatized children is not quick,
a point re-emphasized in recent writings (Crenshaw and Mordock, 2005a,
2005b; Crenshaw and Hardy, 2005).

The Play-Therapy Decision Grid

The pace of therapy should be determined by the child's ego strengths, the nature of the conflict and struggle, and any trauma to which the child has been
exposed (Allan, 1988). When traumatic experiences need to be integrated, it is
crucial to respect the child's pace. The "Play-Therapy Decision Grid" (Crenshaw and Mordock, 2005a) is offered to guide treatment decision making.
With most seriously troubled children, therapy requires ongoing assessment of
an ever-changing process and constant therapeutic adjustment. Sometimes ad-
justments in approach must be made in single treatment sessions. The Decision
Grid allows for this flexibility and encourages therapists to "downshift" when
required by the child's changing needs.

The Coping Track.   The Decision Grid identifies two tracks, "Coping"
and "Invitational." The Coping track is primarily psychoeducational, with emphasis on teaching adaptive defenses, pro-social and problem-solving skills, and
building genuine self-esteem by highlighting strengths. A later chapter in this
book is devoted to specific strategies to build self-esteem and highlight
strengths in children.

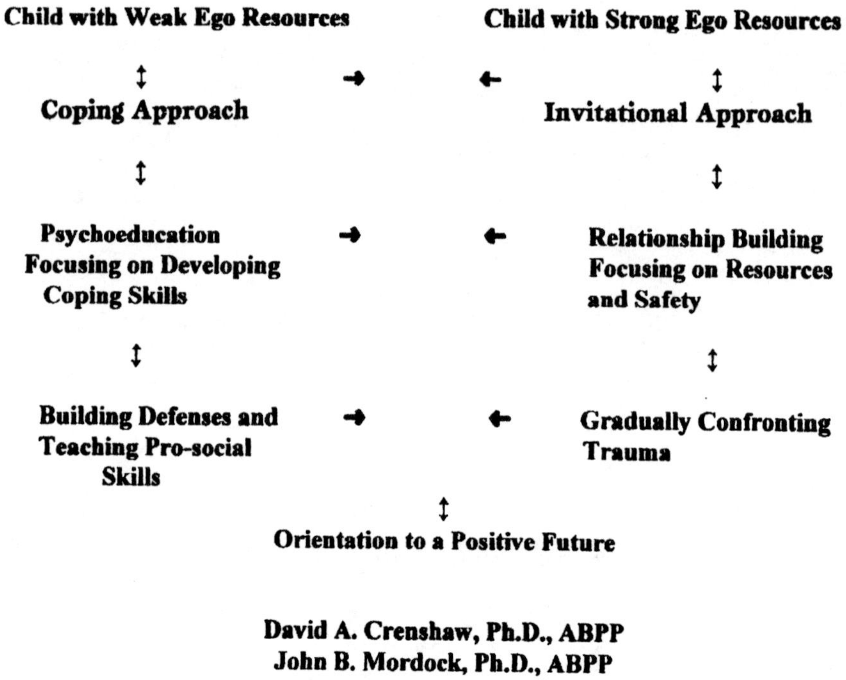

Child with Weak Ego Resources   **Child with Strong Ego Resources**

‡   →   ←   ‡

Coping Approach   **Invitational Approach**

‡   ‡

Psychoeducation   →   ←   **Relationship Building**
Focusing on Developing   **Focusing on Resources**
Coping Skills   **and Safety**

‡   ‡

Building Defenses and   →   ←   **Gradually Confronting**
Teaching Pro-social   **Trauma**
Skills

‡

Orientation to a Positive Future

David A. Crenshaw, Ph.D., ABPP
John B. Mordock, Ph.D., ABPP

Figure 3.1.   Decision Grid for Child Therapy

The Invitational Track.   The Invitational track of therapy gradually involves more direct work with painful or trauma-related events. It should be undertaken only after the child has been carefully assessed and judged to be ready for this more challenging and emotionally taxing level of therapy.

Criteria for Selection of Therapy Tracks.   In addition to the child and family's strengths, the assessment of readiness for the Invitational track should take into account the degree of external stressors in the child's present life. Invitational therapy should not be undertaken when children are feeling unsafe. In a presentation on children of domestic violence Pelcovitz (1999) stated eloquently, "Treating children facing domestic violence while the violence is still going on is like trying to treat PTSD in the midst of a hurricane."

Another benchmark would be the degree of "spillover" when emotionally laden material is addressed in a session. If the child acts out with parents following the session it would be a indicator that the child needs more work in the Coping track or, if in the Invitational track at the time, that there may be a need to cross over to the Coping track for more work on building defenses and coping resources (see Crenshaw and Mordock, 2005a, 2005b, for detailed guidelines and suggestions for developing mature defenses). I once was distressed to learn that one hour after an adolescent's therapy session with me he was chasing his mother around the house with a knife. Clearly, this youngster was not ready to tackle the emotionally laden material that had been activated in his therapy session. It was necessary to readjust the level of challenge in his therapy and work on building coping skills and defenses before returning to the Invitational track.

With the exception of some of the techniques in chapter 11, the evocative strategies in this book are tools appropriate for the Invitational track. They are designed to move the therapy process forward but always with a sensitivity to the issue of safety and respect for the pace at which the child needs to go.

SPECIAL CONSIDERATIONS IN TRAUMA WORK

Childhood Traumatic Grief

Cohen and Mannarino (2004) describe a brief treatment approach for childhood traumatic grief in which two or three sessions are usually devoted to developing the trauma narrative.

> Creating the child's trauma narrative typically takes two to three sessions and encourages the child to gradually face increasingly painful and frightening aspects of the event that led to the death of their loved one. The goals of this component are to gradually desensitize the child to thoughts and reminders of the traumatic aspects of the death, to decrease avoidance of the more horrifying aspects of the experience, to help contextualize these events in the greater schema of his or her own life and the world, and to identify cognitive distortions about the death. (p. 825)

While Cohen and Mannarino demonstrated that brief therapy works for some children facing traumatic deaths, many children would not be able to safely develop the trauma narrative within a two-to-three-session time frame. An important feature of their work is the active involvement of the child's family in the treatment program. In the program described, the children and parents participated in parallel child and parent therapy activities in separate groups but were brought together for joint work on crucial therapeutic tasks, such as sharing the trauma narrative. Involvement of the family can enhance the pace of change because of the mutual sharing, support, and collaboration. The approach is currently being empirically evaluated in an open trial at Allegheny General Hospital in Pittsburgh, where Cohen and Mannarino direct the Child

Psychiatry Trauma Treatment Unit for traumatized children, and also in a randomized controlled trial in New York City (Brown and Goodman, 2005).

Children who have faced extensive losses or major psychological disorders may require interventions that allow for a slower pacing and greater safety by dealing with loss issues within the metaphor, through stories and artistic symbols, prior to creating the trauma narrative. Cohen and Mannarino (2004) add, "At some point the therapist should encourage the child to include the 'worst moment' of the traumatic death in the narrative" (p. 826). Here again, pacing and timing would be essential in order to maintain safety in the therapy context.

Havens (1989) reminds us that therapy can only begin in a "safe place," and this would be even more essential in trauma therapy. It should be noted that Judith Cohen has agreed in discussion (2005) that clinical judgment is crucial in developing the trauma narrative and that Cohen's and Mannarino's brief treatment model, while showing promising results with their clinical population, would not be appropriate for certain children, particularly those with extensive prior trauma. Cohen has also acknowledged the merits of using metaphor and indirect techniques with youngsters who are unable to approach the trauma narrative directly.

Post-Traumatic Stress Disorder

Another important contribution in the trauma treatment literature is a paper that attempts to bridge the gap between post-traumatic stress disorder (PTSD) research and clinical practice (Cook, Schnurr, and Foa, 2004). These researchers and clinicians recognize that exposure therapy for PTSD may not be applicable for complex cases. Foa, Keane, and Friedman (2000) observe that intervention studies on which the International Society for Traumatic Stress Studies (ISTSS) Task Force guidelines for treatment was based have inclusion and exclusion criteria that may limit their generalizability. Specifically, Foa, Keane, and Friedman (2000) note that exclusion criteria for these studies often eliminate patients with "active substance dependence, acute suicidal ideation, neuropsychological disorders, and cardiovascular disease" (pp. 376–77). The paper offers suggestions as to how prolonged exposure (PE) can be altered to make it useful with complex cases of PTSD. Specific examples of these suggestions to address barriers to PE with more complex cases, include the following:

- "Emotional numbing (underengagement)—Prompt for more details of what happened and what the person is thinking, feeling, or sensing" (Cook, Schnurr, and Foa, 2004, p. 378).

- "Overengagement—Allow for short breaks during session for patient to slow down breathing and focus on the present; memories are told with eyes open in past tense and in a form of a dialogue with the therapist" (Cook, Schnurr, and Foa, 2004, p. 378).
- "Severe flashback or distress during exposure—Advise patient to keep eyes open; use past tense in retelling; and make eye contact and converse while retelling. Therapist provides grounding comments (e.g., 'You are safe here')" (Cook, Schnurr, and Foa, 2004, p. 378).

This work is commendable and recognizes the gap between research on empirically supported treatments (ESTs) for trauma and PTSD and their implementation in real-world clinical practice. Cook, Schnurr, and Foa (2004) note that disseminating ESTs through manuals can be viewed as a top-down process. They cite Chorpita (2002), who recommends that if researchers want their treatment manuals to be used in community clinical practice, they should be designing, implementing, and testing them in community clinical practice settings. I could not agree more that "We all have an ethical and professional responsibility to work cooperatively toward bridging this gap" (Cook, Schnurr, and Foa, 2004, p. 363). Only then will our patients get the full benefit of what combined science-based research and rich clinical experience can offer.

Timing and Pacing Especially Critical in Trauma Work

The therapist should not initiate evocative strategies in the second half of the session, when there may be insufficient time to properly process the feelings or allow the child to regroup before leaving the session. While self-calming skills are a core focus in the Coping track, the child in the Invitational track may need reminders and reinforcement in employing these tools when confronting difficult material. If the child shows signs of extreme anxiety, panic, or hyperventilation, or is otherwise disrupted by any evocative strategy in this book, the therapist can assume that a mistake in judgment has been made or that circumstances have changed; the child should be returned to the Coping track for strengthening of defensive resources.

These judgments can be hard to make, but when a mistake has been made it is best to correct it promptly. Therapists, even when doing directive work, need to be responsive to cues and feedback from the child with respect to timing and pacing. Skilled and experienced child therapists will make corrections even in the midst of a given evocative strategy. If a child shows signs of significant anxiety, they will move from direct exploration into metaphor or third-person monologues, or they may simply cut short the evocative strategy, saying, "We will come back to this at another time that is more comfortable for you." The therapist might then do self-calming and self-soothing activities in a collaborative manner with the child or suggest that the child pick a non-threatening activity, such as a favorite activity or game, to do with the therapist.

Treacherous Waters: Therapists Beware

Child and play therapists enter dangerous territory—make the most mistakes in timing and pacing—when they are feeling pressure from parents, schools, courts, or other referral sources for quicker results. Sometimes the pressure to move faster in therapy comes from internal expectations of the therapist. Therapists may feel the work is unproductive, that they are not doing enough. They may feel inadequate and impotent. As a consequence they may push the child onto scary turf that he or she is not prepared to tread. It is essential for therapists to self-monitor and consider whether they are pressuring a child, "Am I doing this because I truly believe that the child will benefit from a more challenging level of therapy? Or am I pushing this child at this time because of some notion that I am not doing good therapy?"

Creating Safety as well as Therapeutic Communication

The strategies described in this book, while evocative, also allow for the symbolic haven provided by remaining in the metaphor until the child gives clear indication that he or she is ready for more direct work with the more painful events and issues. The techniques, if used judiciously, can jump-start the therapy process, enabling and empowering the troubled child to discover and share feelings more easily with an adult whom they have gradually learned to trust. It should be emphasized, however, that without trust all the tools and techniques imaginable are of little help to the child or to the therapist.

4

Themes of Attachment and Loss

Hold On
Hold on to what is good,
Even if it's a handful of earth.
Hold on to what you believe,
Even if it's a tree that stands by itself.
Hold on to what you must do,
Even if it's a long way from here.
Hold on to your life,
Even if it's easier to let go.
Hold on to my hand,
Even if someday I'll be gone away from you

A Pueblo Indian Prayer

EVOCATIVE SCENARIO: "HELLOS AND GOOD-BYES"

*A*ll of life can be viewed as a series of hellos and good-byes to the people we love and who love us. It is the predominant dilemma of human existence. We can only experience the joy of closeness with others if we are willing to suffer the pain of letting go.

Hellos

Let's start with the hellos. Think about a new person that came into your life who has meant a lot to you. It could be a friend, a teacher, a coach, a sibling, or a new neighbor. If you can think of more than one, please describe each of the new persons you have met along the way that have made a positive difference in your life. If you wish to make a

*drawing of one or more of the people, please feel free to do so, or you may wish to tell a
story about each one.*

Good-byes

*Now think about some of the good-byes that have been sad for you, people or pets that
were important to you who died or moved away. It could have been a grandparent or
even a pet to which you had to say a sad good-bye. Or perhaps it was a friend who
moved away. Good-byes can be sad but are part of the natural course of life, and we will
all face them as we journey through life. Tell about one or more of the good-byes that
were hard for you.*

Follow-Up

1. *What were the feelings you experienced at the time?*
2. *What helped you the most to cope with your difficult good-bye(s)?*
3. *What did you learn from your experience(s)?*
4. *Some good-byes are expected and you can prepare for them, like when a
   grandparent is ill for a long time and then dies. Others are sudden and unexpected. Have you had any sudden, unexpected experiences of saying good-
   bye? If so, what was that experience like for you?*
5. *Sometimes the end comes so suddenly there is no chance at all to say good-
   bye. Has that happened to you? What was that time like for you, and what
   did you learn from it?*
6. *What has been the hardest good-bye for you so far?*
7. *Even when a good-bye is expected, when the time comes it still can be a shock
   even though you thought you had prepared for it. Have you had that experience? If so, please describe it.*
8. *Do you think we can grow stronger by facing and surviving the sad good-byes
   that are a part of life?*
9. *What are some of the factors that determine whether people grow from such
   difficult experiences?*
10. *Not everyone grows from such an experience; some become bitter and nega-
    tive. Do you think it depends partly on a choice the person makes? Explain
    your answer.*

Discussion

This strategy focuses children on both the rewards that derive from allowing
new people to become important and close to them, as well as on the pain that
results from loss or separation from someone special. Both hellos and good-

byes are natural features of life. Children who have experienced extensive or traumatic loss will likely find the good-bye portion of this intervention to be difficult. Therapists should use their judgment in terms of how many of the follow-up questions to ask. The therapist should pick and choose follow-up questions or construct new ones that would be specifically appropriate and useful with the child in treatment.

This evocative strategy is intended for kids in the Invitational track who have developed a strong enough therapeutic alliance to explore the issue of painful losses in their lives. The normal developmental progression of therapy is that the issues become more challenging and emotionally taxing as the work proceeds but that at the same time the therapeutic relationship grows stronger and allows the child to tap the strength of the therapeutic alliance in order to face the more difficult, emotionally laden material. This particular technique focuses directly on losses, as compared to relying on metaphor.

THE BRAMLEY STORY SERIES
(FOR CHILDREN AGES THREE TO EIGHT),
ILLUSTRATIONS BY CORRINE NIEKREWICZ

Introduction

Grief and loss has to be faced in everyone's life. It is almost always painful, but it is a natural process, as much a part of the life cycle as birth. It may be indescribably painful, but it need not be traumatic. When young children are faced with the death of someone important to them, it can be very trying for parents to help them, perhaps because the parents may be overwhelmed with their own grief, but also because they may not know how to approach the issue with such a young child. Yet we know from the research and clinical experience that children as young as three can do grief work when given the proper encouragement, facilitation, and modeling from parents. These stories are written for young children from pre-school to eight, to assist child and family therapists to help their young child or children through the journey of grief. They are also designed to educate children and parents about the grief process. Children need to be taught early on that death is a natural expected part of life, certainly sad and painful but survivable. This is especially true if the family faces it with a sense of togetherness and mutual support. The child may learn that when painful events occur the family pulls together, helps one another, together they can face anything. The child and family therapist can be of help in guiding the parents to facilitate the acute grief of young children by educating and supporting them through this process.

The Bramley series consists of stories about a rabbit going through the journey of grief, after his father dies unexpectedly, with the help of his family and friends. It is to be read to the child by a therapist in either child or family sessions. Therapists (and/or parents, if this is done in a family session) will want to help kids process and answer questions as the stories are read. The series is designed to bring into the open the myriad of feelings that arise in even young children as they grapple with these mysteries. It is not as though we have the option of protecting them by not talking to them; it is on their minds, and young children play out fears, conflicts, and worries about death and loss. This was a common theme in the play of children (ages two to eight) in the Baylor studies (Benedict, 2004). Our only choice is whether to join and assist them or to leave them to struggle with these bewildering issues alone.

Story One: Bramley's Longest Day

Bramley was playing with his fellow rabbits in the meadow when he noticed a big fuss going on near his family's underground den. He ran over to see what was going on. All the mother and father rabbits were coming out of the den, and he saw his mother crying.

Bramley started to run toward his mother when one of his buddy rabbits, Sonny, headed him off and said, "Your daddy is dead."

Bramley said, "No! No! It's not true! Why do you tell such a terrible lie? It can't be true."

"It is true," said his friend Spotty. "That's why your mom is crying and so many rabbits are coming to your den."

Bramley went racing toward his mother screaming, "It's not true! It's not true!"

When he reached his mother, she cuddled with him for a long time and then said, "It is true, Bramley. Your daddy has died, and we are all very sad."

Bramley didn't want to make his mother sadder, so he quietly slipped away and went to a hiding place that only he knew about, and he cried and cried. Never before had he cried so hard and so long. He felt very sad. He also felt scared. "How are we going to get along without Daddy?" he wondered. "It won't be the same without him." He also felt angry. "Why did this have to happen? Why did it have to be my daddy?"

Bramley wondered, "Why couldn't it be somebody else's daddy? Daddy was so good, and all the Cottontail rabbits in the neighboring ten acres loved my daddy. Why couldn't it have happened to a mean rabbit that nobody liked?" He couldn't help but feel that it was unfair! His heart was broken.

Figure 4.1.   Bramley talking to Uncle Benny

Then Bramley began to think that maybe it was his fault. Maybe he had been bad and this was his punishment. Then he had the thought, "If I were to be really, really good from now on maybe my daddy could come back."

As he was thinking all of these thoughts and feeling so sad, he left his hiding place and noticed coming toward him a very wise old rabbit by the name of Uncle Bensonhurst, better known as "Uncle Benny." Uncle Benny saw Bramley crying and began to speak to him. Uncle Benny said, "I know that you must feel so sad, because you really miss your father. We all loved him." Bramley continued to cry, and then he told Uncle Benny about his feelings and thoughts.

Uncle Benny listened patiently as Bramley described his sadness, his anger, his wishes that his father would come back, and his feeling that it was his fault. He told Uncle Benny about his idea that if he were extra good maybe his daddy would come back.

As he told these things to Uncle Benny, Bramley discovered how much better it felt to share his feelings with someone he trusted and someone he knew would understand.

Uncle Benny said to Bramley, "I have listened to many young rabbits who have lost someone they loved through death. They too have talked about their sadness, about their missing their loved one and wishing that rabbit could come back. They too talked about blaming themselves and thinking that if they were good the one they loved might come back."

When Uncle Benny said these things, Bramley no longer felt quite so alone in his feelings. Other rabbits have felt the same way, he thought to himself.

Uncle Benny said, "When someone dies, they are dead. When you are dead, you do not come back in this life the way you were. Your body stops working, and your life here on earth is over. Your body is buried in the ground [in the case of cremation, therapists can substitute the body is exposed to heat and turned into ashes; do not say the body is burned], but all of those who are left behind and who loved that Cottontail will remember all the beautiful and good things about his life. In this way we can continue to feel close to the one who has died. Those precious memories are yours to keep, and no one can ever take them away from you."

Uncle Benny continued, "Not all of your memories will be happy. You may remember some times when you did things that made your father angry with you or he did things that make you angry with him, but this did not cause him to die, nor will being good bring him back. It has nothing to do with being good or bad."

Uncle Benny explained, "We die when our bodies completely stop working because of old age or because of very serious sickness or accidents when we are hurt so badly that our rabbit bodies can't keep working. You are a young rabbit, Bramley; you should live a long and healthy life."

Although Bramley still felt very sad, and he realized he would feel sad for a long time, he knew that he was not alone. Uncle Benny said, "Let's go back to the den now." So side by side Uncle Benny and Bramley hopped slowly back to the family den.

Story Two: The Glistening Rock and Bramley's Question

On their way back to the den, Uncle Benny pointed to a glistening quartz in the ground just a few feet away. Uncle Benny said, "Bramley there will be times when you will forget what I have told you today. When it happens, come back to this beautiful piece of quartz and touch it. That will help you remember what is important. Remember, lessons of the heart are never to be forgotten."

Bramley felt comfort from Uncle Benny's words. Then he became very quiet and troubled. He had a question that he was afraid to ask, because he wasn't sure he really wanted to hear the answer, but finally he asked, "Uncle Benny," Bramley said, "May I ask one more question?"

"What is it Bramley?" [Pause] Bramley finally found the courage to ask, "Uncle Benny, will I ever see my daddy again? I didn't have a chance to say good-bye."

Uncle Benny replied, "Bramley, I bet you would give anything if you had a chance to have one more talk with your daddy and to tell him you loved him and to say good-bye. But your daddy knew how much you loved him, he told me this many times; he loved you and was very proud of you. He felt lucky to

Figure 4.2.   Uncle Benny pointing out to Bramley the glistening, quartz rock

have such a fine son! Many rabbits believe that there is a rabbit heaven after we die where we will meet and be rejoined with our loved ones. Some rabbits believe we create our own heaven right here on earth depending on how we live our lives. I know your daddy believed he would live on in the hearts of his family and all who loved him." [It is important at this point for the therapist to ask the child what his or her family believes happens when someone dies, or if the parents are present, turn to the parents asking them to explain to the child what their beliefs are.]

Uncle Benny, added, "You have many good memories of your Daddy. That will help you in many situations, because you have learned a lot from him. Just like your Daddy, you have many friends, your mother, your brothers and sisters, so you are not alone. I will be glad to help too in any way I can. So together we will make it through this." Uncle Benny said, "Now let me take you back to your mother." So side by side Uncle Benny and Bramley hopped slowly back to the family den.

Story Three: Bramley's Nightmare, by Stefanie L. Crenshaw, M.A.

The moonlight shown brightly down on the Burrow in Grover's Field, and crept softly into Bramley's room, throwing shadows on the wall.

It was three o'clock in the morning, and everything was still.

Too still.

Too quiet.

Bramley lay in his bed and swallowed.

He was trying not to breathe, not to move.

He clutched the blanket to his chin.

Only his ears, his eyes, and his little quivering nose were visible.

"You're being silly, Bramley!" he told himself. He was the man of the house now, and he wanted his mother to know she could depend on him. "I can't be afraid," he thought, swallowing again and clutching the blanket tighter.

Bravely, he tried to turn his eyes to the corner, the darkest corner in the room.

All of a sudden there was a creaking sound from somewhere, and he froze, clutching the blanket once more, all his bravery gone. His paws were sweating, his ears were sweating, and his neck was sweating. He was hot. He wanted some water. He wanted his mother, but he didn't dare to move. "Mommy," he tried to call, but his voice got stuck in his throat, and he didn't dare call louder. So he stayed still. He didn't make a single sound, and slowly, ever so slowly, time passed.

It was four o'clock now, and finally Bramley's eyes were growing heavier. He fought to keep them open. He knew if he closed them, the big metal monster would come.

He fought . . .

. . . and fought. . . .

. . . and fought, and his eyelids drooped lower . . .

. . . and lower . . .

. . . and lower.

Finally, the sun started to rise.

Bramley heard the familiar clink and clatter of dishes as his mother padded softly about the kitchen. He heard the low murmuring of voices coming from the TV as she clicked on the news, and he began to breathe easier.

He could not fight anymore. The blanket fell from his paws. He felt cooler, calmer, his eyelids drooped again, and two seconds later Bramley was fast asleep, at last.

Bramley's mother finished setting things in order for breakfast, and then she went softly to Bramley's room and peeked in. Her son was still fast asleep. He was sprawled across the bed, and quietly, she tiptoed in and pulled the wrinkled blanket up over him. It had been kicked into a ball at the end of the bed, and she sighed as she sat next to him. She suspected he had been awake all night.

Figure 4.3.   Bramley waking up to the sounds of his mother in the kitchen

It had been only three weeks now since Bramley's dad had died, and his mom knew he was having a very hard time. She adjusted the blanket again and nuzzled her son's forehead, but Bramley did not even know she was there.

He was far away now. Far away, in a world where his dad could be with him, Bramley was dreaming.

Story Four: Bramley Meets Whiskers

Some time later Bramley was playing in the meadow with other rabbits, and one of the meanest rabbits in the whole area arrived—a real bully, who was known as "Whiskers" and caused pain to others. It was known that from an early age Whiskers had not been able to get along with any other rabbit and lived a very lonely and unhappy life. But he pushed his misery on everyone around him. When he saw Bramley, he immediately attacked in a nasty way with his words.

He said, "Oh, there is that silly rabbit, Bramley. Bramley sent his father to the army by being such a problem that even his own family couldn't stand him."

Bramley was crushed and couldn't really keep it straight in his head that Whiskers was really talking about his own life experience. Whiskers had been separated from his parents and had run off at an early age.

Whiskers said, "I bet your Daddy would rather die than have to put up with you." Whiskers continued with the very hurtful words, "You are so ugly it makes me sick to look at you." Bramley was thinking that the old saying that he had heard grown up rabbits repeat so often, that "sticks and stones can break your bones but words can never hurt you," was complete nonsense.

Words do hurt, he thought to himself. Sometimes they hurt so much that if he had a choice, he might prefer a beating.

Bramley slowly hopped away from the group, but he could still hear Whiskers in the background laughing and telling the other rabbits what a coward Bramley was. He thought to himself, "Whiskers is right. I am a coward."

Bramley thought that Whiskers was also right that he had given his father such a hard time that he probably couldn't take it anymore. Then he just laid flat on the ground and cried and sobbed, and cried and sobbed some more, and mumbled to himself, "I killed my father."

Story Five: Bramley Remembers the Lessons of the Heart

Bramley looked up, and just a short distance away he saw a rock glistening in the sun. It was that magical quartz, that beautiful, glistening rock that Uncle Benny told him to come back to and touch. Then he would be able to remember the important things he had told Bramley.

He hopped quickly over to the rock and lay very close to it and gently stretched out his front paws touching the quartz rock. Bramley then began to remember the comforting and wise words of his Uncle Benny. Uncle Benny had died during the winter, but Bramley could remember his voice and his words as if Uncle Benny were saying them to him right that moment as his paws rested on the granite rock.

In his mind, he heard Uncle Benny say, "Bramley, its not your fault, when a rabbit dies it is not because you are bad. Being good won't bring your father back, because it has nothing to do with being good or bad. Your father knew you loved him, he spoke about it to other rabbits many times." Now Bramley remembered words of Uncle Benny that gave him special comfort: "Bramley, your father also loved you very much. I know because he told me often."

Bramley loved remembering those words of Uncle Benny, and with his paws still on the glistening quartz rock, he focused ever so hard on the words, "Bramley, you loved your father." It was so good to be reminded of his love for his father.

Then suddenly he realized why Whiskers had been so cruel to him. Whiskers had never had a relationship with his own father. Whiskers didn't have any happy memories to call on. Whiskers can't go to a quartz rock, rest his paws on it, and remember that he was loved or that he had loved anyone. Whiskers was truly alone in the world and, sadly, he had decided that the only way he could make his mark in life was to make others suffer the way he suffered.

Bramley made up his mind that he could not change Whiskers and that probably the best thing he could do was just to avoid him. He couldn't help but feel sad that Whiskers wouldn't let anyone get close to him and carried within him all the hurt that he dished out to others.

If he had a chance to help Whiskers he might give it a try, even though he still was angry with him, but Bramley knew that this would probably never happen. Bramley decided he would take a different path. He thought, "I don't want to follow the path of anger and bitterness, because it leads to great unhappiness. Rather, I want to make the most of my life and live it to the fullest. I want to enjoy my family, my friends, and my fellow rabbits."

It came to him as his paws still rested on that beautiful glistening quartz that the best tribute he could pay to his father and Uncle Benny was to live life to its fullest. He knew in his heart that his father and Uncle Benny would want him to do so and that they would be very proud of him for taking the path of living life as if it were a gift, a precious and priceless gift that is his to enjoy as fully as he can.

Bramley gradually pulled his paws away from the granite rock and, having decided his path, hopped off with a new spring in his hop. He knew where he was going, and he also knew he would never be alone.

He would always have within the happy, warm memories of those he loved and those who loved him, and that is something that can never be taken away. Bramley realized that Uncle Benny was right about one more thing: lessons of the heart are never forgotten!

Discussion

My daughter and I have found, in my clinical experience and her teaching experience with children and in previous writing (Crenshaw, 1990a, [1995], [2002]), a serious gap in the guidance given to parents of pre-school and early school-age children and to the children themselves when a family member, particularly a parent, sibling, or grandparent, dies. "The Bramley Story Series" addresses a wide range of issues that pose worry and uncertainty for young children and for their parents who attempt to guide and help them through their grief. In terms of timing, it is likely that the story series, which serves both an educative as well as a therapeutic purpose, would best be introduced between one and three months after the death of a loved one. It would not be appropriate in the immediate aftermath, when children and even adults are in acute grief, perhaps in shock in the case of unexpected death.

It is desirable that the parents communicate with their young children about these issues. Parents and therapists of this age group are often confused as to what to say, how to say it, and how to explain death to such a young child. They often get from well-meaning people conflicting advice that leave them in the end more frustrated and bewildered. It is not the goal of this series to make the argument that parents should turn over their young children to mental health professionals to undertake this work, although a small percentage of children may need professional intervention. The goal is rather to empower parents and families and give them the tools to guide their own children through this natural process in a healing and healthy way. So the preferred and recommended way to read this series would be in a family session with the surviving family present. If the parent's own grief is overwhelming and inhibits the child's expression of grief, it may be helpful in the beginning to have individual child sessions, with separate sessions for the parent(s).

An additional feature of this series that may be helpful to children who have suffered the loss of a parent or a sibling as a result of military action is that Bramley's father died while serving his country in the military. While this is not emphasized, since the majority of children lose parents and siblings in other ways, it does validate the experience of a growing number of children in America and throughout the world. Therapists reading the stories to a child can substitute another cause of death if they feel it would be appropriate and helpful for a specific child.

As a young rabbit, Bramley is in shock after learning of the death of his father. Through the tender care of his mother, the support of his friends, and the wise counsel of Uncle Benny he is able to ask the questions that have confused and perplexed him the most, to express the powerful emotions of grief, and to learn the "lessons of the heart" that are never to be forgotten. Most importantly, he learned that even the most painful losses can be survived and that life goes on, the sun does rise again: his mom is in the kitchen making breakfast, comes to tuck him in, and pulls the blankets up in a loving, tender way to keep him warm and cozy.

While the stories address the pain of loss and some of the secondary issues that arise—for example, being teased and set apart from peers—the series has a hopeful and positive thrust, strongly suggesting that even the worst of life's adversities can be faced and that as a consequence, the person can grow stronger and more able to face future losses and setbacks.

Bramley expresses the range of emotions that young children experience and learn to face as they go through the journey of grief. Bramley discovers he does not need to undertake the journey of grief alone. He has family and friends who accompany him and support him, including a wise "Uncle Benny" who in his long life has acquired wisdom and understanding. Not everyone he encounters on his journey is comforting and supportive. He finds it difficult to deal with a bully who teases and taunts him about the death of his father, but then he is able to remember the important lessons that he learned from Uncle Benny, and thus he finds solace and comfort in one of his most lonely and difficult moments. Bramley exhibits many of the behaviors associated with acute grief, including sleep disturbance and nightmares, sadness, withdrawal, and a desire to protect his mother. But he is able to face these challenges and learns how to live with loss and at the same time honor the memory of his father.

EVOCATIVE SCENARIO: "LIKE A ROCK"

At a time of loss it is vital that young children and adolescents alike be aware of who is still there and available to them. This exercise and the one that follows highlight the rock-solid relationships with family and friends that sustain and comfort a grieving child.

Directives to the Child

At a time when you can't help but feel a great loss over the death of your much-loved [friend or family member] I think it might be helpful to take a moment and reflect on who is still here for you. Think about the people in your life, friends, family, teachers [coaches, minister, priest, or rabbi], and others who are "rock solid" in your corner and that you can depend on. Name as many as you can of these "rock-solid" people.

Evocative Use of Symbols: "Creative Depiction of Rock-Solid Attachments"

Ask children to pick from a wide range of appealing rocks those that best symbolize or stand for or represent those people in their life who are still available to them. Another alternative is to ask children to pick from an assortment of miniatures those that symbolize the "rock-solid" family and friends who support and help them.

Clinical Illustration: Cary (Age Seven)

Cary, whose mother died three months ago, picked a "strong warrior" figure to represent her father, whom she sees as her protector. She picked a religious symbol (a cross) to represent the people in her church who have been helpful to her family. She chose a baby bottle for her younger brother, because "he acts like such a baby, but he still is my little brother." She chose a miniature stove to represent her grandmother, because "she does a lot of cooking for us." She picked a group of miniature boys and girls to represent her friends.

Discussion

I was fascinated by Bessel van der Kolk's presentation (2003) on the aftermath of 9/11. He described how in the days following the horrific tragedy New York City and Washington, D.C., were transformed into communities more like small midwestern towns than the huge, driven, and frenetic metropolises that they are. For that brief period, he explained, people in the two cities were unusually kind and patient with one another, helping and supporting each other in all kinds of ways. Van der Kolk made clear that this kind of behavior is necessary for the survival of the species. If we did not treat each other in these extra kind ways after such a horrible event the species would not be able to take it, people would crack under the pressure. While behavior was dramatically altered after such a major disaster, on a smaller scale this kind of behavior is mobilized in virtually every human community after the death of a loved one.

Typically those who know and care about the family surround them with love and support, and this caring and sense of community are essential for getting through such a personally disastrous time.

EVOCATIVE IMAGERY: "WHO IS NO LONGER IN THE PICTURE?" (PRE-TEENS AND ADOLESCENTS)

Directives to the Child

Have you been to a family reunion when at some point all those attending are rounded up and a family picture is taken by various relatives, who take turns snapping pictures while everyone else lines up for the photo? In some cases the family may be able to assemble only on rare occasions, because the members live in different parts of the country. In some cases it may be years before another such picture can be taken. When you compare the family reunion pictures taken years apart, you will notice new faces, babies and young children who have entered the family, along with daughters-in-law and sons-in-law, brothers-in-law, and sisters-in-law, and when you look closely you will also notice faces that are no longer there. Perhaps they couldn't attend the more recent reunion or, sadly, they are no longer living. Looking at that most recent family picture brings both joy and sadness. Pretend you are looking at a recent family reunion picture and you are happy about the new members of the family but then you notice that some are missing, no longer living. You feel sad and experience a deep sense of loss and of missing those who are no longer in the picture. Tell about the new members added in recent years to your family through birth, adoption, and marriage or love partnerships and then tell about those family members who are no longer in the picture. What is the impact on the rest of the family, including you, of the fact that those members are no longer here? Think about those who have died and tell about the family member that was most special to you. Tell a story about that family member. Tell what you will always remember about that person. Tell a funny story about that person. Is there something that you learned from that person that you would always hold onto and treasure?

Alternatives or Modifications

Evocative Drawing: "The Missing Special Person or Pet" The child may be instructed to draw a picture of the person most significant for the child who is no longer in the picture. Follow-up would include: "Tell me about this person." "What do you miss most about this special person no longer in the picture?"

Evocative Writing: "The Story of Someone Whom I Will Never Forget" Write a story about the person no longer in the picture whom you miss the most. Tell how that special person has influenced your life and what you will always remember about him or her.

Evocative Narrative Stem: "The Family Hub" A close-knit family would gather every year for a reunion and a family picnic in a scenic state park on a river. The children and grandchildren helped the grandmother, but she was always the one who organized the event and looked forward to it with enthusiasm. The whole family was sad when the grandmother died just one month before the next planned reunion. The children and grandchildren decided _____ [child continues from here]. The follow-up should explore the impact on the rest of the family of the grandmother's death and how her loss affected future reunions.

Evocative Positive Memories: "A Happy Family Gathering" Please try to remember a family reunion when members of your family who are now no longer living were there and it was a happy occasion for you. Write about or describe in as much detail as you can that family gathering and why it was a special and a happy time for you.

Discussion

This evocative strategy was inspired by the work of Norman Paul (1967), a family therapist who has contributed to our understanding of the impact of loss on the family system. Paul pointed out that when you sit with a family, it is just as important to understand who is not there as it is the people who are there. Those important members of the family who are no longer there shape the family that is in front of you. All families face loss, but the presence in the hearts of those who loved them of those no longer here is a vital source of both pain and resources for growth and inner strength.

This evocative technique is designed to bring into awareness the feelings of loss and unattended sorrow (Levine, 2005) that can be buried in the hearts of family members long after a cherished family member has died. This technique uses metaphor to introduce the idea of someone important missing but still present in the hearts of those left behind. It invites the child to directly share his or her own experience of loss, and in the case of traumatic death to move closer to developing the trauma narrative, as described by Cohen and Mannarino (2004).

The impact of the death of a central person, such as a mother or grandmother, who served as the hub of the family gatherings may be experienced by multiple generations of family survivors for years to come. In some cases the family gatherings may become infrequent or cease all together, not only because the hub is no longer there to bring everyone together but also because when they do gather everyone feels so painfully the loss of the central, much-loved person.

Children may protect their parents and other loved ones by not bringing up their own grief for fear of making it harder. This technique could be especially helpful for those families whose unattended sorrow relates to unspeakable trauma, such as losing a son to a drive-by shooting. This evocative strategy may contribute to activating the natural healing forces within the family as they unite in the sharing of their grief and sorrow.

EVOCATIVE PROJECTIVE DRAWING AND STORYTELLING STRATEGY: "LETTING GO, HOLDING ON"

The Story

Did you know that when someone important to us dies, even though we have to let go of the physical person, there are special things that we can hold onto? While the physical person is no longer among the living people we see in our day-to-day life, the special things that we can hold onto, we can keep forever. Those things that we keep are those happy and special memories of times we shared with our family member, our friend, or our pet.

We also keep the important lessons we learned from our loved one and his or her influence in our lives. If, for example, our loved one had a good sense of humor, was especially kind to animals or generous to those in need, we may try to develop these same qualities in ourselves. These are all the things we can keep and hold onto, and they are more important to many people than any possessions that the loved one might leave to them.

Drawing Directives

Now please think about a special loved one, family member, friend, or pet who has died. Think about what you can hold onto from knowing that person or animal. Think about a favorite memory, a special quality of that person that you admired or a lesson that he or she taught you, or a way in which he or she influenced your life. When you have that special person or animal in mind please draw him or her as best you can. If you prefer you can draw a favorite memory or pick a symbol to represent a special quality or a lesson learned from your loved one.

Follow-Up to the Drawing

1. *Tell me about your drawing.*
2. *What did you admire about this person or pet?*
3. *Tell me about your favorite memory of him or her.*
4. *Is there a family story about this person or pet that you particularly enjoy?*
5. *What lessons did you learn from this person or pet?*
6. *What would be a good title for your drawing?*

Storytelling Directives

Now that you have thought about someone who made a difference in your life, I would like you to make up a story about the kind of person you would like to be. Pretend that you are much older and have lived a very long life. Imagine that your best friend who knows you better than anyone is telling stories about you at an occasion in your honor. The audience is made up of people who admire and respect you. What story would your best friend tell if you had become the person you want to be?

Follow-Up to the Story

1. *What is it that you would especially want other people to see in you?*
2. *Of the positive things that your best friend in the story said about you, which ones would make you most proud?*
3. *Are there similarities in the story told about you as the person you would like to be and the story you told about your special loved one?*
4. *If so, what are those similarities?*
5. *What would make a good title for your story?*
6. *If your best friend had to describe you at this point in time using just one word, what one word would he or she use?*

Alternatives or Modifications: Evocative Proverb, "We All Can Make a Difference"

Please write about or discuss the meaning of this Chinese proverb: "A child's life is like a piece of paper on which every person leaves a mark."

Discussion

No one is exempt from the inevitable losses that have to be faced in our time-limited journey through life. While no one escapes life's endings, it seems to me that some families do experience more than their share of losses and hardships. This story is meant to emphasize what we gain from risking closeness with others, though the loss of that person is exceedingly painful—that we are often better human beings, our lives richer and more meaningful for allowing that person or even a special pet into the inner chambers of our heart.

PROJECTIVE DRAWING AND STORYTELLING EVOCATIVE STRATEGY: "A BASKET OF MIXED AND CONFUSING FEELINGS" (ADOLESCENTS)

Children don't get to pick their parents. Most parents love their children and do the best they can to provide what their children need. Sometimes parents face difficult situations, hardships like lack of money, loss of a job, or illness that make things hard for the whole family. During these times parents may be irritable, angry, or one or more parent may drink too much. The kids may feel there is too much yelling, either at them or between the parents or both. Sometimes parents never learned the skills they need to be good parents. Perhaps they only learned to punish, not to praise when a child does something well.

The Story

Terrell was thirteen years old. His father had never learned the skill of talking to his wife or kids when he was upset. Instead, he would yell at Terrell's mother and often at Terrell, his younger brother, Wayne, and his little sister, Janice. Terrell was the oldest, so he got the worst of it.

Things got worse when Terrell's father lost his job and started drinking a lot. When he came home late at night, he would almost always start a fight with his wife, and sometimes Terrell. One time, he tripped over a pair of sneakers that Terrell had left in the hall. Terrell's father was furious and yelled so loud that all the kids woke up and were scared. He ordered Terrell out of bed and yelled, "Pick those shoes up and if you ever do that again, I'll kick your ass." Three months later Terrell's dad had a heart attack and died. Terrell didn't cry. On the outside, Terrell appeared as though nothing had changed, but on the inside it was a different story. On the inside, Terrell was carrying a basketful of mixed and confusing feelings.

Drawing Directives

Draw as best you can a large basket and in the basket list as many of the mixed and confusing feelings that you think Terrell was experiencing.

Follow-Up to the Drawing

1. *Do you think anyone in his family noticed that Terrell was really suffering, although he tried to hide it?*
2. *If so, who do you think in his family would be most likely to notice and try to help him?*
3. *If you did not name any positive feelings toward his father, do you think Terrell might have had some warm, positive, or even loving feelings toward his father? Please explain your answer.*
4. *What do you think is causing Terrell to suffer the most?*

Storytelling Directives

Now I want you to think about Terrell and that big basket of feelings, different, mixed, and confusing feelings, that he carries inside. Please make up a story about what happens to Terrell and all those feelings he carries inside.

Follow-Up to the Story

1. *What is the strongest feeling in that basket of mixed and confusing feelings that you think Terrell is carrying inside?*
2. *Can you think of some better ways that Terrell could have handled the feelings that he tried to hide and keep within?*
3. *If Terrell were to turn to someone for help, who do you think it would be?*
4. *Why do you think that Terrell didn't turn to someone for help earlier?*
5. *What can we learn from your story of Terrell?*
6. *Do you think it is better to talk with someone about feelings that are upsetting, or do you think it works better to keep them inside? Tell why you believe that.*
7. *If your story didn't cover what happens to Terrell in the long run, what do you think his life will be like when he is an adult?*
8. *Do you believe it is possible to love someone but also have negative feelings, like anger, at the same time?*

Alternatives or Modifications

Evocative Proverb: "No Sadness, No Joy"   Please discuss or write about the meaning of the following proverb: "The soul would have no rainbow if the eyes had no tears" (Native American).

Evocative Use of Symbols: "Creative Expression of the Loss"   A child faced with loss or the threat of loss or disrupted attachment is asked to pick a symbol from a group of miniatures that would best represent his or her feelings about the loss.

Clinical Illustration: Mindy (Age Seven)

Mindy told me in a session that she was upset and worried about her parents' impending separation and divorce. I asked her to pick from the wide range of miniatures the one that would best symbolize or represent her feelings. She chose a dragon.

Therapist: Mindy, can you tell me why you chose the dragon to represent your feelings about your parents' divorcing?

Mindy (studies the dragon carefully): Because it looks sad. In his eyes he looks very sad.

Therapist: He looks very sad. Was there any other reason you chose the dragon?

Mindy: He is also very angry. You can tell by the mouth and the teeth.

Therapist: He is sad, but he also is very angry. Was there any other reason that you chose the dragon?

Mindy: The dragon breathes fire. When my parents argue it is like they are breathing fire, and I hate it.

Therapist: It makes you angry when they have "fire-breathing" fights.

Mindy: It also makes me sad.

Discussion

When someone dies, no matter how much we love that person or pet, there have always been moments of frustration, disappointment, or resentment. These ups and downs are a given in any significant and long-term relationship, and the accompanying ambivalent feelings are confusing to children. They may feel guilty about the negative side of their mixed and conflicted feelings; this guilt, and often shame, can block the healthy grief response. These same ambivalent feelings are often heightened in a divorce and may cause significant anguish for the child due to their entanglement in conflicted and shifting loyalties.

Therapists will need to carefully distinguish between guilt and shame in the therapy process with a given child. If a child rightly feels guilty for some wrong committed, such as losing his temper with the deceased loved one and saying hurtful things, it would be a mistake for the therapist to challenge this feeling. Rather, based on the research of Tangney and Price (Tangney and Dearing, 2002), it should be validated. Some children may feel exaggerated, excessive, or inappropriate guilt, since pre-school children, especially during what Fraiberg (1959) called the "magic years," tend to feel they are the center of the universe. Children believe that they magically cause all kinds of things to happen, including the really bad things. In these cases of exaggerated, excessive guilt the therapist can use cognitive techniques to challenge such distortions (see Cohen and Mannarino, 2004, for specific strategies).

The therapeutic task is to sort through with the child and family these notions and to validate guilt when it fits the circumstances but to challenge it when it is overdone or derives from distorted notions of cause-and-effect relationships in the young child.

SEPARATION AND LOSS ISSUES

Evocative Drawing and Storytelling: "The Ship Prepares for Voyage"
(Pre-teen and Adolescent)

Drawing Directives.   I would like you to imagine that you are about to take a voyage across the ocean. Now try to picture the ship that will take you across the ocean. Is it a big ship, or is it small? Is it a sailing vessel, a cruise ship, a yacht, a freighter, or some other kind of boat? Is it made out of wood or steel or fiberglass or some other material? As soon as you have a clear picture, please draw your ship as best you can.

Follow-Up to the Drawing
1. *What title would you give your picture?*
2. *What materials is your ship made out of?*
3. *How strong and seaworthy is your ship?*
4. *Would it be able to withstand the worst of ocean storms? How confident are you that your ship will be able to successfully make the crossing of the ocean?*
5. *What kind of equipment does the ship have on board to deal with emergencies?*
6. *How many passengers and crew will be on board your ship?*

The Story.   Now, I want you to pretend that you have your own ship and you are preparing for a voyage across the ocean. Think about what preparations are needed. What supplies will be needed? How big a crew will you need? How experienced will your crew be? Will you be the captain of the ship, or will you hire someone to pilot the ship? How will you prepare for storms and rough seas? Who else will you invite to go on this voyage with you? I want you to think about your voyage across the ocean and what kind of adventure it is going to be for you, your invited guests, and the crew. Think about some of the challenges that you will face as you make your way across the ocean and how you will manage those crises that arise. Make up a story about your voyage, your adventure across the ocean; be sure to give your story a beginning, a middle part, and an ending. Be sure to include some action, drama, and suspense in the story—in other words make it a good story. Children are good at making up interesting stories, and I am sure you will be able to come up with an exciting story of your own.

Follow-Up to the Story

1. *What title would you give your story?*
2. *How did it all turn out in the end?*
3. *What would you do differently on your next voyage?*
4. *How did you feel about your voyage? How did your guests feel? How did your crew feel about the voyage?*
5. *What can we learn from your story?*
6. *If you could give advice to other people starting out on a voyage, what advice would you give after your voyage across the sea?*

Discussion.   This projective storytelling technique invokes the powerful metaphor of piloting or organizing a voyage across the ocean (life journey) with all the adventure, challenge, and crisis that facing the often treacherous seas can entail (life is full of challenges and setbacks). The story also elicits the children's perceptions of their resources both internally and within their interpersonal support system to prepare for the anticipated adversities. The internal or external locus of control of children is likely to be revealed by whether they choose to captain the ship themselves or rely on someone else to pilot the ship. Their choice of guests to accompany them on the voyage may be revealing of whom they regard as significant attachments. The degree of hope or hopelessness and their optimistic or pessimistic explanatory styles will be suggested by the outcome of the trip and how the crises are handled. Water has often been viewed as a symbol of life and a boat/ship as a vessel of life, a crossing as the bridge between life and death, sometimes between good and evil, from life to afterlife. Thus, the story basics contain rich symbolism that offer a unique opportunity to gain access to the child's inner world of thoughts, feelings, and fantasies. The ship leaving its home port to face uncertainties on the high seas is also evocative of themes of loss, desertion, and abandonment for those left behind, fear of never returning to one's home base and of being separated forever.

Clinical Illustration: Terrell (Age Fourteen).   "My crew would probably be me as the captain and there is a friend of mine who is very good with mechanics and cars. I would make him the first mate. I would invite four other random friends. I would get a lot of soda, and candy, and some fruit. I would make a lower deck so I would have lifeboats ready in case there is a storm. We would also have a lightning rod."

Follow-Up.

Therapist: Do you think if you encountered a bad storm you would be prepared to meet the challenge?

Terrell: If we hit a storm, I guess we would work together and try to make everything safe. We would go to the bottom of the boat and play cards or something until the storm passed.

Therapist: What would you do if someone was injured?

Terrell: If someone got hurt we would have to go to the nearest island to get help.

Therapist: What other challenges might you face on your voyage?

Terrell: If a shark were to attack, I guess we would throw a chair or something.

Therapist: How do you think your voyage will turn out?

Terrell: I think we would be able to reach our destination.

Therapist: What advice would you give others who are preparing for a voyage across the ocean?

Terrell: We learned that we needed to work together. We needed a stronger-built boat. The passengers enjoyed it. Make sure you have a good crew, no slackers; you and your crew should try to do things together.

Therapist: What title would you give your story?

Terrell: "The Voyage"

Therapist: What was the greatest challenge faced on your voyage?

Terrell: When the shark attacked the boat. We went to the other side and took off in a lifeboat.

Discussion.   There are many incongruous elements in Terrell's account of his voyage. He insisted that he would captain the ship, with the help of his first mate who knows about mechanics. Yet when the storm hit the whole crew went below to play cards. When a shark attacked, first he guessed they would throw a chair at it and then they abandoned ship in a lifeboat, which, to say the least, does not sound like good planning. Yet in spite of everything, they reach their destination, and the passengers have a good time. Also of interest is his choice of four "random friends." Terrell has a hard time making and keeping friends, and his word choice may reflect his difficulty in knowing what friends he would be able to invite to go on the voyage with him. The story also contains some elements of healthy growth forces, for a child who has frequently been withdrawn, chronically angry, and socially isolated—starting with his deciding not to take the voyage alone and also his stressing the need for everyone to work together. In addition, when asked what was learned from the voyage he expressed the need "for a stronger boat." This may symbolically represent his awareness and insight that he needs to grow stronger as well as learn to work well with others before undertaking such a challenging adventure in life.

Evocative Projective Drawing and Storytelling Strategy:
"Miguel's Endless Search" (Adolescents)

The Story.   Miguel was an angry boy. He was angry with his teachers, his mother, his brothers, his sisters; he didn't keep any friends for long, because he would get angry with them and write them off. Miguel was only thirteen years old. How could a boy so young already be so angry, so bitter, and so unhappy? This question was on the minds of all who knew him and cared about him. Miguel constantly approached others, even strangers he passed in the small sea-side village in Spain where he lived. He asked over and over, "Have you seen what I have been looking for?" Most people just ignored him and kept on walking. The kids at school had long ago stopped paying attention to him, because they had heard Miguel ask the same question over and over. Others were polite and patient. Some kind folks asked Miguel, "What is it that you are look-ing for?" He would always answer, "I am not sure, but I know it is important and I can't find it." Others asked Miguel, "How long have you been looking?" Miguel always answered the last question, "For as long as I can remember."

Miguel's responses puzzled the people of his village and the visitors who greeted him. They would often shake or scratch their heads and then just move on down the street. Miguel was equally frustrated, because it was clear to him that no one had an answer to his question. Miguel was starting to feel desper-ate. He was getting older, and soon he would be fourteen years old. He always thought he would have the answer by the time he reached fourteen. He was beginning to lose hope that he would ever find an answer.

Drawing Directives.   *Now, make yourself as comfortable as you can. Try to get a clear picture in your mind of Miguel. What is he wearing? Is he tall or short, or av-erage height? Is he thin or stocky or just about average weight for his height? Where is Miguel in your picture? Is he at home or school, or in the village or someplace else? Is he alone or with others? When you have a clear picture of Miguel, please draw him as best you can.*

Follow-Up to the Drawing
1. *Tell me about your drawing?*
2. *What would be a good title for your drawing?*
3. *Where is Miguel in your drawing?*
4. *If there are other people in your picture. Who are they and what are their rela-tionships to Miguel?*
5. *Does Miguel remind you of anyone? If so tell me about that person?*
6. *What kind of feeling do you get when you look at your picture?*

Storytelling Directives.   *Now think about Miguel's search for something missing in his life. He has been looking for a long time. Make up a story that includes what he has been searching for, whether he finds it or not, and if so, when he finds it and how.*

Include whoever you feel should be in the story besides Miguel, such as family, friends, teachers, or anyone else. Take your time and think about what could have driven Miguel to constantly search for what was missing. Think about whether he was searching for something he once had but then lost, or something he hungered for but never had. Make up the most interesting story you can. Be sure your story has a beginning, a middle part, and an ending. Be creative; put all the action, suspense, and drama that you wish into your story.

Follow-Up to the Story

1. *Why did you pick _____ to be the missing piece that Miguel had been looking for all his life?*
2. *If he found the missing item, how did that change his life? How will things be different for him?*
3. *If he didn't find what has always been missing, how will that affect him in his later life?*
4. *Will his finding or not finding what he has looked for affect his relationship with others?*
5. *What title would you give your story?*
6. *What feelings come up for you as you think about the story that you told?*

Discussion.   Children are often searching, yearning, longing for that which is missing in their lives, even if they are unable to name it, describe it to another, or explain it. There is an ache in the soul, a sense of incompleteness, a wish to be whole, to find that missing piece that was once there and then lost, or never was there but was always hungered for. Readers are referred in chapter 16 to a detailed clinical example involving Max, a boy who suffered loss, surrounded by secrecy in which "Miguel's Endless Search" was a pivotal strategy in creating therapeutic dialogue about the family secrets.

5

Themes of Power, Domination, and Control

The striving for power serves in the first place as a protection against helplessness, which as we have seen is one of the basic elements in anxiety.

Karen Horney (1937, p. 141)

DIRECTIVE EVOCATIVE INTERVENTIONS IN SYMBOLIC PLAY: "REDIRECTING THE IDENTIFICATION WITH THE AGGRESSOR"

It is important to honor the child's need to be in control and to exercise power but to redirect this into constructive channels. At the first opportunity after the therapist becomes uncomfortable with the extent and intensity of the child's identification with the aggressor, the child should be redirected to empowering roles that entail positive leadership (police chief, fire captain, EMT, rescue squad chief, etc.). In these roles the child can give orders and direct the operations, but the power is being directed to helping, rescuing, and protecting others rather than continuing the pattern that has caused so much pain in his or her life of victimizing others. This shift may be resisted by the child, and it may evolve slowly. The therapist can provide modeling, encouragement, and reinforcement within the metaphor of the play, as can be seen in the dialogue below:

Therapist: What would you like me to do, Chief? Do you want me to arrest this guy?
Child: Lock him up.

Therapist (talking to the offender): You made a big mistake, fellow, when you came to cause trouble in the Chief's town. Let me tell you something about the Chief. He is a fair guy. If you don't break the law, you won't have any trouble with him. But if you try to hurt someone, let me tell you, he will track you down and put you behind bars. Never underestimate the Chief. He always gets his man, and everyone in this town looks up to him and respects him.

Child: That's right. You came to the wrong town.

Discussion

It might require numerous variations of the above scenario before the child is able to accept that there are many constructive ways to exercise power by exerting leadership, by helping and protecting others, but at least that modeling, practice, and reinforcement process is initiated. When children are "stuck" in the role of identification with the aggressor, I do not recommend a nondirective approach. The therapist's passivity could result in consolidation of the child's identity around the aggressor/victimizer role.

Part of the objective of this intervention is to expand the choices for the child in the roles that he can adopt. It is typical of children in clinical settings to rather rigidly cling to narrow, overlearned patterns of behavior; the directive interventions are intended to open up new choices and options for the child. Children with relatively healthy internal resources might well expand on the roles they could take. In that instance, a child-centered approach may suffice. But many children in clinical populations, particularly those who have been exposed to abuse, trauma, and violence, will need the direction of the therapist to accomplish this shift.

The child or play therapist needs to monitor carefully the extent to which the child is gratified by the role of aggressor and to intervene when signs point to over-gratification. Such signs would include the child becoming attached rigidly, even compulsively, to the role of the aggressor. Exaggerated affect, obvious gratification and energy displayed in aggressive, or violent, even sadistic roles in play would be additional signs. Resistance to taking a different role even when encouraged to do so directly by the therapist and redundant, endless repetitions of aggressive, symbolic play with little movement or variation would raise a red flag of concern.

These characteristics are similar to Terr's (1990) delineation of the features of post-traumatic play, and it could be argued that what I am calling over-identification with the aggressor is a variant of post-traumatic play. The crucial consideration is how to intervene in a helpful way. Children will not be easily redirected if they are "stuck" in the role of aggressor, tyrant, persecutor, or dominator. The degree to which a child fixates and clings tenaciously to the aggressor role may reflect the extent that he or she previously felt oppressed by those who exercised power over her or him.

Kevin O'Connor (1995) proposed the essential features of this directive strategy in a presentation on dealing with abused children, although I differ with one aspect of his criteria for strategically intervening with aggression. O'Connor (1995) states that aggression toward the offender/abuser in symbolic play does not require redirection, as compared to aggression directed toward victims. My approach is to intervene with a consistent, redundant pattern of identification with aggressor regardless of whom it is directed toward. This is because the longer this identification persists and is reinforced by the immediate gratification that is derived from exercising power over others, the more difficult it will be to change this pattern and the greater the risk that the child's identity with be consolidated around the role of aggressor and that the cycle that leads to destructive use of power and control will continue.

O'Connor (1995) offers some practical and useful ideas for redirecting the child whose aggression is directed toward a victim. He suggests that the therapist interrupt a repetitive play sequence in which the child is identified with an aggressor in symbolic play. The child, for example, chooses the crocodile puppet and terrorizes all the other animal puppets, especially the relatively helpless, vulnerable puppets like the rabbit. In that case, the therapist would stop the play drama and hand the child a superhero puppet or police chief puppet that brings the crocodile under control or puts it in jail to protect the other animals.

A directive approach is needed, according to O'Connor (1995), in these instances to take charge of the play sequences. After a brief exposure of the child to the role of a superhero or helper, the therapist should once again stop the sequence to avoid the child reverting back to the aggressor role, which is probable if the process is left open-ended. The child experiences briefly the constructive exercise of power. But since the child has an overlearned proclivity to identify with the aggressor, the exposure to these alternative ways of exercising power need to be closely supervised and directed by the therapist.

Evocative Dramatic Scripts: "Constructive Displays of Power"

The child should be reinforced for the constructive display of power in helping, protecting, or rescuing others or in self-protective actions appropriate to the context. During this directive strategic intervention the play therapist acts very much like a movie or drama director who interrupts, re-directs, coaches, encourages, and reinforces.

EVOCATIVE DIRECTIVE SYMBOLIC PLAY WITHIN
THE METAPHOR: "ORCHESTRATING
ROLE-SHIFTS BY REFLECTIONS"

Sometimes the play therapist can do a considerable amount of encouragement, prompting, and reinforcing within the metaphor of the play. In previous writing (Crenshaw and Hardy, 2005) a detailed case of a boy who was severely traumatized by extensive abuse was discussed. This youngster was stuck in the role of identification with the aggressor; in one critical session, I redirected him to the role of police chief but then immediately returned to the metaphor by taking the role of the assistant police chief. In that role I could prompt him, coach him, and reinforce him by saying things like, "That alligator is going to have to learn the hard way that you can't treat frogs, turtles, and bunny rabbits that way. He is nothing but a big bully. Shall we take him away, Chief?" (Crenshaw and Hardy, 2005, p. 185). Some children will respond better to the therapist's direction if it can be done in this less intrusive manner, in the context of the symbolic play drama, via the voice of one of the play characters.

Discussion

It is important for the child therapist to appreciate why children who have a history of being dominated and controlled may not respond well to the directive intervention unless it is embedded in the way suggested above, within the metaphor of the play drama.

Child therapists working with kids who have suffered intrusive and oppressive forms of control would be well advised to anticipate overt or more subtle attempts to defeat what the child will perceive as still another adult authority figure (the therapist) trying to impose his or her will on her/him. Again, from a psychodynamic framework, these attempts to defeat the direction of the therapist are developed as an adaptive attempt to cope with destructive forms of control. In order to manage these now-maladaptive responses to the therapist and therapy process in a helpful way, it is essential for the therapist to adopt this mind-set. In the absence of this mind-set and understanding of the psychodynamics of these children, the behavior may be judged to be resistant, uncooperative, or defiant; the child could even be dismissed, on the grounds that he is not receptive, not ready, not capable of benefiting from therapy, or simply resistant to the well-intended efforts of the therapist.

This mind-set of the child who has experienced various forms of malevolent control is typically reinforced from the outset, because only a small minority of children initiate the idea of seeking therapy; most don't understand or agree with whatever rationale is offered by the referring adults, whether parents, teachers or school administrators, probation officers, or courts. So the vast majority of children are strong-armed into going to therapy, and the process is experienced as disempowering from the outset.

It is also a basic tenet of the psychodynamic framework that a significant portion of these learned ways of responding by the child would be outside his or her awareness. Thus, the therapeutic relationship as it unfolds offers opportunities, not only for a richer, more complex view of the child but also for the therapist to work with the problematic behaviors, thoughts, attitudes, and feelings derived from an overall context that made such behaviors, feelings, thoughts, and attitudes a necessity but that now require modification in order to live in harmony with one's present circumstances.

Evocative Scenario: "When to Take Off the Gorilla Suit; When to Keep It On"

A small but significant number of kids have been hurt so badly in their relationships with key adults in their lives they put on a gorilla suit. The gorilla suit protects them from further harm by keeping adults at a distance. Donning the gorilla suit—pretending to be aggressive, scary, and powerful—will usually keep others away. Although children often feel safer with the gorilla suit on, eventually they feel sad and lonely. The wearing of the gorilla suit isolates the child from others. The gorilla suit doesn't distinguish between friend and foe, between those who can be trusted and those who can't.

Keeping the gorilla suit on is a good idea if those approaching would hurt you further. When those coming near are friendly and trustworthy, it would, however, be a good idea to take the gorilla suit off, because you risk scaring away the very people who want to be your friends.

The important skill that everyone needs to learn for safe passage in their social world is how to tell the difference between those you can trust and those you can't. It can be a lonely and sad passage if you never take the gorilla suit off. It might be an unsafe passage if you never keep the gorilla suit on, regardless of who is approaching.

Directives to the Child

Probably everyone meets someone along the way who is not to be trusted, who is a threat to one's safety. Ideally, everyone meets people along the way who are trustworthy, caring, friendly, and who want to lend a helping hand. What are some ways that you have learned to tell the difference? Try to name at least five signs that you would look for to help you decide, "Is this a person I can trust or not? Do I dare take off the gorilla suit or not?"

Follow-Up

1. *Can you add one or more other signs to your list?*
2. *Can you think of a time when you took off the gorilla suit or let your guard down, when you trusted someone, it turned out to be a mistake? If so, please tell about that experience.*
3. *Can you think of a time when you kept your gorilla suit on and that turned out to be a mistake? In other words, you kept someone at a distance who you later realized was trustworthy and friendly or could have been helpful to you. If so please tell about that experience.*
4. *What did you learn from these experiences?*

EVOCATIVE DIRECTIVE SYMBOLIC PLAY: "THE ALLIGATOR BULLIES THE RABBIT"

The alligator puppet is sitting in the classroom with his classmates: the monkey puppet, the parrot, the dog, the panda, the rabbit, the skunk, and the raccoon. The alligator begins to make fun of the rabbit. He whispers, "Hey, rabbit, you are really dumb; I bet you will never pass." All the other puppets laugh except the little rabbit, who starts to cry. This encourages Alligator to say even more mean things. Alligator says, "Hey, what is that smell in here?" The monkey, the parrot, the dog, the panda, the skunk, and the raccoon all say one at a time, "It is not I." Alligator continues, "I knew it, it's that smelly rabbit." All the animals except the rabbit laugh, while the rabbit cries harder. The teacher, Mrs. Penguin, said, "All right, that's enough. What is going on here?" Everyone was quiet, except the rabbit, who cried louder and louder. Mrs. Penguin said, "Oh, rabbit, when are you going to grow up? You are such a crybaby." The other animals snickered quietly while the rabbit slumped deeper and deeper into her chair.

Alternatives or Modifications

If children don't spontaneously evolve their own puppet plays and dramas, I will often introduce and model one that is based on a relevant theme in the child's life—in the present example, for a child who is being bullied and taunted. After the above drama is played out, the child can be offered the chance to take one of the roles. Alternatively, the child may want to use the puppet drama modeled by the therapist as a springboard to develop a story of his or her own. Still another option would be to ask the child if he or she would like to ask questions of one or more of the puppet characters. The latter strategy would be consistent with the gestalt approach practiced by Violet Oaklander (1988).

Still another approach would entail asking the child to coach either the victim or the aggressor to modify their behavior, to help the alligator tame his aggression toward others, and for the little rabbit to become more self-assertive. Finally, the other puppets could model for either the alligator or rabbit or both more adaptive behavior and ways of coping. The latter would be another example of a child-friendly cognitive behavioral approach. The child would receive practice and reinforcement in socially desirable, more adaptive behavior as well as coping strategies.

Evocative Narrative Stem: "The Dominating Dinosaur"

There was once a dinosaur whose name was _____ [child decides the name] *whom everyone feared. When he was approaching the other dinosaurs and jungle animals the earth would shake and the animals and other dinosaurs would break out in a cold sweat and tremble. One day a family of tigers felt the ground shake beneath them and* _____ [the child continues from here].

Follow-Up

1. *What title would you like to give your story?*
2. *What did this huge and scary dinosaur feel when all the others would shake and tremble when it approached?*
3. *How about the other dinosaurs and jungle animals? What was it like for them to know that this scary dinosaur could be approaching at any time?*
4. *If your story didn't already answer this question, do you think any of the other dinosaurs or animals would ever stand up to this frightening creature?*
5. *If so, which one? Why did you pick that one?*
6. *What other options did the other dinosaurs and animals have to deal with regarding this tough problem?*
7. *What can be learned from your story?*

Discussion

Reflecting the sense of powerlessness and helplessness that children sometimes feel, a significant number of children will identify with the weaker, more vulnerable dinosaurs and animals, while other children will take delight in identifying with the aggressor. Either way, the underlying psychodynamics are similar. Those who identify with the aggressor are attempting to counter or compensate for their feelings of vulnerability, helplessness, and powerlessness.

The problem-solving question (#6 above) is intended to direct their attention to the respects in which they are not helpless, the options and choices available to them through the metaphor of the dinosaurs and jungle animals.

Evocative Writing Assignments: "How Cool Is the Bully on Your Block?"

Please discuss or write about the following topic: "Are bullies in your school viewed as popular or 'cool,' or do bullies have few friends?" Please discuss or write about what you think could help solve the problem of bullying in schools.

Evocative Use of Symbols: "Artistic Depiction of a Bully"

The child is asked to pick a symbol from an assortment of miniatures to represent a bully who picks on him or her.

Clinical Illustration: Tommy (Age Twelve)

Tommy, who had been taunted and tormented by bullies, picked a grotesque-looking monster from the miniatures to symbolize the bully who picked on him the most. Tommy explained, "He tries to destroy everyone—he tries to show that he is the boss, the most powerful and can rule the other kids." He picked a "gladiator" to represent the principal at his school, because "he takes care of the bully and puts him in detention."

EVOCATIVE IMAGERY: "SPEAKER'S CORNER"

In London there is a famous corner of Hyde Park that is designated "the Speaker's Corner." There any person, regardless of age, occupation, class, or race, can stand on a platform and have their say. Usually there are several speakers speaking to small groups who gather to listen to the different speakers. Some talk about politics, some about religion, the environment, any subject they choose. It is the ultimate symbol of democracy, of which free speech is one of the most treasured cornerstones. The speakers might be controversial or conservative, but typically the speakers display strong emotions and convictions behind their words.

Directives to the Child

Now let's pretend that we pick a corner of this room to be our speaker's corner. Think about a subject that you have strong feelings or beliefs and convictions about. It could be a topic that you think you have not had the chance to speak your mind on. Or it could be something important for you to say that you don't feel that others have been willing to listen to fully.

You may also do this at anytime during our work together that you think of something that you wish to say that you think has not been fully heard by others or me. I will tell you the maximum amount of uninterrupted time you can have to say what you want, and I promise to listen fully. If there are one or more family members who you think should be here to listen to what you have to say, I will do my best to arrange it.

Discussion

This evocative strategy is particularly of potential value to those youngsters who have been silenced by social toxicity (Garbarino, 1995), oppression (Hardy and Laszloffy, 2005), or sociocultural trauma. It will also potentially benefit youngsters who feel they have never been truly heard. I will never forget an eleven-year-old girl who was angry beyond what is typical even for abused children. In working with Charlotte, her father, stepmother, and stepsiblings in family sessions it became clear that part of what drove this striking rage in Charlotte was that no one in the family ever seemed to listen to her. Her voice was repeatedly invalidated, and her anger rose accordingly. Now it has reached the point that Charlotte no longer talked in the family, she shouted. That further guaranteed that no one would listen to her.

I pointed out to the family that Charlotte doesn't believe that anyone in the family will listen to her if she speaks in a calm voice, so her only choice was to be silent or to keep raising her voice, to the point that now she only shouts. Since Charlotte is a spunky kid with a fighting spirit, being silent is not an option for her. But no one wants to listen when someone yells all the time.

I said to the family, "I am going to ask Charlotte to speak to you as calmly as she can manage, but I want you to understand that if someone believes that no one will listen to them, it may come out more angry and louder than they intend until they are convinced that people really do want to hear what they have to say. So no matter how loud she gets I ask you to make a commitment to do your best just to listen, not to interrupt, just try to hear what she needs you to understand. Charlotte, you can speak until you feel you have said what you need to say? If we run out of time I will have to stop you, but you can continue where you left off next time. When Charlotte is convinced that she can have her say and will be heard by her family, she can learn to speak to you more calmly."

One of many valuable lessons that kids have taught me over the years is that children will not tell their story unless they are convinced the adults *are able and willing* to hear it. They absolutely will not tell their story if they believe the parents are unable to hear it, if it will be too upsetting to them, if they believe it will make their depressed mom more depressed, if it will make their alcoholic father drink more. I find truly amazing the lengths that kids will go to protect their parents or even their therapist (if they feel the therapist is not capable or ready to hear their story). They simply won't talk. Likewise, if they feel the family (or therapist) is unwilling to hear their story or, worse, if they believe it will result in the family (or therapist) responding in anger, perhaps even blaming them for what happened, they will not share their story.

The way I approached this therapeutically was to "put the ball in the family's court" by stating, "Charlotte will not tell you what she needs to tell you unless you are able to convince her that you truly want to hear it. If you want Charlotte to tell you what is on her mind, please talk to her and try to convince her that you sincerely want to know. I would like each member of the family to speak with Charlotte; do your best to show her that you sincerely want to hear what she has to say."

The family did the best they could, but Charlotte was at best only partially convinced, so she only shared a small portion of what was on her mind—but it was a beginning. Creating a time and space to talk and be heard became a regular part of our family sessions. The family, in good humor, would say, "When Charlotte speaks, everyone listens." What was more important the family began to recognize that when Charlotte's anger was rising it was time to stop and listen to what she had to say. Gradually she developed trust that they were truly interested in hearing what was bothering her, and she told them more, and because most of the time she said it in a calmer voice they were able to listen better.

Eventually she was able to tell her family how much of an outsider she felt she was, that she felt not only that she did not have a voice in her family but that she had no place in her family. She was the one who, after her father remarried, didn't fit, didn't belong. This was an extremely sensitive issue for Charlotte, who had become very close to her father after her mother died when she was seven. When her father remarried two years before, she experienced a great loss; she had not only lost her mother but also, she felt, the special relationship she enjoyed with her father.

Now that she was able to openly talk about these losses, her feelings, her worries, her fears, and her family was finally able to listen, her anger dramatically diminished. It was then possible to do important work on restoring the connection between her and her father. I saw Charlotte's family before I started using "the Speaker's Corner" as an intervention, but the principles of laying the groundwork for the child to be truly heard are the same.

EVOCATIVE PROJECTIVE DRAWING AND
STORYTELLING TECHNIQUE: "THE INTIMIDATOR"
(PRE-TEENS AND ADOLESCENTS)

Bullying is a major concern of students, parents, teachers, and school administrators. Surveys by Garbarino and DeLara (2002) reveal that high school students believe that school staff does not take the problem seriously enough. The
students also indicated that in their judgment female teachers were more aware
and more likely to intervene in cases of bullying than male staff. The long-term
results of bullying indicate that both the victim and bully are at greater risk for
psychopathology, with the greatest risk applying to bullies–victims. These children suffer the consequences both of the victim and the victimizer.

The Story

Big Jim Reardon struck fear in the hearts of male students at South Platte High
School. He was a tall guy, about six foot three, and a star on the high school
basketball team. But Jim had a mean streak, and he was intimidating. Billy Rut-
gers found this out the hard way. Billy was proud to be the only freshman to
make the varsity basketball team. He was a good point guard, but at five feet
ten inches he was not as tall as many of the older varsity players. One day during a scrimmage with the starting team against the reserves, Jim, after a spec-
tacular dunk shot, picked up the ball and instead of tossing it to Billy walked
over to him and slammed the ball into his midsection with extreme force. Billy,
doubled over, the wind knocked out of him, was totally bewildered by Jim's
actions.

After the first game of the season, a game that South Platte won, Jim came
into the section of the locker room reserved for freshmen, where Billy was
changing. Billy didn't notice Jim at first, but when he turned around to see
who was there, Jim landed a hard right to Billy's jaw, knocking him into the
locker and then to the floor. Jim towered over Billy and, his eyes darting ven-
omous rage, he shouted, "You stay away from my girl or I'll kill you!"

Jim's current girlfriend was Liz, a pretty blond girl in Billy's class who had
always been friendly to Billy, but as far as Billy knew the idea of her becoming his girlfriend had never entered the heads of either one of them. Billy, in
fact, considered her "out of reach," as she was popular and was attracted to
older guys. Billy had no idea how Jim came to believe that he was trying to
steal his girlfriend, but Jim's harassment of Billy continued through the end of
that school year.

Billy dreaded going to school, because he never knew what he would face
that day. On some days, he would turn the corner in the hallway lined with

lockers only to see Jim and his friends approaching. They would take turns slamming him into the lockers. Other days he would escape with just a hard punch in the stomach. Some days they would let him pass and then take turns kicking him hard in the butt. Billy often woke up in the morning with knots in his stomach and wishing that he could think of an acceptable excuse to avoid school. Billy drew comfort only from the thought that Jim was a senior and that when the school year ended he would never have to deal with Jim again.

Fearful that he would make the situation worse, Billy never told anyone about the situation. As a sign of his determination not to let Jim intimidate him, Billy also did not miss a single day of school. Jim did manage, however, to make the rest of the school year a nightmare for Billy.

Drawing Directives

Now try to get a picture of Billy and his encounters with Jim. What picture comes to your mind of the different ways that Jim bullied and intimidated Billy? Does the scene that you picture take place in the hallway, locker room, basketball court, or some other place? What is happening between Jim and Billy in your picture? When you have a clear picture, please draw it as best you can.

Follow-Up to the Drawing

1. *If others were included in the picture, what are they doing?*
2. *What do you think about Billy's decision not to tell anyone what was going on?*
3. *What is your reaction to Billy's determination to go to school every day in spite of his fear?*
4. *Who do you think will suffer the most in the long run, Billy or Jim? Why do you think so?*
5. *How would you explain the problem of bullying in school?*
6. *Do you believe adults in school take the problem seriously enough?*
7. *What do you think would help solve the problem of bullying in school?*
8. *If you had a chance to talk to Billy, what advice would you give him?*
9. *What advice would you give to Jim?*
10. *Have you ever known anyone who was either a bully or victim of a bully?*
11. *If so, describe your relationship to that person or those people.*

Storytelling Directives

Now I would like you to share your own story about bullies who threaten or intimidate others. This can be a completely made up story or something that actually happened to you or someone you know. Do not, however, use a story that comes from TV, the movies, a book, or from video games. Use your own creative imagination to tell the most interesting story you can. Be sure that it has a beginning, middle, and ending part and include a lesson that can be learned from your story. When you are ready, please tell me your story.

Follow-Up to the Story

1. *What feelings come up for you as you reflect on your story?*
2. *What can be learned from your story?*
3. *If you were a victim of a bully or intimidator, would you turn to anyone for help? If so, to whom would you turn?*
4. *Are there things that adults don't really understand about the problem of bullying?*
5. *Do you think girls who bully do it in the same way that boys do? If not, what are some of the differences?*
6. *How big do you think the problem of bullying is in your school? On a ten-point scale with 10 the worst it could be and 1 the best it could be, how would you rate the problem in your school?*
7. *Using the same rating scale, how would you rate the teachers in your school in terms of how well they respond to the problem?*
8. *On the same ten-point scale, how would you rate parents in terms of how well they understand the problem of bullying?*
9. *How seriously do you think adults take the problem of bullying? Again, use the ten-point scale and tell me why you chose the rating.*
10. *How interested and concerned are school administrators (principals, assistant principals, deans of discipline) with respect to the problem of bullying? Use the same rating scale and explain the rating you give.*
11. *How seriously do you think hall monitors, bus monitors, lunchroom aides, and bus drivers take the problem of bullying? Use the same rating scale and explain the rating you pick.*
12. *How would you summarize your feelings about the degree to which adults take the problem of bullying seriously?*

Clinical Illustration: (Brittany, Age Thirteen)

Therapist: What title do you choose for your picture?
Brittany: "The Intimidator."
Therapist: What do you think Jim is feeling?
Brittany: He is mad, but also happy because he realizes he is stronger.
Therapist: What is Billy feeling?
Brittany: He is scared, really scared.
Therapist: What do you think about Billy's decision not to tell anyone?

Figure 5.1. "The Intimidator" talking to Billy

Brittany: Bad decision, because no one knew it was going on and no one could stop it.

Therapist: What is your reaction to Billy's determination to go to school every day?

Brittany: Good, because Jim would know he was really scared if he stayed home.

Therapist: Who do you think will suffer the most in the long run, Jim or Billy? Please explain your answer.

Brittany: Jim, because when he looks back when he is more mature he will realize what a jerk he was in high school and how he wasted his time, and he will feel bad.

Therapist: How would you explain the problem of bullying in school?

Brittany: Maybe they are jealous of the kids or they are just mad and looking to take it out on somebody.

Therapist: Do you believe adults in school take the problem of bullying seriously enough?

Brittany: Not in high school, in middle school a little more, but not really even in middle school.

Therapist: What do you think could help solve the problem of bullying?

Brittany: Nothing, people will always do it. If they control it in school it will just happen out of school.

Therapist: If you had a chance to talk to Billy what advice would you give him?

Brittany: Tell a guidance counselor or a principal, but tell some other kid to go in and tell the principal for him.

Therapist: Have you known someone who was either a bully or a victim of a bully?

Brittany: My friend, who got beat up bad by a high school student.

Brittany's Story

"At around 9:56 AM there was a lot of commotion in the halls when I saw James crying and dripping blood down the hallway. I saw many teachers taking him away. He was punched, knocked out, and then stomped on. A little while later I saw cops and an ambulance arrive in the school parking lot. James was wrapped in cloth from head to feet. He was taken away to the hospital. Johnny, who beat him, was sent out of school and still hasn't returned. Today if you were to ask James what happened, he would not be able to tell you, because he was knocked out and he doesn't remember anything that happened to him."

Therapist: What title do you choose for your story?

Brittany: "The Third Period."

Therapist: If you just picked one word for your title, what would it be?

Brittany: "Chaos"

Therapist: What feelings come up for you as you reflect on your story?

Brittany: Scared, sheer panic.

Therapist: No wonder, it must have been very scary. What can be learned from your story?

Brittany: Don't tell rumors because that's what started the fight.

Therapist: If you were the victim of a bully would you turn to anyone for help? If so, whom would you turn to?

Brittany: A friend, the principal, adults at the school.

Therapist: How well do you think schools do in dealing with the problem of bullying?

Brittany: Not too good. They just send the kid out. It is not going to teach him anything.

Therapist: How aware do you think the teachers are in your school of the problem of bullying?

Brittany: Not good; they just don't know what is going on.

Therapist: How about the school administrators; are they aware?

Brittany: The school principals understand it more.

Discussion

Emotional violence can be devastating to the psyche of children and adolescents. It is a source of secret and hidden woundedness in many children who suffer in silence due to shame, embarrassment, and humiliation. Garbarino and

DeLara (2002) explain that the costs of physical and emotional violence at school include "the 160,000 children who avoid school every day and the thousands who drop out of school altogether because they are always afraid at school" (p. 43). Children are often fearful to report taunting or verbal abuse, sometimes physical violence, for fear of retaliation. Those who bully the victims often bear wounds as well. The inner pain they suffer is inflicted on others, and their long-term futures are marred by higher than normal rates of arrest and violence well into their adult lives (Andershed, Kerr, and Stattin, 2001; Kaltiala-Heino, Rimpela, Rantanen, et al., 2000). Some children who were victims of abuse and harassment reach a point when they decide to become the aggressor and seek their revenge by targeting other vulnerable kids. These bully-victims have the worst prognosis of all (Haynie, Nansel, Eitel, et al., 2001).

Children are harassed for a wide range of differences from the prevailing norm. Race, gender, nationality, ethnicity, regionalism, size, and disability of any kind can all be triggers to intimidation or harassment. Some bullies are reactive (hotheaded) and some are proactive (cold-blooded) in their bullying patterns (Arsenio and Lemerise, 2001). The hotheaded bullies may react impulsively in a fit of anger and lash out at weaker, vulnerable targets. The cold-blooded bullies are more likely to target victims in a more systematic and calculated way.

As an example of the cold-blooded pattern, Jim and his friends instilled fear and anxiety in Billy, who never knew what to expect from one day to the next from their campaign of harassment, which lasted the majority of the school year and consisted of repeated incidents of intimidation and aggression. Billy lived in a perpetual state of fear and anxiety but showed strength and determination by going to school each day in spite of his fear. It is important to note the degree of outrage expressed by children in response to the story of Billy's victimization. Those who view such treatment as something to be expected and endured may in fact lack a vital, fighting spirit, which has somehow been dampened or silenced in them.

In addition, it is crucial to monitor the level of empathy shown toward Billy in particular. However, some with an unusual capacity for empathy may be able to appreciate that Jim's life is likely to be beset with serious problems as well and that he may have been victimized at some point. The capacity for empathy is a key factor in breaking the cycle of violence (Crenshaw and Mordock, 2005b). The development of self and other empathy should be a cornerstone of any comprehensive child therapy intervention. A previous writing (Crenshaw and Mordock, 2005a) detailed empathy practice exercises utilizing role-playing and perspective taking in individual, group, or family therapy. Chapter 12 in this book is devoted to additional strategies to facilitate the development of empathy.

6

Themes of Aggression, Rage, and Violence

> To suffer the loss of love from others, by being rejected or aban-
> doned, assaulted or insulted, slighted or demeaned, humiliated or
> ridiculed, dishonored or disrespected, is to be shamed by them. To
> be overwhelmed by shame and humiliation is to experience the
> destruction of self-esteem, the self collapses and the soul dies.
>
> James Gilligan (1996, p. 48)

EVOCATIVE IMAGERY AND DRAWING: "A CHILD-FRIENDLY THREE-STEP AFFECT MODULATION STRATEGY"

Many children seen in clinical settings are not having trouble expressing their feelings but rather in controlling their feelings. The child therapy and play-therapy literature is saturated with techniques to enable children to be more expressive of their feelings, and those are helpful to an internalizing, anxious, depressed, or inhibited child. Children who act out or externalize their feelings, however, don't need help being more expressive; they need help in being expressive in an appropriate way. This three-step drawing strategy was developed to teach the crucial skill of modulating anger for externalizing kids whose presenting problem is reactive-impulsive anger and aggression.

- The Volcano Speaks—the child is asked to depict the extent of their anger about a specific event by the symbol of a volcano in the various stages of eruption.

81

- The Storm Clouds Gather—the child is directed to symbolically represent the degree of anger through the artistic depiction of an approaching storm.
- The Angry Monster Roars—the child reveals the intensity of anger through an artistic rendition of an angry monster.
- The Dragon Breathes Fire—the child uses the symbol of the dragon breathing fire to represent the level of anger.

Alternatives or Modifications

Children may choose to use clay to mold the volcano or the other symbols, or to construct scenes in a sand tray using miniatures depicting their anger; some children may wish to do a collage using pictures from magazines to artistically depict the degree of anger. Of course, the child may choose other symbols of anger/rage as well. It is essential even in directive–play-therapy interventions to offer the child choices.

Step One: Scaling through Artistic Depiction

Using metaphors from nature, ask the child to make a picture of a volcano or a storm (thunderstorm, tornado, hurricane) that would show just how angry the child was on a particular occasion (such as when he/she was thrown out of the baseball game). Alternatively, they can draw an angry monster or a fire-breathing dragon that would depict how angry they felt in the given situation (e.g., when he or she hit a teacher). This step involves the child scaling his experience. If the picture shows a passing thunderstorm, it is relatively low on the anger-thermometer scale; if on the other hand the tornado or hurricane blasts through and levels the town, or the volcano erupts and spews hot lava that engulfs neighboring villages, the anger thermometer is off the scale. By emphasizing that there are degrees of anger, this step can teach children that anger-control problems need not be all-or-none propositions. The artistic expression of their anger also offers practice in a safe and socially acceptable way of expressing anger.

Step Two: Verbal Mediation

The most crucial skill in developing the ability to modulate anger is learning the use of verbal mediation. When children are able to express anger through words instead of biting, kicking, or hitting they have taken a big step toward expressing their anger constructively. The child can be instructed: "Pretend that the volcano [or storm or angry monster] can talk and give words to the anger it feels. What would *it* be saying?" The child can write directly on his picture

Figure 6.1.   Volcano drawing

the words the volcano, storm, or angry monster would use to express its feelings. If they prefer the therapist, parent, or other adult to do the writing, that
is no problem. It is important, however, to allow them to use their natural language for expressing raw emotion. This is no time to insist on use of the
"King's English." Remember, we are trying to move from biting, kicking, or
punching to verbalization; that is a major accomplishment. We can work on

finding more appropriate use of language at a later time. A child may be sent to the principal's office for using foul language but won't be in nearly as much trouble as they would if he or she had belted another child in the mouth.

It is also important to try to get them to verbalize as many ways of expressing the anger of the chosen metaphor (volcano, storm, angry monster) as possible. "What else would the storm say about how angry it is?" Pushing the child for additional ways of expressing the anger into language gives them vital practice in verbal mediation.

Step Three: Problem Solving

This is a crucial step in which the therapist engages the child in problem solving and finding alternatives to exploding, erupting, destroying everything in one's path, etc. The therapist or other adult can say to the child, "Suppose the volcano noticed it was starting to get angry at this early point [indicating a lower point on the volcano far from the erupting top], or suppose the storm before it became a Category 2 storm was able to find a way to calm itself, what do you think are some ways it could do that?" It is important to use language that teaches children a vocabulary for these lower-level angers; this once again teaches that there are many degrees on the scale. You can say, "Let's pretend that the volcano was only irritated or annoyed at that point, or that the storm clouds are just beginning to gather, not really that angry, describe what it could do to calm itself." Children are being asked at this step to solve problems. As they propose an option, such as "talk to someone," or "think about something else," or "take a deep breath," it is crucial to follow up and ask how they think that would have worked out. "Could all that destruction have been avoided?"

If a child blocks and is unable to think of alternatives, the therapist should offer a menu of coping strategies for the child to pick from: "Could it get more information, clarification?" "Could it turn to a friend for support?" "Could it take a time-out to think the situation over?" "Could it take three deep breaths and try to just relax and stay calm?" "Could it just say to itself, 'It will pass, everything will be okay, I will get through this?'" The therapist is modeling for the child some important CBT coping strategies. The prime deficit for an impulsive-reactive aggressive child is an inability to stop and reflect on his or her impulses and feelings. This is an important way in which the child can practice developing these crucial problem-solving skills.

Clinical Illustration: Pete (Age Eleven)

> *Therapist:* Tell me about your angry monster.
> *Pete:* He is ready to do some serious damage. He is going to kick ass.

Figure 6.2. "The Angry Monster"

Therapist: On the anger thermometer, is he in the blue [irritated, annoyed] zone, the yellow zone [angry but still in control], or in the red zone [meltdown, rage, out of control]?

Pete: He is in the red zone, off the chart.

Therapist: Is this as angry as he could ever get?

Pete: This is it. He is ready to break up the earth.

Therapist: What words would express how angry the enraged monster feels?

Pete: I hate you!

Therapist: What other words could express his rage?

Pete: I hate you so much that I want to crush you!

Therapist: Are there any other words that would express how angry the monster feels?

Pete: Feel like breaking earth.

Therapist: I notice the angry monster has horns.

Pete: Yeah, the angry monster is the devil. He has the power to do the worst kinds of evil, and no one will be able to stop him.

Therapist: Do you think the angry monster/devil wants to be stopped?

Pete: Nobody would dare.

Therapist: It can be scary to be out of control to that degree; maybe he wants somebody to stop him.

Pete: Nobody can stop him.

Therapist: Can he stop himself?

Pete: Not at this point—he just wants to kick ass and break earth.

Therapist: What if he tried to stop himself when he was in the blue or yellow zone before the anger got out of control, would he be able to stop himself at that point?

Pete: Maybe in the blue zone, but it is too late once he gets to the yellow zone, and forget it when he gets to the red zone, he just goes nuts at that point.

Therapist: What could he have done when his anger was in the blue zone to calm down?

Pete: I am not sure he wanted to calm down.

Therapist: I am not sure either, but I do know that it is not a good feeling when you are completely "nuts," as you put it, when you are totally out of control and the anger has control of you instead of the other way around. Let's pretend that he did want to keep control of his anger. What could he have done while he was still in the blue zone?

Pete: I guess he could have done what we practice together; he could have taken three deep breaths.

Therapist: What else could he do?

Pete: He could count to ten.

Therapist: What else?

Pete: He could talk to someone, maybe another monster that is not so angry.

Therapist: Are there other things you can think of?

Pete: He could take a walk.

Therapist: Are there any calming things he could say to himself?

Pete: He could say, "Forget it; it is not that big a deal."

Therapist: What else could he say?

Pete: He could say, "To hell with it, let it go."

Therapist: Are there any calming pictures or images that he could go to in his mind?

Pete: Well, he could think about all the souls he can torture.

Therapist: Will that be calming for him?

Pete: For the devil it probably would be great fun.

Discussion

Pete identifies closely with his angry monster/devil, and as is the case with his angry monster his only hope of controlling his anger depends on his skill in catching it early, because even when it hits the yellow midrange of intensity, he tends to lose control. The significance of the angry monster depicted in the form of the devil is that it reveals his moral conflict with his angry outbursts, which have been severe enough at times to injure other children. On such occasions he has experienced genuine remorse. That the devil derives enjoyment from torturing the souls of others points to Pete's own suffering as a result of his hurting others. He is a good example of a child who fits the Ross Greene (1998) classification of "explosive kids," who tend to be inflexible and have extremely low frustration tolerance. These children tend to be impulsive and over-reactive to slights or provocations from others, but they do not want to hurt others; they simply lack reliable internal controls.

Alternatives or Modifications

Evocative Proverb: "The Wisdom of Reflection" *Tell or write about the meaning of this ancient proverb: "When anger rises, think about the consequences" (Confucius).*

Evocative Writing Assignment: "Calm in the Midst of a Storm" *Tell or write about a time when you were angry but you were able to find ways to stay calm and find a constructive way to express your anger.*

EVOCATIVE USE OF THE SELF OF THE THERAPIST:
"JOHN WAYNE MOVIE"

This intervention requires experience, a high level of skill, careful timing, and a healthy degree of self-awareness and self-monitoring in the therapist. This intervention is grounded in the theoretical view that some projections of the child onto the therapist are properly viewed as "projective communication" (Hoxter, 1983). Viewed from this perspective, the feelings aroused in the therapist from the projective communication of the child, particularly when redundant and experienced over a period of time, may be an unconscious attempt on the part of the child to communicate painful facets of her/his internal world. The therapist in sessions with a child, for example, finds his or her mind wandering to a John Wayne movie.

It is crucial to rule out contamination from the therapist's own issues and then to decide if it would be helpful or not to share the hunches with the child.

Clinical Illustration: Tony (Age Fifteen)

Therapist: Tony, I don't know why this is, but over the last few sessions during my time with you I have found myself feeling sad. This may be way off the mark, but I am wondering if there is some sadness in you that you have not been able to talk about with me?

Tony (looking stunned): How did you know?

Therapist: How did I know what?

Tony: My girlfriend broke up with me. I haven't even told my parents. I kept hoping that it was just one of those fights we sometimes had, but this time I think it is really over.

Please note that it is essential that such "clinical hunches," if shared with the child, be conveyed in a tentative way that invites the active collaboration of the child or teen in exploring whether there is any merit in such hypotheses. It should be done only when a strong therapeutic alliance is in place.

DIRECTIVE EVOCATIVE SYMBOLIC PLAY SCENARIO:
"TOMMY TURTLE'S PASSWORD-PROTECTED COPING CLUB"

This is another "Child-Friendly CBT Technique." Tommy Turtle tells the other animal puppets about a new coping strategy that he has learned that helps him to deal with his anger. He explains that when he gets mad he just pulls into his shell long enough to cool off, think things over, and decide on a helpful way to express his anger. Tommy Turtle is so pleased with his new coping skill that he decided to start a new Coping Club. He tells the animal puppets that in order for them to join his new Coping Club they have to know the password. The password is a new coping strategy that each one of them had learned. Each puppet is given a chance to join the club by approaching Tommy Turtle and giving the correct password, which would be a new coping strategy to deal with anger.

Discussion

This directed puppet play scenario allows for practice and reinforcement in self-calming, anger management, and coping skills that provide the password for gaining entry to Tommy Turtle's Coping Club. It is difficult to motivate young kids to rehearse and practice self-calming and coping statements, but when they are interwoven into playful puppet interaction with the colorful puppet characters, it is possible to accomplish a number of repetitions, rehearsals of desired behaviors, and practice and reinforcement of crucial pro-social skills. These puppet dramas will likely appeal to youngsters eight and younger, but some older kids who have experienced developmental deficits and/or arrests due to deprivation or trauma may also join in with enthusiasm.

EVOCATIVE DIRECTIVE SYMBOLIC PLAY INTERVENTION: "THE ALLIGATOR FLIPS ITS LID"

The therapist models the alligator's wicked temper, which spins out of control, making for scary and wild displays of anger. All of the other puppet animals pass by after Alligator finally calms down and offer to him the coping strategy that works best for each of them. The Bumblebee, for example, comes along and says, "Relax pal, take a deep breath. It is going to be okay." Mr. Turtle passes by and adds, "When I get angry, I go into my shell and think things over, it helps me to calm down." Mr. Panda Bear shares, "When I get really mad I run toward the nearest swimming hole and jump in. It cools me down." The "Wise Ole Owl" explains, "I think it over and decide if it's a big deal or not."

Discussion

Initially the therapist models the above puppet scene, but as soon as the child shows an interest in taking over the voice of one of the puppets, he or she become part of the drama and eventually may be willing to become the voice of all the animal puppets who are attempting to help the alligator tame his explosive temper. The child then gets practice in articulating a variety of calming and coping strategies. This represents another child-friendly way of working on essential anger-management skills.

RAGE AND SEEKING REVENGE

Children who suffer extreme privation of basic needs tend to be enraged. These are children who missed out on the essentials of love, nurture, food, shelter, and protection, or for whom these basic needs were met inconsistently and unpredictably. Such deprivation or inconsistent provision of these vital needs impedes the development of a sense of basic trust.

Evocative Story: "The Girl Who Is Mad at the Whole World"

The Story.   Katrina is now fourteen years of age, but ever since she was a first grader she has been known as the "girl who is mad at the whole world." When her classmates would say, "Good morning Katrina," she would snap back, "Don't talk to me." If a concerned child would ask, "What's wrong, Katrina?" she would shout back, "Mind your own business!" Nobody could ever be Katrina's friend for long, because sooner or later she would get mad at him or her and refuse to speak to them. The other kids didn't know what to think or how to act around Katrina. Some of the kids thought that maybe something was wrong at home for Katrina, but no one had ever been invited to her house, and she never mentioned her family, so no one knew for sure.

Follow-Up

1. *What are three possibilities as to why Katrina seems to be mad at the whole world?*
2. *Have you ever known anyone like Katrina?*
3. *Do you have any ideas about how to help a kid like Katrina?*
4. *Can you remember a time even if it were for just a short period when you felt like Katrina? If so, please tell about that time.*
5. *Are there things that adults don't seem to understand about kids like Katrina?*
6. *Are there things that adults don't seem to understand about kids in general?*

Evocative Projective Drawing and Storytelling Strategy:
"A Tale of Revenge" (Pre-teens and Adolescents)

Going for revenge is part of the natural response to being hurt or wronged by another. The wish to seek revenge is understandable. Whether it solves or ends the problem is another matter. All too often it simply keeps the grudge going, with no hope of resolution. Where does it end? What does it take to settle the matter once and for all? How many people are hurt in the meantime? Is it worth it, or is the price too high? Is revenge really sweet, or is it a bitter dead-end?

The Story.   Miguel will never forgive James as long as he lives. He has said so many times. James told the kids in Branch Creek Middle School that Miguel was gay. Miguel denied it, but the more he denied it and the angrier he became the more the other kids thought it must be true. Miguel was teased on the playground, in the hallways, on the bus, in the lunchroom, and in gym nearly every day of his seventh-grade year. He hated James and thought often about how he would like to get even with him. By the time Miguel was in eighth grade, most kids had forgotten about it, but not Miguel. James was truly sorry for the pain he had caused Miguel, and before the school year ended had tried to tell the other kids it wasn't true, but by that time they didn't care whether it was true or not; they just enjoyed teasing Miguel because it upset him so much. James even tried to apologize, but Miguel was not in the mood to hear it. He told James that he would settle the score with him, so he better watch his back.

Drawing Directives.   *Now try to picture James and Miguel facing each other in the hallway of the school building. Try to picture what that face-to-face meeting would look like. Who else is there? What is happening between the two boys? Would anyone step in between the two boys, or would they just be allowed to fight it out? When you have a picture in your mind of the two boys facing off with each other, draw it as best you can. If others are there, feel free to include them in the picture.*

Follow-Up to the Drawing
1. *Tell about your picture.*
2. *What do you think about the action that the boys took?*
3. *Do you think it will solve the problem?*
4. *What are the boys' feelings in your picture?*
5. *What are the other people feeling in your picture?*
6. *If you were given a chance to talk to the two boys before anything violent happened between them, what would you say to them?*
7. *Does this situation remind you of anything that has happened in your life?*
8. *What would be a good title for your picture?*

Storytelling Directives

Now I want you to think about revenge and make up your own story about it. Be sure to include in your story what happened that caused someone to hold a grudge and what they did to seek revenge. What happened as a result? Did getting revenge solve the problem? How long did the person hold the grudge? What did it do to the person holding the grudge for that long? Did the person who caused hurt in the first place want to make it up to the other person or did he or she really not care how much the other person was hurt? How did it all turn out in the long run? Make up the most interesting story you can.

Follow-Up to the Story

1. *What made the hurtful actions so hard to forgive?*
2. *Did seeking revenge solve the problem for the person who held the grudge?*
3. *Who do you think ends up paying the greater price, the person who caused the hurt or the person who holds the grudge?*
4. *Have you ever held a grudge against anyone? If so, please explain what happened. Do you still hold a grudge against that person? If so what would have to happen in order for you to forgive the other person?*
5. *If someone apologizes and really means it from the bottom of their heart, does that help the other person forgive?*
6. *What is the longest time anyone in your family has held a grudge?*
7. *Has anyone in your family stopped talking to someone else in the family? Are there any other cutoffs [people refusing to talk or see one another] in your family? Are these cutoffs still going on?*
8. *Sometimes family members carry their grudges right to the grave. What do you think about this? What do you think a person's life would be like if she/he continued to not communicate with someone else in the family right up to the time he/she died? Do you think that would ever happen to you or anyone in your family?*
9. *What would be a good title for your story?*

Clinical Illustration: Carlos (Age Fourteen)

Carlos drew a picture of two boys squaring off to fight with bystanders cheering them on by shouting, "Fight, fight!"

Therapist: Tell me about your picture.

Carlos: Miguel is hitting James in the jaw. There are three people in the background cheering them on to fight.

Therapist: What do you think of the action that the two boys took?

Carlos: It's not right to call someone "gay." Revenge is sweet, but it can sometimes hurt the hand.

Therapist: Do you think it will solve the problem?

Carlos: Depends on what you think will solve the problem. Yes, somewhat gets it off your back—that's worth something.

Therapist: What are the boys feeling in your picture?

Carlos: James is feeling sorry for the wrong he has done to Miguel. Miguel is good and pissed off.

Therapist: What are the others feeling in your picture?

Carlos: The bystanders are happy because they get to see a fight.

Therapist: If you had a chance to talk to the boys before anything violent happened, what would you say to them?

Carlos: To Miguel, I would say, "You have the right idea." To James, I would say, "You better hope someone dials 911."

Therapist: Does the picture remind you of anything that has ever happened in your life?

Carlos: Not really.

Therapist: What would be a good title for your picture?

Carlos: "The Rumble."

Carlos's Story.   "There once was a boy, thirteen years old, he was at school one day and he did not expect to be confronted by his cohort. His cohort thought this boy was acting 'like a prick' back to the boy. Now the cohort wanted to seek revenge, so the cohort stopped talking to the boy, and he is currently not talking to the boy. The boy is befuddled because the cohort is still acting like a 'prick.' Richard was befuddled by these strange ways of his cohort Andy. Andy is still acting like a 'prick' and does not talk to Richard. He will always remain a 'prick.'"

Follow-Up to the Story

Therapist: What makes what Andy did so hard for Richard to forgive?

Carlos: Because Richard thought Andy was his friend.

Therapist: So Richard felt betrayed?

Carlos: That's right. He turned his back on Richard.

Therapist: What is it about betrayal that is so hurtful, so hard to forgive?

Carlos: It is like being stabbed in the back. Someone you counted on to be a friend turns on you, it hurts a lot.

Therapist: Has anything like that happened to you Carlos?

Carlos: More than once.

Therapist: What was the most hurtful betrayal?

Carlos: When a girl I liked, but to her I was a joke, started a rumor in seventh grade that I was gay. Everyone was making fun of me.

Therapist: I bet that was not only hurtful but also enraging.

Carlos: I couldn't believe she would do that to me. She seemed like a nice girl, but I was sure wrong. I don't know if I will ever get over it. For two years kids were always making jokes and laughing at me.

Therapist: In your story did Richard seek revenge against Andy?

Carlos: No, I think he was secretly wishing that he could have his friend back.

Therapist: Was that also the case with the girl who betrayed you? Do you secretly hope that someday she will like you?

Carlos: I hate to admit it, but I think you might be right. I hadn't thought about it that way, but as much as she hurt me and as much as I hate her sometimes, I guess I do hope someday she will see me as one of the "cool kids."

Therapist: It can be painful to like someone who doesn't seem to like you. But it is also hard to let go of the wish that it could be different if you like that girl a lot.

Carlos: I really liked her a lot, and I guess part of me still does.

Therapist: Do you think revenge is a good solution when someone hurts you?

Carlos: Sometimes I do, but I guess it would just make a real mess of things. It would only make things worse, I guess.

Therapist: Has anyone in your family held a grudge against another family member to the point that they don't talk to each other?

Carlos: My father hasn't talked to his brother in ten years.

Therapist: Do you know why this has happened?

Carlos: He won't talk about it. I just know it has something to do with money.

Therapist: You haven't seen your uncle in ten years?

Carlos: I was only three when I last saw him. I can't remember anything about him.

Therapist: What do you think about holding grudges in the family?

Carlos: I don't like it. I have never met my cousins, and I don't remember my aunt and uncles. It stinks.

Therapist: Sometimes you have been troubled about your relationship with your Dad. Do you ever worry that something would go wrong and your Dad wouldn't talk to you for ten years or more?

Carlos: I am very scared about it. Dad has a bad temper, and he is very stubborn. He is one of those guys who would carry a grudge right to his grave.

Therapist: That must be really tough to have that worry in the back of your mind, that you could be permanently cut off from your Dad. What do you think about my trying to set up one or more sessions with you and your Dad to see if we can work on this together with him?

Carlos: Maybe, but I am a little scared about that idea.

Therapist: What scares you?

Carlos: That I will say something that will make him mad and I will never hear the end of it.

Therapist: I can understand that, especially if you have the worry that you could say or do something that would lead to a complete cutoff from him. What if we work up to this and do it when you are ready and more comfortable with the idea?

Carlos: I think that is a good idea.

Therapist: What would be a good title for your story?
Carlos: "The Double-Cross"

Alternatives and Modifications: Evocative Proverb, "Forgiveness or Revenge?"

Please discuss or write about the meaning of the following proverbs "To understand all is to forgive all" (French), and "When you start out on the journey of revenge, dig two graves, one for your enemy, and one for yourself" (Native American Proverb)

Clinical Illustration: Susan (Age Thirteen)

If you live by the sword you will die by the sword. Violence leads to more violence and it never ends. Everyone in the end loses.

Evocative Narrative Stem: "Balancing the Scales of Justice"

If children are blocked on telling a story of his or her own, the therapist may help them get started by the following narrative stem: "Once there was a girl who was angry and couldn't let it go. She could only think about the ways she was going to get even with the person who had hurt her so badly. One day she decided _____ [the child continues]."

Discussion

Revenge plays an insidious role in the cycle of violence. While it is a natural human response to wish to seek retribution, it only keeps the chain of violence going. The code of honor upheld with ironclad conviction among many urban poor minority youth is, "I'd rather die than be dissed" (Hardy and Laszloffy, 2005; Garbarino, 1999; Gilligan, 1996). Hardy and Laszloffy (2005) observe that the violent act is sometimes triggered by what would appear to an onlooker to be a minor provocation, but, they point out, these teens "live in a world where the opportunities for validation and respect are amazingly sparse, and almost every aspect of their identities and lives is denigrated. In their world, respect is a rare commodity of such value that many are willing to kill or die to obtain it" (p. 43).

An assault on one's dignity can become the trigger for an act of revenge; it is deemed unforgivable, because what shreds of self-respect remain is perhaps all that youth have left that is worth fighting for or even dying for. Gilligan (1996) observes that behind nearly every violent act in the prison population is some form of disrespect, an insult to one's tenuous and shaky sense of self-worth. It is essential that we understand what underlies the life-and-death importance that is attached to this issue among teens who live under socially toxic conditions (Garbarino, 1995). Hardy and Laszloffy (2005) explain,

> To be devalued is to be disrespected. One of the central features of those who have been devalued is that they suffer from an exaggerated, all consuming concern with obtaining respect. Ironically, perpetual efforts to obtain respect often becloud the devaluation that underpins the need for respect. When all of one's energy becomes focused around respect, it is easy for those around to lose sight of the devaluation that drives the need for respect in the first place. In particular, the ways in which many adolescents strive to obtain respect distracts others from appreciating the underlying devaluation that resides at the heart of their unrelenting quest for respect. (p. 45)

The evocative drawing and storytelling strategy brings into focus a highly prevalent form of peer harassment that derives its devastating effects on kids from homophobia. Garbarino and DeLara (2002) reported that kids with same-sex orientation, gay and lesbian teens, constitute about 10 percent of the adolescent population. Garbarino and DeLara (2002) state, "Kids as early as elementary school use 'gay' as a kind of conversational or universal insult, even when it does not specifically have a homosexual reference. Even for kids who are not gay or lesbian, homophobic taunting takes a toll. Boys particularly live in fear that any act of same-sex kindness or affection is going to be interpreted as a homosexual gesture and thus invoke homophobic sexual harassment" (p. 91). The potential violence that can result from this insidious taunting is alarming. Garbarino and DeLara (2002) further state, "When teachers and other adults at school do not stop verbal bullying of gay, lesbian, or bisexual teens, such abuse can easily move to physical violence. Research finds that homosexual youths are five times more likely to miss school for fear for their personal safety or to have been threatened with a weapon at school" (p. 92).

Carlos suffered significant learning disabilities, consisting of language-processing deficits combined with a significant degree of attentional deficits. He was targeted from early grades on, because he frequently could not follow the conversations of classmates, often made inappropriate remarks, could not understand jokes the other kids thought were funny, and was socially immature. When he reached middle school, a girl he liked but who was not interested in him started a rumor that Carlos was gay. Carlos was devastated. Although quite tall for his age, Carlos was a nonviolent, rather passive kid. After this experience in school, however, Carlos became obsessed with body building, acting tough and street-wise, and doing everything he could to project a "macho image" to prove that he was not gay. No one took him seriously, however, and after two years he gave it up. At that point he was so much taller and muscular than most of his peers, however, that the taunting largely stopped. The two years of intense suffering and trying to convince others that he was not that gentle, kindhearted kid he truly is was painful to witness. It is an example of the homophobic minefield that even kids who are not gay or lesbian sometimes encounter. Carlos's suffering parallels the deep sense of shame and humiliation of Miguel in the story, who became obsessed with seeking retaliation toward James.

Another cardinal feature of this story is the objective to provoke thought and feelings in adolescents regarding the insidious effects of obsession with revenge, not only on the target of wrath but on the revenge seeker as well. What price will be paid to seek retribution? What will it ultimately do to the target of the revenge and the enraged party seeking his or her "pound of flesh?" The biblical references to "an eye for an eye" and "a tooth for a tooth" underline that the motive for revenge runs deep, perhaps to the very tissues and sinews of the human being. Throughout human history it has been often the prime justification for wars that have killed hundreds of thousands of human beings. It is important to raise the consciousness of our youth regarding this issue and to ask the question: Is revenge sweet, or does it exact a price that is prohibitive?

7

Themes of Anxiety, Fear, Terror, and Seeking Safety

Children's fears fall on a continuum from the common childhood fears of ghosts and monsters that inhabit their dreams and imaginations to unspeakable terror characteristic of trauma events. The research literature has demonstrated the effectiveness of exposure treatment to enable children to desensitize themselves to the typical fears of childhood. Special considerations apply to trauma-based fears, which require utmost sensitivity to create and maintain a sense of safety for the child while undertaking the exposure training.

SEPARATION FEARS

Evocative Story: "Elfy's Rainbow Bridge"

Separation fears are common among children, especially among four-to-seven-year-olds but sometimes even into middle school. Many of these children became panicked and hysterical if their parents, or just one of their parents, even goes out for a short while, perhaps to the grocery store. Some young children will find it hard to separate from parents when dropped off at pre-school or even in the early elementary grades. This story addresses these fears.

The Story

There once was a baby elephant named Elfy who became separated from the circus. He was sad, confused, and lost. He was walking down a country road, and he noticed some horses lining the fence on a farm he was passing. The horses were curious, because they had never seen a baby elephant walking

99

down the road. The horses called out to Elfy, "Where are you headed?" Elfy said, "I don't know, I am lost. I don't know which way to go, can you help me?"

"Well," the horses said, "we will tell you a secret. There is a path that leads into the woods just beyond the bend. Take that path, and it will eventually bring you to a rainbow bridge. It is called the 'rainbow bridge' because when the sun hits the gleaming stainless-steel bridge at a certain angle it reflects at that magic moment all the colors of the rainbow. The bridge may seem scary at first, because it is very high above the water. It may make you nervous when you start across it, but if you can find ways to stay calm, like thinking about how good you will feel when you get to the other side, you will be able to cross the bridge. When you make it across the rainbow bridge you will come to a thick curtain of shrubs, densely planted. On the other side of the shrubs you will find yourself in a safe place."

Elfy didn't know what to think. He didn't know if the horses were playing tricks on him, but he thanked them and continued down the road. When he rounded the bend, he saw the path that led into the woods. Elfy wondered if the horses were laughing at him and thinking what a fool that elephant was for taking the path through the woods that perhaps led to nowhere. He thought to himself, "After all, who ever heard of a rainbow bridge?" Nevertheless, Elfy admitted he didn't have a better idea, so he took the path into the woods.

Elfy walked and walked. He was very tired and sad. He could still picture in his mind the horses still laughing at the foolish, silly elephant on "a wild goose chase" on the path through the woods. He was so tired he didn't know if he could take another step, but he did, one at a time. His tired legs and feet kept going.

Suddenly, he looked up and saw in the distance a gleaming stainless-steel bridge. He shouted with great excitement, "There is the rainbow bridge!" He began to move faster, and he soon came to the foot of the glistening bridge, arching high over the water.

Elfy stood still and admired the beautiful bridge, gleaming in the sun like a precious jewel in Mother's Nature's crown, and then he saw all the colors of the rainbow beautifully reflected off the bridge. But then Elfy suddenly felt nervous as he looked up at the steel structure rising tall over the water. He said, "I can't do this. I would not survive the fall, and even if I did the swift currents of the river below would pull me under." He started to shake and tremble, but then he remembered what the horses said: "If you find a way to stay calm, such as thinking about how good it will feel when you reach the other side, then you will make it across the bridge and find yourself in a safe place."

Elfy felt like giving up on the long path that led to the bridge, but he didn't. As tired as he was, he had kept going, and now he was at the foot of the bridge. Elfy said, "I can do this. I will put one foot in front of the other and keep going until I reach the other side." Thinking these positive thoughts, Elfy started across the bridge. Every time he started to get weak in the knees and scared he thought about how he could have given up long before now, but he hadn't, and now he was so close to his safe place. He kept going, putting one foot in front of the other, taking one step, then another. Finally, with a huge sigh of relief, he reached the other side of the bridge. Immediately in front of him was the thick curtain of brush and hedges, just like the horses had said. When Elfy pushed through the thick brushes and hedges, *he saw the* circus people and animals waiting for him. Everyone was so happy, and they all celebrated together Elfy's safe return to his circus family.

Discussion

This story is written in the Joyce Mills and Richard Crowley (1986) tradition, based on the work of Milton Erickson, in the sense that the story is intended to stand alone; no follow-up or discussion of its meaning is considered necessary. According to Ericksonian theory, the symbols and metaphors of the story speak directly to the healthy, positive, and healing forces of the child's conscious, as well as unconscious, mind, and it may even detract from the therapeutic value of the story to discuss it or to analyze it. After reading the story to the child or family the therapist can simply state, "I just wanted to share this story with you," and then go on to other matters. While the story features a magical "rainbow bridge," readers will note that Elfy still has a long and tiring journey to reach the bridge and he has many doubts along the way but he perseveres, fueled by hope of reunion with his circus family. When he reaches the narrow and high bridge he has to reach deep inside for courage to cross it.

Alternatives and Modification

Evocative Writing or Storytelling: "Brief Separations from Parents" Please write *or tell about a time when you were separated from your parents, even for a brief period of time. What was that experience like for you? How did you cope? What did you do?*

Evocative Narrative Stem: "Distracted and Lost at the Mall" A little girl went *with her mom to the mall. Her mother was looking at shoes, and the little girl whose name was* _____ [child supplies name] *saw the cutest stuffed animal, a little rabbit, she had ever seen. She went over to look at it and cuddle it. As she held the little bunny tightly she looked around, but she did not see her mother. She turned around and* _____ [child continues]. Follow-up questions appropriate to the child and the child's story can then be asked.

Evocative Directed Symbolic Play: "A Lost and Scared Rabbit"   *Let's pretend that the rabbit puppet is lost. She goes up to each of the other animal puppets and asks for help. She is scared and lonely. The other animals may be helpful or not. You decide that. Do you want to be the rabbit or to take the voice of the other animals?*

What follow-up is appropriate would depend on whether any of the other animals were helpful. If so (and if the therapist is playing those roles she/he can model helpful behaviors), there can be a discussion of calming, coping, and problem-solving skills. If the child takes the roles of the other animals and portrays them as unable or unwilling to help, or insists that the therapist taking the part of the other animals behave in an unhelpful manner, the therapist can engage the child in a discussion of whom to turn to for help or what signs to look for in deciding if someone should be approached for help. If the child can't engage in direct discussion of these issues, the therapist can remain in the metaphor and interview each of the animal puppets regarding these issues.

Evocative Role Playing: "Lost at the County Fair"   *Let's pretend that you are lost at a county fair in a huge crowd. Somehow you get separated from your family. Let's role-play what to do in a situation like that.*

Note that the child can be instructed to approach the therapist, who can take a number of roles, including policeman, employee at the fair, complete stranger, an unsavory character, etc. The child practices not only asking for help but also exercising good judgment as to whom to approach or not to approach for assistance.

EVOCATIVE PROJECTIVE DRAWING AND STORYTELLING STRATEGY: "THE TRAIN HAS LEFT THE STATION"

The Story

Michael and his sister Michelle were traveling with their grandparents on a trip to the western states. Their grandparents had planned this trip over a long period of time, and Michael, twelve, and his sister, Michelle, ten, had been looking forward to it for the past year. Since Michael was a tiny tot the grandparents had talked about taking him and his sister on a trip out West by train. Michael and his sister lived in Washington, D.C., and this was their first chance to see the magnificent Rocky Mountains.

The family changed trains in Denver, and since the grandparents always liked to board trains as early as possible, they had been sitting on board for twenty minutes when Michael told his grandparents he wanted to go to the bathroom. As he was returning to his seat he remembered a sporting goods store in the terminal that sold Colorado Rockies baseball caps. His grandparents had told him when they passed the store, "We don't have time now," but Michael figured that he could make a quick run and return with plenty of time to spare.

He ran to the store and quickly paid for his baseball cap. As he left the store, however, he saw a backpack with the Rockies' insignia. It was just what he had been looking for. He had wanted to bring a backpack on the trip, but his was pretty beat up, so he had left it at home. It took a while before the sales clerk could wait on him, and he was getting a little nervous, but he reminded himself of how early his grandparents always boarded the train.

In a few minutes he had paid for the backpack and ran as fast as he could back to the train. When he reached gate 48A, however, he panicked. The train was moving. He raced to catch it, but he couldn't; the train had left the station.

Drawing Directives

Please picture Michael in your mind. You can picture him on the train with his sister and grandparents, in the sporting goods store, or racing to catch the train. When you have that picture in mind, please draw it as best you can.

Follow-Up to the Drawing

1. *Tell me about your drawing.*
2. *What is Michael feeling in your picture?*
3. *What title would you choose for your drawing?*
4. *What mistakes did Michael make?*
5. *Do you think that Michael might be a kid who often acts before thinking the situation through?*
6. *Please give the reasons or signs that made you answer the above question the way you did.*
7. *What do you think Michael's sister and grandparents felt when they realized he was not on the train?*

Storytelling Directives

I want you to think about how Michael was feeling, his total panic, when he realized the train had pulled out of the station. Please make up a story about what happened next. Tell in your story what Michael did once he realized he had missed his train. Describe the feelings of all the people involved in the story. Consider the different options that Michael has and which one you think he picked. Give your story a beginning, a middle part, and an ending.

Follow-Up to the Story

1. *What title would you give your story?*
2. *What feeling comes up the most strongly for you as you think about your story?*
3. *What do you think about the choices that Michael made in your story to solve the problem?*
4. *What can be learned from your story?*
5. *Has anything like this ever happened to you?*

Clinical Illustration: (Natasha, Age Twelve)

Nastasha drew a picture of Michael chasing the train with his shopping bag and his Rockies cap sticking out of the bag and in the hand his new Rockies backpack.

Therapist: Tell me about your picture.

Natasha: That's Michael running toward the train; he doesn't catch it.

Therapist: What is Michael feeling in your picture?

Natasha: Mad—mad at the cashier for taking a long time.

Therapist: What title would you give your picture?

Natasha: "The Last Step"

Therapist: Can you explain your title to me?

Natasha: The picture shows him taking his last step before he realizes he is not going to catch the train. He knows he is too late.

Therapist: What mistakes did Michael make?

Natasha: Not seeing the backpack earlier, not listening to his grandfather, going back to get the backpack anyway.

Therapist: Do you think Michael may be the kind of kid who makes a habit of doing things without thinking them through?

Natasha: Yeah, probably, because when he decided to get the backpack he didn't go back to see if he had enough time.

Therapist: What do you think Michael's sister and grandparents felt when they realized he was not on the train?

Natasha: Very worried, mad—because it will prevent them from seeing the Rockies—because they will have to go back and get him.

Alternatives and Modifications

Evocative Directive Symbolic Play: "Missed Connections"   The following scenario will serve as an example. The child is asked to choose two puppets and pick the one he or she wishes to use. Then the child is told, "Let's pretend that these two play characters had made a plan to meet somewhere. Where should we have them meet? Okay, they will meet over here at the post office. Now let's pretend that the little boy shows up but his father is not there. The little boy looks all around, but he is not there. Now let's play out what happens next."

The therapist titrates the level of challenge in reuniting the child with the parent; the reunion should happen quickly in the case of a highly anxious child but made increasingly challenging for a less anxious child. This symbolic-play scenario would allow the therapist, through the play characters, to model and reinforce coping, calming, and problem-solving skills.

Evocative Narrative Stem: "Baby Tiger Looking for His Mother"   *Once there was a baby tiger separated from his mother. He was tired, sad, and lonely. He had cried for his mother and looked for her until his tired legs gave out. He decided to lie down for a while and then* _____ [child continues]. Follow-up questions should remain in the metaphor unless the child initiates direct discussion.

EVOCATIVE SCENARIO: "FRIENDS SEPARATED IN THE CITY" (ADOLESCENTS)

"Once there were two young teenage girls who were excited because their parents had given them permission for the first time to go to New York City together on the train to see a show. The parents based their permission on the clear understanding that the two girls would stick together and neither would wander off even for a short time. The two girls readily agreed, and when the day came they had a good trip to the city on the train. When they arrived at the station Mary wanted to stop at the restroom, and Jenny said, pointing just a few feet away, 'I will meet you at that newsstand.' When Mary came out of the restroom, Jenny was not there. She looked over at the newsstand, but there were no signs of Jenny. She started to panic, and her mind went blank. She could hardly move."

This evocative scenario can be followed up with questions like, "What happened next?" or "How did this story end?" The questions could also focus on strategies for Mary to use to stay calm, to problem-solve, and to seek assistance. The adolescent could be asked, "What are five steps that Mary could take that would be helpful in this situation?"

Evocative Writing or Stories: "Separation Panic"

The teen is directed to write or tell a story about a time when he or she or an acquaintance missed connections with someone and it triggered fear or panic until the reconnection was made.

Discussion

This story captures not only the anxiety and sometimes panic associated with separation from loved ones or friends but the psychologically potent theme "of being left behind." In America schools are under pressure to keep up with the federal mandates of "No Child Left Behind." Many children *are* left behind, however, not just for academic reasons but also due to emotional, social, and sociocultural factors. Children of extreme poverty understand early on that they are "not on the same train" as their more privileged peers. Some kids are academically on target but lagging significantly behind their cohorts socially. Others are emotionally immature or significantly impaired due to mood disorders, behavioral disturbances, or more serious forms of emotional disturbance consisting of thought disturbance. Others may suffer from various developmental disorders, such as Asperger's syndrome or nonverbal learning disabilities. A significant number of children are left behind in one way or another.

Another evocative theme implicit in the original story is "missed connections." ADHD (attention deficit hyperactivity disorder) children and Michael certainly exhibit some of those characteristics, such as impulsive behavior, poor planning, failure to anticipate consequences, and poor time estimation. Missed connections for these children often include being late for school or for class; failing to bring home the books they need; forgetting to turn their homework in or to study for a test; losing their textbooks; and so on. Their life is a steady stream of "missed connections." They miss the point of a joke and laugh at the wrong time. They miss teachers' instructions and get most of their assignments wrong, and understanding only part of the question the teacher asks they say something that is embarrassing in response. These cumulative "missed connections" are humiliating and heartbreaking for these kids.

Children with Asperger's syndrome also are prone to" miss the train," particularly in their interpersonal relationships. Their rigidity and social oddities leave them vulnerable to being "out of sync" with their social world and a target for teasing and sometimes bullying by peers. They, like all the other children left behind in one way or another, experience frequently the pain of missing out on something important that they see others able to enjoy. These children experience almost daily the anguish that their "train has left the station," and no matter how fast they run to catch it, the attempt is futile, the train has already departed. Also implicit in this story is the underlying theme of loss. The children who are left behind experience losses that tend to be cumulative and compounded throughout their developmental years.

EVOCATIVE CBT "CHILD-FRIENDLY" STRATEGIES:
"THREE STEP FEAR/TERROR MODULATION"

The work of Bruce Perry (1997) has demonstrated that aggression/violence is often driven by the neurobiology of chronic fear and terror. The brain literally gets shaped and organized around the perception of threat and danger for youngsters who grow up in environments where danger is constantly lurking around the next corner.

- *The Fear Monster*—the child artistically expresses the degree of fear experienced in a frightening situation through the metaphor of the fear monster.
- *The Tidal Wave of Terror*—the symbol of a tidal wave, perhaps the most terrifying of all natural catastrophes, depicts the level of fear.
- *Petrified Bunny*—bunnies are typically viewed by children as particularly defenseless and vulnerable in the animal world, so they serve as particularly rich symbols of fear. Alternatives would include a lamb, kitten, or puppy.
- *The Voiceless Parrot*—this can be a powerful symbol, since the parrot is usually quite talkative, but we know terror often leaves a person voiceless.

Step One: Scaling through Artistic Depiction

The child is asked to pick one of the metaphors above to depict fear or terror. The bunny is offered as an example because it tends to evoke feelings of relative helplessness and vulnerability. The voiceless parrot is offered as an example of the "mute with terror" phenomenon, well known in trauma work. Van der Kolk (1999) and others have explained the neurobiological basis of such voicelessness by describing how the Brocchia area of the brain, responsible for language, tends to shut down in emotional states associated with trauma. The fear monster allows the child considerable leeway in artistic depiction of the degree of experienced fear, and the tidal wave is often a symbol of the worst of nature's destructive forces.

The child is instructed to pick a symbol and to show in an artistic creation just how scared he or she felt in a particular situation or "when the worst or scariest thing happened." Obviously, this strategy, like most of the strategies in this book, would be used only in the Invitational Track, after the child has a solid relationship with the therapist. The goal is to facilitate graded exposure to fear, anxiety, and panic. This strategy also teaches scalability, an essential feature of affect modulation, by emphasizing degrees of fear. Children learn that emotions need not be experienced in an all-or-none fashion.

Step Two: Verbal Mediation

The child is encouraged in this step to put the intense fear or terror into words. The therapist can say, "If the parrot could speak, what would those words be?" If the child agrees, the therapist writes the words on the child's picture of the parrot. If the child prefers, use a separate sheet of paper for either the child or the therapist to record the words to be used.

It is crucial to facilitate as many alternative verbal expressions of the fear/terror as possible. Don't accept the first meager offerings as the best the child can do. The child may need the therapist to model some choices, or in some cases to offer a menu of options, but it is critical that the child get practice and reinforcement in using language to express these powerful affects. Framing her/his experience in words helps to integrate the fragments that are the remnants of terrifying experiences, and especially traumatic experiences.

Step Three: Problem Solving

In fear modulation, the problem-solving step is focused on ways to create safety. The therapist and child/family collaborate to develop a safety plan. Steps are defined to be followed when threats of various levels of danger emerge. A protocol can be developed that might include such steps as:

- Stay calm.
- Remember that you think more clearly when you stay calm, so take a deep breath.
- A reminder of competence ("I've handled tough situations before").
- "Is this a situation that I need to call 911?" "Who else should I notify?"
- "Is there a place I need to go that will enable me to be safer at this moment?"

The child and/or family become co-architects of the plan and have stakes in it. The child is helped to be aware of internal, interpersonal, and community resources that she/he can call on. Evocative strategies to highlight these resources are detailed in chapter 11. It would also be a good time to utilize the Projective Drawing and Storytelling Strategy of "The Ballistic Stallion" (Crenshaw, 2004), which is one of my favorite techniques for honoring the courage and fighting spirit of children. "The Ballistic Stallion" focuses the child on past triumphs in overcoming adversity. As Bonime (1982) pointed out, "Reassurance is empty, of little or no help; true help derives from locating genuine strength and inner resources in the client." Then the subject's strength is not dependent in any way on the therapist.

Alternatives or Modifications

The child may prefer other mediums and materials, such as clay, collages, sandplay pictures, or watercolor painting to artistically portray the intensity of fear. Also, they may come up with their own symbols that may capture the level of fear more vividly than the ones suggested above. Children have taught me most of what I know about how best to reach them. We should always listen and honor their choices.

Evocative Use of Symbols: "What Fear Looks Like?" The children are asked to pick from a collection of miniatures the symbol that best reveals their degree of fear in a specific situation. They are then asked to explain why they chose that particular object to symbolize their fear.

Evocative Imagery, Fantasy, and Drawing Strategy: "A Super-Safe Home" *I want you to try to imagine a home so safe that kids never worry about harm to anyone in the family. The home is so safe that kids never have any problems going to sleep; in fact, they fall asleep in their super-safe home as soon as their head hits the pillow. The home is so safe and secure that the children in the house only have pleasant dreams, never bad dreams. Just hold that image of your completely safe, comfortable home for as long as you want. When you are ready, if your eyes are still closed, you may gradually open them.*

Drawing Directives

I would like you to please draw your super-safe home in whatever way you picture it in your mind. If you pictured the house from the outside, or the inside, or just a particular room in the house, please draw it as best you can in whatever way you imagined it.

Follow-Up

1. *Tell me about your safe home.*
2. *Who else lives in the home with you?*
3. *Is there anything else you can think of that would make it safer for you?*
4. *What are the three most important features of this home that make it super safe for you?*
5. *Is there anything you would like to add or change about the way you imagined your super-safe home or the way you drew it that would make you like it better?*

EVOCATIVE PLEASANT MEMORIES:
"MY MOST PLEASANT DREAM"

Directives

Please try to replay in your mind the most pleasant dream you can remember. Take your time and try to remember as much as you can about your most pleasant dream. When you are ready please describe your most pleasant dream.

Follow-Up

Is there anything you would like to add or change about your pleasant dream that would make it even more pleasant?

Evocative Drawing: "My Favorite Dream"

Please draw as best you can your favorite dream. Put in as many details as you can.

Follow-Up to the Drawing

1. *Tell me about your drawing.*
2. *What is your favorite part of the dream?*
3. *Is this a dream you have often?*
4. *Have your tried rehearsing in your mind your favorite dream before going to sleep?* [Kids are often surprised how well that works.]
5. *Do you think you could use your rich imagination to create a dream even more pleasant than the one you described? If so, please do so now, take your time, and when you are ready please describe it to me.*
6. *Feel free to draw a picture of your new, creative dream if you wish.*

Alternatives or Modifications

If children can't remember a pleasant dream, ask them to make one up. Tell them to describe the most pleasant dream they can imagine, the kind of dream they would like to have every night.

EVOCATIVE NARRATIVE STEM: "A BEAUTIFUL SUNSET"

If children have a hard time remembering or creating a pleasant dream, the therapist can help get them started: "I was lying on the beach watching a beautiful sunset, my whole family was there, and we were all looking at the beautiful sky, and _____ [the child continues]."

Alternatives or Modifications

Evocative Rituals: "Shield of Safety" Some children develop rituals of their own at bedtime in which they create their own shields of safety. They may arrange stuffed animals in a specific configuration that provides a sense of comfort before sleep, or they may cuddle a special blanket that serves as a transitional object providing comfort when separated from their parents at night during sleep. Other children may need direction from the therapist and/or parents to develop such rituals. Children may draw comfort from objects that symbolize safety. They may wish to hold a "safe stone" or "magic stone" or some other object symbolizing safety or protection, which they hold in a leather or felt pouch and clutch tightly during the night. A picture of their parents next to their bed may be helpful to some children; holding something that belongs to Mom or Dad may provide comfort. Some may adopt a "guardian angel" that looks after them through the night. These symbolic representations of safety and security are more likely to be effective with children whose terror originates from internal sources, fantasized demons and monsters. If the problem originates in fantasy, so can the solution (Furman and Ahola, 1992).

Traumatized children, in contrast, have experienced in reality events too terrifying to assimilate within the psychic at the time of their occurrence. Their sense of terror does not arise from fantasy or a vivid imagination, although the fear derived from direct experiences may be intensified by fantasy embellishments or distortions of perception or memory. They too may develop, either spontaneously or with the help of caregivers, nighttime rituals that are helpful to going to sleep. They are likely, however, to be more assured by concrete reminders of their safety, such as accompanying the parent who locks up the house or sets the security alarm, or observing the dog lying at the foot of the bed, or being reminded that adults are just a few feet down the hall.

Evocative Drawing and Imagery: "Protective Shield" A modification of this intervention consists of inviting the child to draw a picture of a big shield with the names of all his or her protectors on the shield.

Evocative Drawing and Imagery: "Survival Badge" As a way of honoring and highlighting ways that kids have learned to keep safe, they can draw and cut out a large survival badge. They can write on their survival badge all the ways they have learned to keep safe. For kids who have experienced trauma, this is a way of accentuating what they have learned in the way of survival skills, skills that they did not have at the time of the trauma events. Kids who face violence as a part of their everyday lives will be able to share the street-wise savvy that has enabled them to stay alive.

Discussion

Children who are overwhelmed with nighttime fears or frequent bad dreams, and traumatized children, whose shield of safety has been shattered, lose sight of the people, including family members and pets in their own house, who are there to protect them. Their fears, their heightened sense of vulnerability, leads them to believe that threat and danger is ever present. This is true whether the imminent threat is a product of an overly anxious child's imagination or due to the demolished sense of safety that results from exposure to trauma.

Concrete reminders of those people who are present in their lives, perhaps just a few feet down the hall, while they are sleeping—or in the case of a pet, at the foot of their bed—can be helpful. They can keep the visual reminder of their "Protective Shield" and refer to it just before bedtime or any other time they need reminders that they are surrounded by people who love and care about them. This technique can be used even with children in out-of-home care by asking them to name the people in their present living situation who are there to help and protect them.

FEAR AND TERROR RELATED TO VIOLENCE

Evocative Drawing: "The Tidal Wave"

If ever a picture was worth a thousand words, this one certainly is. No words could come close to adequately depicting the intensity of the fear experienced by this child as she witnessed a terrifying incident of domestic violence that she was helpless to prevent, as illustrated by the huge tidal wave approaching the tiny, vulnerable depiction of self. Yet expressing their intense fears in the realm of symbolization provides for children natural modulation and a sense of mastery.

Projective Drawing and Storytelling Technique: "The Dog Who Hid beneath the Cabinet"

A note of caution—children who have been maltreated may find this story disturbing. I would recommend that the therapist tell the child before reading the story that it is a story about a dog named Sammy that was adopted by a nice family but was very scared because it had not been treated well in the past. Ask

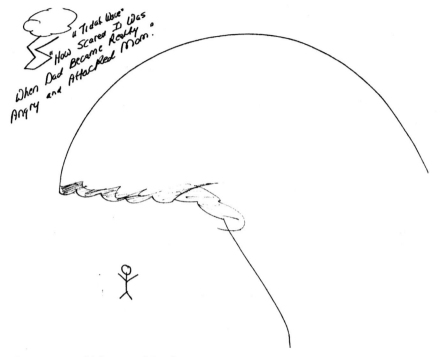

Figure 7.1.   "Tidal Wave of Fear"

if the child wants to hear the story; if they say, "No," I would recommend going on to another story or strategy. I would not try to talk them into it. Their defenses need to be honored and respected in order for therapy to be a safe place. If they later want to hear the story when they are stronger and ready for it, it can be read at that point.

The Story.   A kind and warmhearted family by the name of Meadows took in a dog they found at the animal shelter. The dog had been mistreated. Its name was Sammy. He was a beautiful dog, with a mix of German shepherd and black Lab. Sammy was also smart and learned quickly the routine and proper behavior expected in the Meadows family.

The Meadows had two daughters, Linda, who was twelve, and Glenda, who was ten. The girls, like their parents, loved all animals. In spite of the love this family gave, however, Sammy would often hide under a cabinet in the utility room next to the kitchen. Other times he would startle at a sudden movement or a loud noise. It was sad for the family to see. They understood that Sammy had been mistreated, but they hoped that with all the love they gave him that those scars would gradually heal. Most of the time, in fact, Sammy seemed happy and loved to romp with the two girls in the backyard. He loved to take walks in the evening with Mr. and Mrs. Meadows, but when there was a loud noise in the neighborhood or a sudden movement, even by family members, Sammy would still jump in a startled, frightened manner and seek refuge under the cabinet in the utility room, where he felt safe. Each time he did the Meadows family was sadly reminded of how badly he had been treated in the past.

Drawing Directives.   Try to picture Sammy living with the Meadows family. What is he doing? Where do you picture him? Is he out in the yard romping with the girls? Is he taking a walk with the parents? Is he hiding under the cabinet?

Follow-Up to the Drawing

1. *Tell me about your drawing.*
2. *What title would you give your drawing?*
3. *What is the strongest feeling that you experience when you look at your drawing?*
4. *What are some of the ways that Sammy shows that he was mistreated before he came to the Meadows' home?*
5. *Why do you think the love of the Meadows' family is not enough to make Sammy feel completely safe?*

Storytelling Directives.   Think about Sammy for a moment and how you think things will turn out for him in the long run, living in the Meadows family. Do you think someday he will feel completely safe and no longer run to his hiding place beneath the cabinet? Make up a story about how it turned out for Sammy and the Meadows family after Sammy had been with them for three years.

Follow-Up to the Story

1. *What title do you choose for your story?*
2. *What is the feeling that you experience the most strongly in reaction to your story?*
3. *Why do you think that love is not always enough to heal the scars of animals that have been mistreated?*
4. *How do you think the Meadow's family felt when they were trying their best and yet they could not make Sammy feel completely safe, at least for a long time?*
5. *Have you ever known of an animal that was mistreated like Sammy?*

Alternatives or Modifications

Evocative Scenario: "The Bear Cub Who Was Too Rough"   "There was once a bear cub that was bigger and stronger than the other bear cubs, and he was too rough with the little ones. He sometimes hurt the little bears because he didn't know his own strength. The papa bear took the bear cub aside and did some roughhouse play with him and showed him how easy it is to overpower another cub if you are bigger and stronger. Under the watchful eye of his papa the bear cub gradually learned to play with the other cubs without hurting them, and they all began to have more fun."

Discussion.   It is important to stay in the metaphor when dealing with issues of violence and abuse unless children demonstrate their capacity to deal with it more directly. The above scenario is less threatening than some alternatives that could be used, because the story implies that the bigger cub was not intentionally hurting the smaller cubs. Follow-up questions could include, "What are the things the cub needed to learn before he could play safely with the other cubs?" "If you could talk with the bear cub, what advice would you give him?" "Why did the papa bear continue to watch the aggressive cub play with the others?"

Evocative Narrative Stem: "The Papa Tiger with a Bad Temper"

"Once there was a papa tiger that had a bad temper. When the little tigers would wander off, he would smack them with his giant paws and send them rolling down the hill. The mama tiger was worried about this and one day took the papa tiger aside and said, _____ [child continues from here]."

Discussion.   While still remaining in metaphor, this technique would be more threatening than the previous one, because the papa tiger had a bad temper and mistreated his cubs. Follow-up questions could include: "Did the papa tiger learn not to hit the cubs?" "What did the tiger cubs do after the papa tiger hit them?" "What do you think the tiger cubs felt when this happened?" "How did things turn out in the long run?"

Evocative Directive Symbolic Play: "Help for the Papa Tiger"   The above narrative stem could be used for a directed symbolic-play scenario in which not only the mama tiger but the other animals pass by, one by one, and try to help the papa tiger find other ways to discipline his tiger cubs.

Evocative Role-Playing Scenarios: "The Tiger Cubs Find Their Voices"   Let's pretend the papa tiger could talk and the tiger cubs also. Let's pretend the papa tiger is in a good mood and each of the tiger cubs, one by one, talks to him about how they feel when he hits them. The therapist may need to go first and let the child observe as he or she assumes the voice of each of the tiger cubs expressing how it feels to be mistreated.

Evocative Drawing Strategy: "The Tiger Family in the Future"   Draw a picture of the papa tiger and the little tiger cubs together as you imagine them to be six months after the mama tiger took the papa aside to talk to him about how he was treating the cubs. This picture would likely reveal the child's view of how likely change is when a parent or other caregiving adult has a problem with anger.

EVOCATIVE WRITING OR STORY:
"WHEN AN ADULT LOSES IT" (ADOLESCENTS)

Please write or tell about a time when you witnessed an adult who was out of control with anger. If not covered in the story, the follow-up would include questions like, "What did you do?" "What did you feel?" "Did you turn to someone for help?" "Did you tell anybody about what happened?"

Projective Drawing and Storytelling Technique: "The Land of No Harm"

The Story.   There was once upon a time in a faraway land a place known as "The Land of No Harm." The people who lived in this land were in most ways like folks everywhere; the kids went to school, and their parents went to work and raised their children, paid their bills, and mowed their lawns. One thing, however, was special about this land—no one had to worry about being harmed. Every citizen, regardless of age, gender, or race, could walk the streets of their cities and towns without fear, even at night. Those who lived in this special land had the usual problems of the rest of us—the children had school-related problems, the parents worried about money problems—but one problem they did not face was violence, because they lived in The Land of No Harm.

Drawing Directives.   Picture The Land of No Harm in anyway you wish. There is no right way. When you have a picture clearly in mind, please draw it as best you can.

Follow-Up to the Drawing
1. *What would be a good title for your drawing?*
2. *What would be a good one-word title for your drawing?*
3. *Why do you think violence is such a concern in our world?*
4. *Do you have some ideas about how to reduce violence in the world?*
5. *How would your life be different if you lived in "The Land of No Harm?"*
6. *Do you fear being a victim of violence?*
7. *Has anyone you know ever been a victim of violence?*
8. *Have you ever hurt someone in a fit of anger?*
9. *If so, how did you feel afterward?*

Storytelling Directives.   If you have known anyone whose life has been affected by violence, please tell the story of what happened. If you have not known anyone who has been a victim of violence, make up a story about the kind of violence you worry about the most.

Follow-Up to the Story
1. *On a ten-point scale with 10 the best and 1 the worst, rate how safe you feel in the world.*

2. *Can you think of any changes that would make your world safer?*

3. *Do you think we could ever live in a world like "The Land of No Harm?" Please explain your answer.*

4. *Do you think that we have to live with some amount of risk as just a part of life? Please explain your answer.*

5. *Is there a person in your life who you consider to be "a safe person," someone who makes you feel safe when he/she is with you?*

6. *Have you ever made anyone else, perhaps a little brother or little sister, or younger child or friend, feel safer? If so, please tell about that experience.*

Clinical Illustration: "Follow-Up to Pete's Drawing"

Pete drew a picture of a charming, quiet-looking village.

Therapist: Tell me about your drawing.

Pete: Everyone is a nice person, no harm, no violence, no policemen; people are friendly. No one has weapons. There is a fireman, but no police, because there is no violence. People are happy here.

Therapist: What title would you choose for your picture?

Pete: "A Crime-Free City."

Therapist: Can you think of a one-word title?

Pete: "Harm-Free."

Therapist: Why do you think violence is such a big concern in the world today?

Pete: The world is not like "The Land of No Harm." Some people are full of hatred and will hurt others.

Therapist: Do you have some ideas about how to reduce violence in the world?

Pete: Try to make laws that everyone is happy with, eliminate racism, avoid wars. It seems nearly impossible to have a world like that.

Therapist: How would your life be different if you lived in "The Land of No Harm?"

Pete: I would worry less about the unexpected things happening, like someone trying to kill me.

Therapist: Sounds like you fear being a victim of violence?

Pete: Sometimes, like when I go to New York City. Sometimes people get mugged when they least expect it. I worry about terrorists a lot.

Therapist: Has anyone you know ever been a victim of violence?

Pete: I don't think so.

Therapist: Have you ever hurt someone in a fit of anger?

Pete: I hit a younger boy in a fit of anger when he wouldn't share the TV.

Therapist: How did you feel afterward?

Pete: I felt sorry; he is just a little boy.

Pete's Story

This boy lived in New York City, and he was a worry-free kid. One day when he was fifteen, he was on the way to a store to buy a video game for a kid who was having a birthday. This man pulled him into a storefront, an abandoned building, and he said, "Give me your money!" The kid said, "What?" The man said, "Give me your money!" The guy was really scary. The kid was shocked, and said, "What?" The man shouted, "Give me your money!" The kid gave him his money and the man yelled, "Get out of here!" and kicked him out of the store. He told his mother but they never caught the man.

Follow-Up to the Story

Therapist: On a ten-point scale, with 10 the best and 1 the worst, rate how safe you feel in the world right now.
   Pete: 7.
   Therapist: Can you think of any changes that would make the world feel safer?
   Pete: Increase in police, who could move with the speed of light. Also, keep a cell phone with you at all times. Have an emergency shelter that would protect from bombs.
   Therapist: Do you think we could ever live in a world like "The Land of No Harm?
   Pete: Not very likely; there are too many people full of anger and hate.
   Therapist: Do you think that some amount of risk is just a part of life?
   Pete: There really shouldn't be, but I guess it really is, and we should do our best to avoid it.
   Therapist: Is there a person or persons in your life who you consider to be a safe person or safe persons for you, someone who makes you feel safe when you are with them?
   Pete: Mom and Dad, and policemen. They know how to deal with it.
   Therapist: Have you ever made anyone else, perhaps a little brother or sister, or younger child or friend, feel safer?
   Pete: I don't believe so.

Alternatives or Modifications

   Evocative Drawing: "Your Safe Place"   Please draw a picture of a "safe place" that either exists in the real world or one that you create in your mind. It might be a *tree house or a fort you built in the backyard or an imaginary cave or secret hiding place. When you have a picture of your "safe place" please draw it as best you can.*

Evocative Writing or Story: "Shelter from the Storm"   Pretend that a bad storm was coming and you had to create a "shelter from the storm." Write or tell about your safe shelter. What would it consist of? What would it look like? Who else would you want to have with you to ride out the storm? Tell in your story how things turned out.

EVOCATIVE DIRECTIVE SYMBOLIC PLAY: "MAKING A SAFE PLACE"

Let's pretend that we need to make a safe place in case of danger. Just pretending, what kind of danger should we protect ourselves from? Using the materials in the room, let's see if we can make a really safe place. Do you think one of us should be the boss, or can we work together as a team on this project? Okay, let's get to it.

Discussion

The terror events that are a part of our current world are frightening to kids as well as adults. The fantasy of a place of "no harm" has great appeal to kids. Since kids seen in clinical settings have typically been exposed to more than their share of frightening events, these particular strategies may offer comfort and also offer tools for self-calming, using symbolization and fantasy to create "safe spaces," even if only in their minds, to counter the diffuse anxiety that is a part of contemporary life. "The Land of No Harm" and the alternatives are appropriate strategies for kids in both the Coping and Invitational tracks of therapy.

EVOCATIVE SCENARIO: "WHEN THE UNTHINKABLE HAPPENS" (ADOLESCENTS)

Directives to the Adolescent

Now I want you to take a deep breath and try to remember what you were doing on September 11, 2001, when you first learned that the Twin Towers and Pentagon had been hit by planes. Where were you when you heard the news? Were you in school, at home, or somewhere else? Who told you the horrible news? You can share your experience in any way you like. You can draw it, write about it, or simply tell about it.

Follow-Up

1. *Tell about the picture* [if the child made a drawing].
2. *What did you feel when you first heard the news?*
3. *Did you know anyone who died in the New York City or Pentagon attacks?*
4. *Were you afraid for your family's safety on that day, no matter how far away they were from the areas that were hit?*
5. *Did you watch the replays of the planes hitting the buildings on TV? If so, did you have nightmares afterward?*
6. *What helped you the most to cope with these tragic events?*

Directives to the Child

Now I would like you to think about the stories you have heard about people helping other people when 9/11 occurred. Besides the heroic acts of firefighters and the police, ordinary citizens did brave, kind, and helpful things for their fellow citizens. Can you tell or write a story or draw someone you know or heard about who did something brave, kind, or helpful to others on that day or the days that followed?

Alternative Directions

If you don't know of such a story please make up a story about how you or someone else could be helpful to others after such a disaster.

Follow-Up

1. *Why did you pick this particular story to tell?*
2. *What would be a good title to your story?*
3. *If this story is about someone else, can you remember something you did that was kind, thoughtful, or helpful to someone else right after 9/11?*
4. *Can you remember anything kind or helpful that someone did for you* [unless this is contained in the child's story] *after 9/11?*
5. *Who was the person or pet that was most helpful to you at the time?*
6. *Do you feel safe in the world now? How long after 9/11 did it take for you to feel safe again?*
7. *Many people who help others cope with such horrible things believe it is helpful to talk about or draw what happened. Others believe it is best not to think or talk about it. What do you think?*

Alternatives or Modifications

Evocative Writing or Stories: "Helpful to Others"   *Write or tell a story of someone you know or heard about who was helpful to others on that terrible day.*

Evocative Narrative Stem: "Heartwarming Tales" There were many inspiring stories told about the brave men and women who put their own lives on the line in order to help or save someone else. The story that touched my heart the most was the story of _____ [adolescent continues].

Discussion

I, along with millions of Americans, will never forget the day President Kennedy was shot or the terrible day when the planes hit the Twin Towers and the Pentagon and the heroic passengers forced down the plane in Pennsylvania. When President Kennedy was shot, I was on my way home from college. I was halfway home when I got a flat tire. After I changed the tire my favorite radio station broadcast a news bulletin from Dallas. A whole generation of Americans will always remember those fateful words: "President Kennedy has been shot." I arrived home and turned on the TV just in time hear Walter Cronkite announce the dreaded news: "President John F. Kennedy is dead."

Lenore Terr (2003), an expert in psychic trauma of children, noted that 9/11, because of the repeated exposure on television to the graphic scenes of the planes hitting the buildings and the Twin Towers collapsing, produced in some children *distant trauma*. These children may have lived on the West Coast, several thousand miles away from the disaster, but because of the replay of the horrific scenes on television nevertheless experienced traumatic reactions. When trauma events occur, one of the most disturbing effects can be the shattering of core assumptions and beliefs held by a person. The world no longer feels safe. Parents, police, and government are unable to protect us from such atrocities. Children may feel betrayed and angry because the safety net some of them took for granted is suddenly pulled out from under them. This evocative technique is designed to stimulate dialogue about the issue of the uncertainty and potential terror that is part of our contemporary world and a source of anxiety, worry, and fear for many children and adults alike.

While this exercise focuses on the vulnerability that is part of modern life, it also focuses on potential coping strategies and one of the most important traits in resilient children, *helping others*. Giving to others counteracts feelings of helplessness and powerlessness, and it elevates self-worth. It can also help children achieve a more balanced perspective by realizing that while there are terrorists capable of producing great harm to many, there are also many people in the world who are kind, compassionate, and go out of their way, sometimes taking great risks, to help others. In terms of meaning and perspective, many of us learned on that horrific day what is truly important in life—but how quickly we forget.

8

Themes of Conflict, Struggle, and Shame

*Y*oung children in play therapy often play out bitterly fought battles, conflicts between good and evil, life and death, power and helplessness, strength
versus vulnerability, love versus hate, to name just a few of the polarized forces
that permeate the life struggles of a child. The strategies in this chapter capture
some of these issues in the form of projective drawing and storytelling techniques as well as other evocative strategies.

SIBLING RIVALRY

A Projective Drawing and Storytelling Strategy:
"Who Is Sitting in the Front Seat?"

The Story.   There once was a girl named Sue who had a sister named
Ellen. Sue was eleven, and Ellen was twelve. Sue and Ellen fought about almost
everything. In fact, when they did not fight for a whole day their parents were
shocked and felt like celebrating the occasion. Their fights took many forms,
such as who was going to sit in the front seat of the family's minivan or who
was going to take the dog out for a walk. Other times they would fight over
whose turn it was to wash the dishes or to clean the cat litter box. They were
creative in their ability to invent new situations to fight about. But basically
their fighting was about who was going to win out over the other. Who would
have more privileges? Who would have the nicer clothes? Whom would their
mom and dad favor? Who would get away with something that the other got
punished for? And so the fighting continued, on and on.

123

Drawing Directives.   Close your eyes if you are comfortable doing so, relax, and try to get a picture in your mind of the two sisters, Sue and Ellen. What are they doing? Where are they? Are they at home? Are they at school? Are they on the playground? As you picture them in your mind, what is happening between them? Who else is there? What are the others doing? When you are ready, draw a picture of Sue and Ellen and show what is happening between them. Include others in the picture if you wish.

Follow-Up to Drawing

1. *Tell about your picture.*
2. *What is happening between the girls?*
3. *If others are included, what are they doing?*
4. *What title would you give your picture?*
5. *What are the girls feeling in your picture? How about the others who are there?*

Storytelling Directives.   Now I would like you to fast-forward a few years and imagine that the girls are now no longer fighting. In fact, they support one another, and each considers her sister to be her best friend. Make up a story about what has happened in the meantime that has changed the two girls so that they have given up their fight and now are close as sisters. Try to imagine what could have happened over the past few years to cause such a positive change. After you have reflected on it for a few minutes, please tell me the story.

Follow-Up to the Story

1. *What title would you give to your story?*
2. *Explain why the girls no longer fight.*
3. *Can you think of any other possible explanations?*
4. *Do you think one or the other could have ever won the fight?*
5. *What lessons can be learned from your story?*
6. *Is there anything you would like to add or change about your story?*
7. *Have you ever known anyone who fought as much as the two sisters in the story?*
8. *Suppose you were the guest speaker at a junior high school and you were asked to speak on the topic of why fighting doesn't pay; what are the main points you would make?*
9. *Are there any times when it makes sense to fight? Describe those times.*

Clinical Illustration: Hector's Story (Age Eleven)

"Their mother dies and there is a terrorist attack on the Empire State building. They are very sad and they tried to comfort each other and they realized they had a lot in common with each other."

Follow-Up to Hector's Story

Therapist: What title would you give your story?

Hector: "Caring."

Therapist: It took some terrible events, the death of their mother and a terrorist attack, to bring the two sisters together. Do you think there could be any other way they could have ended their battle?

Hector: I can't think of any.

Therapist: Do you think their fight could ever be won by either one of them?

Hector: Nope.

Discussion.   Sadly, Hector's story is played out in real life; family battles and feuds can be taken right to the grave. In Hector's story the two sisters fought the battle "that could not be won" until their mother died and another terrorist attack occurred. He did not feel that anything less catastrophic could have united the sisters.

THE BATTLE OF WILLS

Evocative Projective Drawing and Storytelling:
"The Head-On Collision at Meadows Elementary School"

The Story.   Not that long ago in a rural school district in the Northeast, there were two classmates: Sally, who was stubborn; and Willy, who also was strong-minded. They butted heads in the classroom, during recess, lunch, art, music, and also on the bus going to and from school. When at home with their families, Sally and Willy both engaged their parents in power struggles and fought with their brothers and sisters. No one who knew the pair could figure out why Sally and Willy couldn't resist battles with each other, or their families, or most others in their lives.

To other people, it seemed to make no sense. Sally and Willy were always trying to win the battle against each other, but it was clear to everyone who observed that no one was winning; in fact, they both were losing out on a lot. Both spent their days angry at each other, trying to figure out new and different ways to get back at the other. As a result, neither Willy nor Sally were having much fun. During recess, when other kids in the fifth grade were playing games or chatting with their friends, Willy and Sally were shouting threats at each other and calling each other insulting names. The other kids found the whole scene boring and were growing weary of it. Jake, a good basketball player and a likeable fifth grader, lost his patience one day at recess and shouted, "Why don't you two knock it off!"

That didn't stop Sally and Willie, however, because being right, showing the other who was boss, was more important than having fun. Sally's and Willy's teacher, Mrs. Jones, knew even before the school year started that she was going to have her hands full. The teachers who had had Sally and Willy in prior years said, "Those two fight like cats and dogs."

Another past teacher said, "Even though they are not brother and sister they fight more than any brother or sister I have ever known." Mrs. Jones was once standing in the middle of the playground and heard Sally yell at Willie, "You are a blooming idiot!" Willy quickly returned the insult by shouting, "You are dumber than a doorknob." As Mrs. Jones called the two over for yet another time to sit out the rest of recess, she tried to picture in her mind what Sally and Willy's lives would be like five years in the future. Since they were then eleven, she focused in her mind on what these two kids would be like at age sixteen. Would they still be fighting with each other? Would they still be fighting with their brothers and sisters? Would they still be battling with their families? Would they still have no friends? Would they still not be having any fun? Mrs. Jones wondered if their need to be right, to be the boss, to win every time would keep the fight going strong five years from then.

Drawing Directives.   *Try to get a picture of Willie and Sally in your mind. If you wish you can include other people in your picture. You can include scenery, like a school or a playground, if you like. It is your drawing, so do it anyway you choose. When you have a clear picture of Sally and Willy in mind, please draw it as best you can.*

Follow-Up to the Drawing
1. *Tell me about your drawing.*
2. *Where does your drawing take place [if not obvious or already explained above]?*
3. *What is the feeling you experience the most strongly when you look at your picture?*
4. *Is this a drawing of Willy and Sally when they are eleven or sixteen?*
5. *Does Willy or Sally remind you of anyone?*
6. *What title do you give to your picture?*

Storytelling Directives.   *I want you to think about Mrs. Jones standing in the middle of the playground and wondering what life would be like for Sally and Willy five years later when they are sixteen. Make up a story about Sally and Willy at sixteen. Think about the questions that Mrs. Jones was asking in her mind: "Would they still be fighting with each other?" "Would they still be fighting with their families?" "Would they still have no friends?" "Would they still be having no fun?" "Would their need to be right, to be the boss, to win every battle, keep their fight going strong even five years later?" Make up a story that answers these questions.*

Follow-Up to the Story
1. *What title would you give to your story?*
2. *If the fight is still going on, what do you think it would take to end it?*

Figure 8.1. "The head-on the collision at Meadows Elementary School" (Sally and Willy insulting each other)

3. *If the fight is continuing five years later, what price do you think Willy and Sally have paid to keep it going?*
4. *If you had a chance to talk with Sally and Willy what would you say to them?*
5. *Have you ever been in a battle with someone that you couldn't give up?*
6. *If so, and the battle is over, what ended it? If the fight is still going on, what would it take for you to let it go?*

ENSNARED IN THE PARENTAL CONFLICT

Evocative Projective Drawing and Storytelling: "Caught in the Crossfire" (Pre-teen or Adolescent)

The Story.   Sherry walked out of her bedroom into the hallway after her parent's yelling awakened her. She quickly realized that her parents were in the middle of another ugly fight. She felt cold shivers throughout her body. Sherry was seven years old; her brother Ivan, five years old, was still sleeping in his bed. Sherry clasped her hands over her ears to block out her parents' angry insults to each other. But covering her ears did not completely block out the hurtful words. She heard her mother yell, "Why don't you get out?"

Sherry heard her father yell back at her mother, "If anyone is going to leave, it is you!" At that point Sherry slipped back into her room, crawled back into bed, pulled the covers over her head, and sobbed. The next morning, Sherry was tired when she appeared for breakfast. Her mother, looking even more tired, said, "Your father was drunk last night, and he kept me up half the night." As she walked out of the room her mother told Sherry she would have to make her own breakfast; then, turning to Sherry, she said in a stern voice, "Don't you dare say anything to your father."

Drawing Directives.   *Try to picture Sherry in your mind. Where do you picture her? Fixing her breakfast? Listening to her mother? Outside her parents bedroom listening to her parents argue? In her bed crying? When you have a picture in your mind of Sherry, please draw your picture as best you can.*

Follow-Up to the Drawing
1. *What would be a good title for your drawing?*
2. *What is the strongest feeling Sherry is feeling in your picture?*
3. *Why did you choose to picture Sherry in this particular scene?*
4. *What do you think Sherry's day at school will be like?*
5. *When Sherry comes home and walks through the door after school, what do you think she will be worried about?*
6. *What do you think will happen in Sally's family over the long run?*

Storytelling Directives. *I want you to think about the crossfire that Sherry is caught in. Make up a story that begins when Sherry walks back into the house at the end of her school day after her parents' fight the night before. In your story talk about the situation that Sherry is in and how best she can cope with it.*

Follow-Up to the Story

1. *What title do you give to your story?*
2. *What do you think Sherry worries about the most?*
3. *Do you think it would be best for Sherry to keep her worries to herself or find someone she trusts to talk about them?*
4. *If you could give Sherry advice what would you tell her?*
5. *Do you think Sherry feels safe in her family? If not, what do you think she could do?*

Alternatives and Modifications

Evocative Directive Puppet Scenario: "Mommy and Daddy Arguing" *Let's pretend the mommy and daddy dolls are arguing. The little girl doll is listening in her room with her ears against the door. Let's play out what happens next.*

Evocative Writing or Story: "Overhearing the Parental Battle" *Please write or tell a story about a time when you or someone you know overheard mom and dad arguing. Include in your story how you or the child felt at the time this was happening and how it turned out in the end.* Note that by including the option of making the story about another child it allows for "safe distance" for the children who need it.

Evocative Narrative Stem: "Waking Up to Family Arguments" "The little boy woke up and he thought he heard noises downstairs. He walked out in the hall and he heard his mom and dad arguing. He decided to _____ [child continues]." Follow-up questions should remain within the metaphor unless the child initiates direct discussion.

Discussion

Children worry about their parents, but the fear that they will separate and break up the family is one of their most disturbing worries. Children caught in the destructive, emotional crossfire when the parental relationship hits the rocks are the innocent victims. The emotional atmosphere becomes poisonous. The children breathe every day the toxic air, polluted by the hostility between the two people they depend on the most. Their loyalty to both parents invariably puts them right in the crosshairs of parental hostility, because they can't be loyal to one parent without feeling disloyal to the other.

Figure 8.2.

EVOCATIVE IMAGERY: "THE 140-POUND WEIGHT ON MY BACK" (ADOLESCENTS)

Teens sometimes feel weighed down by their worries and concerns for parents or siblings. An adolescent who was quite worried about his depressed father after his mother left the home for another man told me that he felt he was carrying a 140-pound weight on his back. In the photo above of the "140-pound weight" it is interesting that the "weight" is actually a tombstone. He told me that he was afraid his father would kill himself. It became a useful metaphor throughout therapy. In early stages of the therapy this teen was surly, hostile, and angry at the whole world. He acted out aggressively and was frequently in trouble at school, but when he gained enough trust to share with me the heavy load he was carrying, I gained an appreciation of how depressed he was under the mask of his aggressive posture. Throughout therapy I would frequently check with him about how heavy the weight was that he still carried on his back. If he said, "About a hundred pounds," I would know that we were making progress but that he was still carrying too heavy a load. By the time of termination, he said, "It is about ten pounds, and that much I can carry without a problem—after all, I am a pretty strong kid." I said, "I agree with you."

Directives to the Adolescent

I want you to pretend that you could roll up all of your troubles, worries, fears, and hurts into a bundle that you could then carry on your back. Now try to picture that bundle. How big is it? How heavy is it? If you put it on a scale, how much would it weigh in pounds? What would it be like to carry that on your back at all times? Would it be too heavy? Or do you feel you can carry it without any discomfort?

Follow-Up

1. *If the load is too heavy, do you have some ideas about how to lighten it?*
2. *Are there some worries that you feel you could dump that you don't need to carry on your back?*
3. *Could you talk back to some of the worries, fears, hurts, and troubles and tell them to get off your back?*
4. *If so, what would you say to each one?*
5. *Who else in your family carries a heavy load?*
6. *Can you picture your load being lighter?*
7. *If so, how much would it weigh at that point?*
8. *What would have to change in order to make the load that much lighter?*
9. *What will be the hardest part of the load to let go?*

10. *If we were to view our work together as a way of lightening the load that you carry, do you think we are heading in the right direction, or do we need to change directions?*

Alternatives or Modifications

Evocative Drawing: "The Heavy Load"   "Draw a picture of that heavy weight on your back and show in your drawing if possible how hard it is to carry that much weight."

Evocative Narrative Stem: "A Bundle of Worries"   "An adolescent girl named Lynn was quite pretty and likable, but she did not have a boyfriend, nor did she have any close friends. She didn't really have a social life, because she was worried about her mother, with whom she lived. Her parents were divorced, and her mother drank heavily. She always worried about her mother when she was at school. One day Lynn _____ [adolescent continues]."

Evocative Writing or Story: "When the Load Is Too Heavy to Carry"   Write or tell about a time when the troubles you carry on your back just seemed too heavy. Tell in your story about what you did, how you felt, and how it turned out for you.

Evocative Saying: "Self-Imposed Burdens"   What are your reactions to the saying, "The heaviest burdens to carry are the ones we put on ourselves?" Do you agree with this saying? Please discuss why or why not. Do you think this is always true or just sometimes? What can be learned from this saying?

Discussion

I will always be grateful to my adolescent patient for teaching me this powerful metaphor. It immediately changed the way I viewed him and eventually the way he perceived himself. Clearly, he was not simply "just a bad kid." This metaphor is easy for most kids to relate to and can serve as a way of taking the child or teen's "emotional pulse" at different points in the therapy. One adolescent boy who had been violently abused by his father told me the weight on his back felt like "a thousand tons." The above follow-up questions are only beginning points in exploring the meaning of the weight that a given child carries on his/her back. When a teen uses a metaphor that clearly has significant meaning for him or her, it can be used to communicate in a condensed way throughout the therapy the degree of emotional pain the kid is experiencing.

EVOCATIVE DREAM SYMBOLS: "METAPHORS FOR THERAPY"

At times these metaphors may emerge from revealing dreams that the child shares with the therapist. A dream symbol such as "the car going off the cliff" may capture the terror of a child who feels his or her life is dangerously out of control. Throughout the therapy the therapist can inquire if that car is able to negotiate the curves on the cliff or if it is still in danger of going over the side. The therapist should use metaphors with powerful meaning for a given youngster but should never assume what the symbol means, instead exploring the meaning for the specific child.

Projective Drawing and Storytelling Technique:
"The Storm in the Night" (Pre-teens and Adolescents)

The Story.   Marsha awoke in a startle to the screams of her parents yelling hateful things at each other. What she tried to block out, but could not, were the words of her mother, "F——k you. I can't stand you anymore. Why don't you get the hell out?" Marsha also couldn't block out the equally angry response of her Dad, who shouted back, "Go to hell. You can't make me leave this house until I am good and ready."

Marsha rolled over on her side; she tried to cover her ears between the pillows to drown out the frightening noises and started to cry. Marsha was thirteen, and she had heard her parents fight numerous times, but it was always scarier when she woke up to the shouting in the night. Marsha was especially frightened this time, because the fights were getting worse. She was worried that her father might hurt her mother, and she also was petrified that they might split up. She wondered what would happen to her and her little brother Tommy, age four, if her parents got a divorce. Where would they live? Would they have to move? Would they have to change schools? Would she have to leave her friends? These were the questions that were hard to put out of her mind.

Finally, still unable to block the angry words from the downstairs living room, Marsha, with her heart racing and hands sweaty, got out of her bed and slowly made her way quietly downstairs. With each step down toward the battle scene her heart was beating so hard she feared it would jump out of her chest. When she reached the bottom step, she saw her mother on the couch, her face covered by her hands, sobbing loudly. Her Dad towered over her Mom, still yelling loudly until he saw Marsha out of the corner of his eye, at which point he stopped and yelled, "Marsha, go back to bed!" But Marsha impulsively ran toward her sobbing Mom, threw her arms around her, and tried to comfort her. At that point it was hard to say who was crying the hardest, her Mom or Marsha.

The site of mother and daughter huddled together comforting each other made her Dad angrier. He shouted at them, "Oh sure, it is always my fault, the two of you always blame me for everything. Thanks a hell of a lot. I guess I know where I stand in this family. And Marsha, for the last time, I am telling you to go back to bed. Right now!"

Marsha reluctantly let go of her mom and raced upstairs, crying louder than ever. When she reached her bed she dove under the covers and cried some more. The thoughts swirling in her head were, "Now I have made things worse. Daddy is really mad at me. If he leaves it is my fault. Why did I go downstairs? It was bad enough, but I made it worse." She eventually cried herself to sleep on a pillow wet from her tears.

Drawing Directives.   Please picture Marsha in whatever way comes to mind. You could picture her in her room, going down the stairs, or in the living room. When you have a picture clearly in mind, please draw it as best you can.

Follow-Up to the Drawing

1. *What is the strongest feeling that you get when you look at your picture?*
2. *What are the emotions that Marsha is experiencing in your picture?*
3. *Do you think Marsha made things worse between her parents by going downstairs and getting involved in her parents' fight?*
4. *If her parents separate, would it be Marsha's fault?*
5. *Suppose you had a chance to talk with Marsha, what advice would you give her? What would you say to her that might be helpful to her?*
6. *Have you known of anyone who was in a similar situation to Marsha's? If so what helped that person cope with such a difficult situation?*
7. *Why do you think young children often blame themselves for bad things that happen in the family?*

Storytelling Directives.   Now think about Marsha's difficult situation. Make up a story about what happens to her and her family. Do her parents eventually work out their problems, or do they go their separate ways? Make up the most interesting story you can.

Storytelling Follow-Up

1. *How do you think Marsha's parents' fighting affected her relationships with others?*
2. *What can be learned from your story?*
3. *What do you think are the best ways to cope when the parents often fight?*
4. *Can you think of some things that kids can say to themselves if they hear their parents fighting?*
5. *What helps you cope with a stressful situation?*
6. *Are there things that you have discovered that don't help?*

Alternatives or Modifications

Evocative Narrative Stem: "Trying to Stay out of the Middle"   "Michael tried his very best to stay out of the arguments between his parents. His parents fought a lot and sometimes he worried that someone would be hurt. One night when he was trying to go to sleep he heard _____ [child continues the story]."

Clinical Illustration: Tyrone (Age Thirteen)

Tyrone drew a picture of Marsha lying on her bed awake listening to her stereo.

Therapist: What would be a good title for your drawing?

Tyrone: "Drowning Out." She is trying to drown out the noise of her parents fighting by turning the stereo up loud.

Therapist: What is Marsha feeling in your drawing?

Tyrone: Nervousness.

Therapist: So she is unable to completely drown out the sounds of her parents' fight?

Tyrone: Nothing will completely block it, because you can hear it in your mind even when it is no longer coming in your ears.

Therapist: So a kid like Marsha can't really get away from the knowledge of her parent's fighting even if she can't hear it?

Tyrone: That's right. She knows what is going on downstairs.

Therapist: Does that mean that kids like Marsha would worry about their parents' fighting when they are not home to hear it—like when they are at school or over at a friend's house?

Tyrone: They can't get away from it. They might worry even more, because they are not there to make sure things don't get out of hand.

Therapist: That's a heavy load for a kid to carry.

Tyrone: It's not fair. She is just a kid. She shouldn't have to worry all the time.

Therapist: Do you think kids like Marsha get angry about the load that gets put on them?

Tyrone: It would really piss me off.

Therapist: Do you ever worry about your parents?

Tyrone: They fight just like Marsha's parents. Things get pretty scary sometimes.

Therapist: So you know firsthand what kids like Marsha go through.

Tyrone: I sure do.

Therapist: What was the scariest time for you, Tyrone?

Tyrone: When my mom left and didn't come back for three days. It was the longest three days of my life.

Therapist: Were you scared that she wasn't coming back?

Tyrone: Not at first, but she never did that before. I thought she would be back the next day. When that didn't happen, I was really upset. I was really mad at my dad for upsetting her so much that she left.

Therapist: What did you do to cope with those three longest days of your life?

Tyrone: I called my grandmother a lot. She kept saying, "Now, Ty, your mom will be home soon, don't you worry. I know she will be back soon."

Therapist: You were angry with your dad when this happened, but do you ever blame yourself when your parents fight?

Tyrone: Sometimes. I guess I have to blame someone.

Therapist: Is it helpful to blame yourself or someone else?

Tyrone: Not really. I just don't know what to do.

Therapist: What advice would you give to kids like Marsha when their parents are fighting?

Tyrone: Unless it gets really bad, stay out of it. You will only get blamed if you try to stop it. It is like stepping in front of a freight train to stop it.

Therapist: It sounds like good advice, and I believe you are telling us that not only will it not work but also it can be dangerous.

Tyrone: That's for sure.

Discussion

One of the most disturbing events in the young child's life is awakening in the night to the sounds of parents screaming at each other. All problems are magnified in the dark. Problems that seem quite manageable during the day can seem overwhelming in the night. Children may fear that the ominous shouting coming from downstairs may escalate into violence or culminate in the family breaking up. Some children will not be able to tolerate the anxiety; their hearts racing, palms sweating, they may quietly slip out to the hallway, where they may be able to hear better what is going on. This will be especially true of "parentified" children, who, because of their keen sensitivity to parental conflict, take on the role—sometimes assigned, at other times adopted—to "keep an eye on the situation."

CONFLICTS OF GUILT AND SHAME

> There is no witness so dreadful, no accuser so terrible as the conscience that dwells in the heart of every man.
>
> Polybius (c. 200–c. 118 BC, *History,* Book XVIII, p. 43)

Evocative Narrative Stem: "Too Embarrassed to Tell"

"A child came home from school feeling great conflict about whether or not she should tell her mother about something that happened at school. She was embarrassed and ashamed and worried about how her mother would react. It was bedtime, and she still hadn't decided whether to tell when her mom came in to say good night. The little girl, who was eight years old, heard her mother come into the room and she _____ [the child continues from here]."

   Follow-Up

    1. *What do you think this little girl was worried about the most if she told her mother what happened?*
    2. *What are some other reasons that sometimes make kids reluctant to tell parents about bad things that happen?*
    3. *If a kid can't talk to his or her parents who else could help?*
    4. *You don't have to tell what happened if it is too private, but have you ever been too embarrassed or ashamed to tell your parents about something that happened?*
    5. *Again, you don't have to give the details if you don't want to, but is there something you have felt guilty about for a long time?*
    6. *Are there any steps that you can think of, such as making up for what you did, that would help you feel better about it?*
    7. *What advice would you give someone who suffers silently about something they did, too ashamed to tell anyone?*
    8. *Do you believe there is such a thing as "a bad kid?" If so, why? If not, please explain.*
    9. *Do you see yourself as a "bad kid?" If so, why?*
   10. *If so, what would it take to convince you that you are not?*

   Clinical Illustration of Completion of the Narrative Stem: Lenny (Age Eight)

   "She was still thinking whether she was going to tell her mom or not. So she decided she should, because she knew if she didn't it would build up and be much worse, so she decided to tell her mother. She told her mother that people at school were making fun of her. And her mother said, 'Don't worry about that. If you stay away from the people who are making fun of you they won't bother you. If you get your mind on something else it won't bother you so much, because they will realize it is not working. What is your favorite thing to do?' said her mother. She said, 'Play board games and sports.' Her mother said, 'Then do what you enjoy doing and eventually the kids bothering you will give up. Good night.'"

   Therapist: What worried the girl most about telling her mother?

Lenny: That her mother wouldn't have any idea whatsoever how to help her. She might tell her she just has to get used to it.

Therapist: What are some other reasons that children don't tell their parents when something bad happens?

Lenny: Maybe it might change things that happen. The child might not like what the parent tells them to do about it; it could make the situation worse, it could make it tougher for the kids.

Therapist: If a child can't tell his or her parents, whom else could they tell?

Lenny: A friend or a relative. Maybe someone who will play sports or a board game with the kid, that makes it easier for the kid to tell what is troubling her. If she tells a friend, the friend may have other friends in the group that are making fun of her and perhaps influence them to stop it.

Therapist: What advice would you give to a kid who suffers silently about something they did, too ashamed to tell anybody?

Lenny: They should tell somebody that they think could really listen and help them. Maybe discussing it while playing a game, like a board game.

Therapist: Do you believe there is such a thing as a "bad kid?" If so why, and if not, why?

Lenny: No.

Therapist: Why?

Lenny: Because it is a mixture of things that cause a kid to react the way he or she does. It may have a lot to do with the way the kid has been treated. Lots of things affect the kids' behavior that makes it tough for them to control their temper. It is not simply a bad kid.

Therapist: I couldn't agree with you more, Lenny, and I couldn't say it any better than you just did. Do you see yourself as a "bad kid?"

Lenny: No. I sometimes feel that way, but more of the time I think I am a pretty good kid.

Therapist: Once again, I couldn't agree more.

Discussion.   Lenny acknowledged that he used to feel that he was a "bad kid," but now most of the time he does not. He has a history of explosive behavior that he has gradually learned to contain, and consequently he feels better about himself. For an eight-year-old child, he explains why there is no such thing as simply a "bad kid" in an impressive way. He understands what some adults fail to understand, that when a kid gets into repeated trouble the explanation is complex and multidetermined. It is also interesting that he made repeated reference to helping children talk about difficult matters by an adult or peer engaging the child in a board game; while playing and having fun the child might be able to talk things over more easily. This is a method that seems to work best with Lenny, who is an action-oriented child.

Evocative Scenario: "Hands in the Cookie Jar"

Tommy woke up around midnight. His brother, eight years old, two years younger than Tommy, was snoozing away in the bottom bunk. As quietly as he could, Tommy went down the ladder from the top bunk. He then slowly and quietly crept downstairs. He was hungry. Although his mom had told the boys repeatedly that they were not to get into the cookie jar without permission, this time Tommy could not resist. He just had to have some more of those yummy chocolate chip cookies that mom had freshly baked. He reached into the cookie jar and quickly gulped down two of his favorite cookies. He then reached in for two more but was startled by his dad's voice: "I see that someone has helped himself to some chocolate chip cookies." "Not me," said Tommy as he turned around his face covered with chocolate chip cookie crumbs.

  Follow-Up
  1. *Why do you think Tommy lied even when he was caught with his hands in the cookie jar?*
  2. *What do you think leads some kids to make a habit out of lying?*
  3. *Do you think it ever makes sense to lie? Should we always be truthful even if the truth will be hurtful to someone?*
  4. *What do you think the following expression means? "If you tell lies, you better have a good memory"?*
  5. *What do think the phrase, "little white lies" means?*
  6. *What was the most trouble you ever got into for telling a lie?*

Clinical Illustration: (Charlie, Age Nine)
Therapist: Why do you think Tommy lied even when caught with his hands in the cookie jar?

Larry: It is just the first thing that comes to your mind. He also probably didn't know that he had cookie crumbs all over his face. But it is not good to lie.

Therapist: What do you think leads some kids to make a habit out of lying?

Larry: Well, by starting to do it and getting away with it, they may try it again and again. Tommy probably won't make a habit of it, because he got caught. The more you get away with it the more it will become a habit.

Therapist: Do you think it ever makes sense to lie? Should we always tell the truth even if it will be hurtful to someone?

Larry: Sometimes you need to lie; certain things are not good to say that would really hurt someone even if true.

Therapist: What do you think the following expression means? "If you tell lies, you better have a good memory."

Larry: It means that if somebody catches you it would be important to remember the lies you told, it could trip you up. You could get caught in your own trap.

Alternatives or Modifications

Evocative Quote: "Telling the Truth"   Mark Twain was known for his wise and humorous sayings. Please discuss or write about the following Mark Twain quote: "Always tell the truth. That way you don't have to remember what you said."

Discussion.   Larry had plenty of experience with telling lies and getting caught in his own trap. As a nine-year-old boy he had learned the hard way that lies have a way of coming back to bite you. Andrew Fussner (1986) has pointed out that sometimes when kids tell lies; they are really creating fiction, because the harsh realities, the nonfiction, of their lives are intolerable. They create these small works of fiction to weave a more palatable reality, one that is easier to live with than the actual harsh circumstances of their lives.

Regardless of how outlandish the tales or works of fiction are that children create, there is a kernel of truth, of reality, that can be instructive to adults who are listening with "the third ear." If a child says he beat up a bunch of kids, he is often saying that he is afraid of a bunch of kids or perhaps that he is being harassed by a group of kids. If a child says he is the best athlete in his class, he may be saying that he feels inadequate in sports. Children who tell us they are not afraid of anything may be telling us that they are afraid of many things. Of course, it is not helpful in these cases to correct their reality; it is important to read the underlying motive and feelings and respond in a way that helps the child feel more competent in the specific area of concern.

If the child says he is the best athlete in his class, the adult might join him or her in a game of shooting hoops and help the child to develop more confidence in athletic skills. If a child says, "I can beat up a bunch of kids," but the real message is that he or she is feeling threatened by other kids, it may be helpful to suggest to the parents that they encourage him or her to join a martial arts or self-defense class or do assertion training with the child. In other words, the implied communication is responded to by "the third ear" and acted on without further humiliating the child or increasing the destructive sense of shame. While it may not always be a true assumption, it is therapeutically useful to assume that the child is lying because the reality of the situation for the child is painful. The therapist is more likely to respond in a helpful manner to increase skills and/or confidence in the areas in which the child feels defeated.

An Evocative Story: "The Lie That Haunted Alfredo" (Adolescents)

The Story.   The boys and girls in Alfredo's third-grade class always seemed to have exciting things to share when it was their turn for show and tell. Alfredo dreaded the day it would be his turn, because he could not think of anything interesting that he could share with the class.

Just the week before, Brad had brought in a miniature totem pole that he had bought in Alaska. Susie the week before told about her family's trip to England and all about Stonehenge and the Tower of London. Alfredo's family had never taken a trip like that. They were more likely to drive five hours and spend a week with grandma. Alfredo was certain that his classmates would not want to hear about that. Mrs. Everly announced one day that next week it would be Alfredo's turn for show and tell.

Alfredo was in a panic. "What will I tell them that won't make me look stupid?" he kept asking in his mind. One day that week he passed a travel agency in town, and in the windows he saw some brochures. He went inside and asked the nice lady if he could take some brochures home to his parents. The lady said, "Sure, take as many as you want, and if your parents have any questions, just tell them to call me."

Alfredo was excited; he hatched in his mind a plot that he thought just might work. He would tell his classmates that his family was planning a dream vacation for next summer. Alfredo told himself he wasn't really telling a lie, since anyone can dream about a vacation. He also counted on the kids and Mrs. Everly forgetting all about it by next summer.

Alfredo stuffed the brochures into his backpack. That night in the privacy of his room he looked through the brochures to see which one was the most exciting and likely to impress the kids and Mrs. Everly. He finally decided on a ten-day cruise from Vienna to Venice, partly because he couldn't remember anyone ever reporting on such a cruise.

Alfredo was nervous when he told about the dream vacation his family was planning. He decided at the last minute to put in a "maybe" to soften the blow when other kids found out later on that the family didn't go on any such trip. He said, "If everything goes right, we will maybe take the trip next summer, if not we might have to wait longer to go."

One thing that made Alfredo a little uptight while talking about his dream trip was that he noticed a rather puzzled look on Mrs. Everly's face. The second thing that made Alfredo even more nervous was Elizabeth's question. She asked, "What do you mean by 'if everything goes right?'" Alfredo had not expected this question, and it was a sensitive matter for him. He had learned early on when he entered school that most kids in his school came from families that had more money than his family. His father was a truck driver whose work was not steady. During some periods when his Dad was making money the family didn't worry too much, but there were other times when money was a huge worry and Alfredo's parents would fight more.

Alfredo could not think of any way to answer Elizabeth's question that would dodge the issue, so he hesitantly said, "It depends on how much work my Dad gets." He got the words out but he felt embarrassed and humiliated.

Some of the kids snickered but stopped quickly when Mrs. Everly glared at them. Alfredo finished his presentation and sat down. Alfredo was relieved and hoped he would never hear anything more about his dream vacation cruise from Vienna to Venice.

How wrong Alfredo was. His classmates frequently asked questions like, "When do you leave?" "What ship are you going on?" "What shore excursions are you going to take?" Alfredo was not happy about all of this attention. Whenever he went out to recess he tried to get involved as quickly as possible in a game, so other kids wouldn't have a chance to ask him any more questions.

Alfredo was afraid to invite kids to his house for fear that they would ask him about the dream cruise from Vienna to Venice. He realized his lie was going to haunt him, with no end in sight.

Follow-Up

1. *What motivated Alfredo to make up an elaborate lie to tell his classmates?*
2. *What kind of problems did Alfredo's story make for him?*
3. *What advice would you give to Alfredo to cope with his problem?*
4. *Do you think Alfredo should keep the lie going, or would he be better off to tell the truth to his teacher, his parents, and his classmates?*
5. *If Alfredo decides to tell the truth to his classmates, how do you think they would respond? How do you think his teacher would react? His parents?*
6. *Do you think Alfredo would sleep better at night if he told the whole story?*
7. *What is the worse trouble you ever got into for telling a lie?*

Discussion.   Alfredo's story is a tale of a boy desperately wanting to be accepted by his classmates. It is also a story of devaluation. He was sensitive about his lower-class status in relation to his classmates and was mortified when attention was drawn to his family's money problems by questions. Poverty causes scars that are often carried into adult life. As Hardy (2004) points out, no matter how successful you are in adult life, if you were raised in poverty, a part of you will still feel poor.

Some children and families are in a daily struggle for survival, with urgent concern as to where their next meal will come from. Alfredo created the fiction of his dream trip because in reality the likelihood of his family ever making such a trip was nearly zero. He comforted himself from the distress of creating such a fictional account to impress his classmates by reminding himself that "everyone can dream." But sadly, all too often the dreams of kids like Alfredo who grow up under difficult economic circumstances, and especially those facing extreme poverty, are crushed somewhere along the way. Alfredo created fiction because the reality was too painful. The factors that influence lying in children can vary and are often multidetermined, but it is important to consider that kids, especially those who have experienced sociocultural stress or trauma, may be motivated in part to create fiction because their world of truth is so harsh and depriving.

Evocative Scenario: "What's Yours Is Mine!" (Pre-teens and Adolescents)

Jackie was a first grader. To the shock of her teacher and her parents she kept taking little, inexpensive items from her classroom and stuffing them in her knapsack and taking them home. Most of the items taken from her teacher's desk were magic markers, crayons, even paper clips. Both of Jackie's parents were police officers. Neither they nor her teacher could understand why this kept happening.

    Follow-Up

1. *How would you explain the mystery of Jackie's "stealing" these small, inexpensive items? Her parents could easily afford these items—in fact, she already had all of these things—so she did not need to steal any of them. Do you have some ideas?*

2. *What other explanations can you think of that might lead kids to take items that don't belong to them?*

3. *What do you think the significance is of Jackie's parents being police officers?*

4. *Jackie's story is similar to a number of children who engage in minor shoplifting. Often kids who stuff a candy bar or a CD into their pockets or a coat could easily afford to pay for it. What then could explain why they try to steal these items?*

5. *What are the likely consequences of sneaking something out of a store without paying for it?*

6. *What are some of the excuses that kids give for doing this?*

7. *Have you known of anyone who got caught trying to shoplift from a store?*

8. *Do you think that Jackie or someone who shoplifts something from a store is likely to become a criminal as an adult?*

9. *What is wrong with taking something that does not belong to you if it is small and inexpensive?*

Discussion.   Small minorities of kids who steal things do so because they desperately need them. I have worked with kids in residential treatment who while living in extreme poverty would steal food or take food thrown in a garbage can, because they were hungry. The reasons for stealing from a psychodynamic framework, however, can be complex and varied. I have known kids who shoplifted when the unconscious motive was to be caught, because they were internally in distress. Others were driven by the desire to seek help for their parents or their families. They paid what they considered a reasonable price in their psychic economy to obtain help for either themselves or their families.

Still other children appear to engage in minor theft to send their parents a wake-up call. Children whose parents are preoccupied with other matters, such as the struggle to make a living or, in the case of families struggling to survive, the necessity to focus on day-to-day needs for food and shelter, may be unable to provide children the attention and nurture they require. Other children grow up in relative affluence where the preoccupation of the parents has nothing to do with the struggle to survive but rather with such pursuits as occupational prominence, social status, acquisitiveness, and so on.

Sometimes parents of children who engage in minor delinquency or theft in the community are leaders in that very same community, serve on boards of various charitable and nonprofit agencies, giving generously many hours per month to these worthwhile causes, but their own children may feel neglected, cheated, and robbed. Andrew Fussner (2001) stated in a family training seminar, "Kids who steal have been stolen from." Children in these last two groups tend to be angry kids. Stealing for these youngsters is driven by the rage they feel that in spite of their affluent and privileged circumstances they feel emotionally deprived.

Viewing the symptomatic behavior of privileged children as metaphors not only reflects, as Fussner pointed out, that "those who steal have been stolen from," but angrily indicts their parents as "frauds." No matter how much status their parents enjoy in the eyes of the community, the kids feel they have been robbed, cheated, and defrauded. Stealing in the community symbolizes the robbery they have felt emotionally but also serves to embarrass their high-profile parents, particularly if both parents, as in Jackie's case, are police officers.

Still another way of viewing stealing is from an attachment-theory framework. Often when children steal minor items it is important to look at the relationship between the child who takes and the person taken from (Fussner, 1999). It is not unusual, particularly among insecurely attached children, to want or need something from that particular person. Sometimes it serves as a transitional object for those kids, who are extremely sensitive to separation or loss. This is one of the reasons that children will frequently request to take toys out of the therapy room to keep until the next session. This need for security can be met without frequent loss of therapy room supplies by suggesting a collaborative art project that they can take home with them. In the case of minor theft, within an attachment theory framework, the object taken is a way of holding on to a piece of the person they will be separated from, even if for a short period of time.

AN EVOCATIVE DIRECTIVE INTERVENTION: "MATCHING THE EMOTIONAL INTENSITY OF SHAME-BASED BELIEFS"

Negative messages from childhood are recorded with high emotional intensity (James, 1993). If a child is told that she or he is "fat," "stupid," or a "slut," or if the child is told he or she is "lazy," "worthless," or "no good," those messages even in adult life can be embedded within and backed by strong emotional conviction. The reason is that children are dependent on the important adults in their life for their very survival. The evaluations they receive from the adult caretakers and their teachers carry enormous weight. If later on you try to dispute these negative messages in the older child in a calm, logical manner, you will not make a dent in their belief system. Children who frequently received negative and emotionally laden messages in childhood will need to do emotionally focused work before the positive self-statements or cognitive restructuring will have any significant effect.

It is essential to show strong affect in disputing these negative self-perceptions, based on these emotional early life experiences. If, for example, I am working with a child whose father is in jail for committing a heinous crime, the child may be convinced that he or she too will be a criminal. I might move close to him or her, look him or her right in the eye, and with strong affect challenge that belief, on the basis of positive qualities I see in the child. I might say, "No way! I don't know how you got that idea. Maybe because you have been told things like that or maybe because you believe that you have no choice—that your life will just go in the same direction as your father's. But I am here to tell you that you do have a choice. Your life does not have to take the same path as your father's. You are not the same person as your father. You are the same kid that found some kittens last week and took care of them in a gentle, caring way until a home could be found for them. You have a heart! You cared what happened to those kittens. That doesn't sound like a heartless criminal to me!"

I do not wish to imply that one animated and emotional conversation like this can turn the corner in a child's beliefs about self, but a series of such challenges may make it harder for these beliefs to operate automatically. Over a period of time children may reach the point that they can challenge and dispute themselves these negative and self-condemning beliefs, ideally with the same emotional conviction expressed and modeled by the therapist.

9

The Quest for Identity and Search for Meaning

*W*ho am I? How did I get here? What am I doing here? What will happen to me? Where is my place in the world? What is the purpose of it all? These are questions typical of adolescents, because the search for identity and quest for meaning are uniquely human traits. As far as we know, animals are not plagued with such questions about their existence. Although such questioning can be agonizing to adolescents and young adults, as well as some precocious younger children, it also presents an opportunity for growth and change. Adolescence, however, also involves negotiating successfully an obstacle course with many potential hazards: drugs, alcohol, unsafe driving or riding in vehicles, early sexual activity with both health and emotional risks, and, for teens growing up poor in urban neighborhoods, a daily struggle to survive.

WHAT DOES IT ALL MEAN?

Evocative Projective Drawing and Storytelling:
"The Steep, Winding, and Narrow Road"

Roads can be fascinating to contemplate. When you enter onto a road, do you ever wonder where it begins and where it ends? It can be daunting to think of all the vehicles that had one time passed up and down the road carrying passengers to their destinations. For some who drive or walk it, the road may be a familiar or habitual route. They have traveled in both directions on the road numerous times but perhaps have never traveled the entire route. Others may be passing through on this road and traveling it for the first time. They may be hesitant at first about which direction to go to reach their destination. Others unfamiliar with the road may be cautious, not knowing what curves lie ahead.

Each road has a history, but few, if any, can recount it. Roads deteriorate as a result of harsh winters, and wear and tear, and they require repairs. Some roads are better maintained than others. Some roads are superhighways or interstates and bear a heavy volume of traffic, while others may be country roads, perhaps even unpaved, gravel roads that carry only light traffic. Each road bears the scars of the accidents that have occurred throughout its history. How many people have died, been injured, and/or traumatized while traversing this particular road? Each road has its own story to tell.

The Story.   There was a narrow, paved road with many sharp curves and steep hills. When folks traveled this road they were warned to drive slowly. Some people paid no attention to the warnings and traveled too fast; their journeys ended in sorrow and pain. This made the road sad. Others who traveled the road took their time, paid attention to the dangers of the sharp curves, steep hills, and narrow places and were able to safely travel the road to reach their destination. Along the way, they were treated with beautiful views of the valleys from the top of the hills.

Most people respected the road, but some dumped their garbage beside the road or even threw their junk onto it. This made the road angry. Many who traveled the road enjoyed the beautiful flowers growing on the side of the road, but some folks trampled them or threw their trash on them, and this disappointed the road.

Over the many years of the road's history, it has witnessed many things. Countless cars, trucks, and people have come and gone. When the road was first built, horses and buggies traveled it; other travelers walked. The first automobiles to travel the road did not go too fast over the dirt road, which later became a gravel road, and finally a paved road with a line down the middle and a white stripe on each side. The road is proud of how many people have traveled it over its life to reach their destination. The road has so many stories to tell.

Drawing Directives

Please picture in your mind that narrow road with the steep hills and sharp curves. How do you picture the road in your imagination? Do you picture it as it was in its early history as either a dirt or a gravel road? Or do you see it in your mind as a paved road? Do you picture it going around a curve or up a steep hill? Do you picture it at its beginning point or its ending point or somewhere in the middle? Are there side roads coming into your road? How much traffic is on the road? When you have a picture clearly in mind, please draw it as best you can.

Storytelling Directives

Every road has many stories to tell if it could talk. Some stories would be happy, some sad, others disappointing, while still others may stir anger. Be the voice of the road and make up a story that your road could tell. Make up the most interesting story you can. Be sure that the story has a beginning, middle, and ending part.

Clinical Illustration: Nicky (Age Nine)

Nicky is nine, and he struggles with separation/loss and abandonment fears. During his preschool years he was aggressive, but he has learned to re-channel his aggression into more constructive pursuits, such as sports and karate. He was adopted from an Eastern European orphanage when he was nineteen months old. He suffered extreme deprivation during this time. Minimal information is available about the birth parents, other than that his birth mother was quite young, only seventeen. The birth father, slightly older at nineteen, had a history of abusing drugs and a violent temper. The child was surrendered for adoption at birth. His adoptive parents are a young couple, who are devoted to him as their only child. Nicky has some neurodevelopmental deficits that interfere with learning, and he struggles in school to keep up with his peers. He receives remedial reading and math and visits the resource room one hour a day. His learning deficits are extremely frustrating to him, because he does not want to be perceived as different in any way from his peers.

Nicky's Drawing

Therapist: Tell me about your drawing.

Nicky: This is the road, it is mad because these beautiful flowers are being ruined by the garbage thrown out, the coke bottle, a dead fish hanging out of a grocery store bag. A car did not pay attention to the warning signs and is bouncing off the road.

Therapist: What title would you pick for your drawing?

Nicky: "The Long History of the Road" or "The Road's Warning" or "The Destruction of Humans."

Therapist: Which one do you like the best?

Nicky: "The Road's Warning."

Therapist: Does your road show its beginning point in the picture?

Nicky: No, it is somewhere along the way.

Therapist: Is the ending point of your road shown in your picture?

Nicky: No, it is along the way out of the city into the countryside.

Therapist: Do the cars and the people in the cars on your road reach their destination?

Nicky: No, the one car in the picture has gone off the road.

Therapist: Do the people in the car pictured on your road show respect for the road?

Figure 9.1. Picture of narrow, steep, and winding road

Nicky: No, the car was going too fast and did not pay attention to the warnings. They think they are "cooler" than the road and they can just beat it up.

Therapist: Is your road dirt, graveled, or paved?

Nicky: Dirt.

Therapist: So it was early in its history?

Nicky: Yes.

Therapist: Is the road in your picture a real road that you have been on or a make-believe road?

Nicky: It reminds me of a road somewhere, but mostly it is make-believe.

Therapist: If it is a make-believe road, where would you like it to take you?

Nicky: I am not sure: I guess home.

Therapist: Do you make it there?

Nicky: I am not sure.

Therapist: What makes you unsure?

Nicky: I have a long way to go yet.

Therapist: Why so far?

Nicky: It is a long way back to home.

Therapist: What do you have to do to get back home?

Nicky: Get around all those sharp curves and steep hills.

Therapist: How far have you come already?

Nicky: A long way, but I still have far to go.

Therapist: But you have come a long way already, so you have already managed a lot of sharp curves and steep hills.

Nicky: You can say that again.

Therapist: You are right, Nicky, it is worth saying again. You know something about going around sharp and dangerous curves and climbing up steep hills. You have already faced many challenges, and you have come a long way. You have learned how to travel your road safely, even when faced with dangerous obstacles.

Nicky: I guess I really have.

Therapist: So in traveling your road, you have learned to be careful but also to face the challenges along the way. Do you consider your road to be safe or dangerous?

Nicky: Safe, if you pay attention and show respect for the curves and hills, dangerous if you do not.

Therapist: You really have learned a lot about how to make headway on your journey home.

Nicky's Story

"One time there was some teens in a monster truck, and they hit a large bump in the road and bounced. When the truck came down it damaged the road, because the gas tank sprang a leak and the smelly gas went all over the road and into a nest of baby rabbits alongside the road. It left a trail of smelly gas along a long stretch of the road. It disturbed the nest of rabbits, which had to move someplace else."

Therapist: If your road could have feelings, what feelings would the road have about the story you told?

Nicky: It would feel sad that the rabbits had to move and angry that the monster trucks cause so much damage to the environment.

Therapist: What percentage of the people traveling the road take time to enjoy the scenery along the way?

Nicky: A small number.

Therapist: You, Nicky, however, are very sensitive to the environment and care a lot about flowers and little rabbits beside the road. Do you think there are people who travel the road every day and never see the beautiful flowers and trees alongside the road?

Nicky: Maybe a guy carries a briefcase and makes a lot of money and doesn't care about or even notice the flowers.

Therapist: If the road could speak to the people before they traveled it, what do you think the road would want to tell them?

Nicky: That he doesn't like it when people litter or throw out trash or trample the flowers.

Therapist: Far too many young people have accidents on narrow roads or sharp curves because they are not experienced drivers. What would the road say to them before they traveled on it?

Nicky: Pay attention! There are speed bumps and warning signs to remind them to go slower.

Therapist: Sadly, way too many young people are injured or die in alcohol-related accidents. What would the road like to say to young people about drinking and driving?

Nicky: You should only drink alcohol on special occasions, not to get drunk. If you are going to drink, stay off of my road!

Therapist: What are the important lessons the road can teach us?

Nicky: The road feels very sad when people don't drive safely and when people think it is more important to be "cool" than to respect the road and the environment, and how stupid it is to drink and drive.

Therapist: Those are important lessons. Nicky do you think you have ever put yourself or others in danger by doing something reckless?

Nicky: I don't think so.

Therapist: You have learned to be safe in your journey, and there is a lot that folks can learn from your story of the road.

Alternatives or Modifications

Evocative Quotes: "Pursuit of Meaning" (Pre-teens or Adolescents).   Please discuss or write about the meaning of one or more of the following quotes.

- *"The best use of life is to spend it for something that outlasts life" (William James)*
- *"Go confidently in the direction of your dreams! Live the life you've imagined" (Henry David Thoreau)*

- *"The man is the richest whose pleasures are the cheapest"* (Thoreau)
- *"Our life is frittered away by detail. . . . Simplify, simplify"* (Thoreau)
- *"I went to the woods because I wished to live deliberately, to front only the essential facts of life, and see if I could not learn what it had to teach, and not, when I came to die, discover that I had not lived"* (Thoreau, Walden, 1970, p. 75)
- *"Character cannot be developed in ease and quiet. Only through experience of trial and suffering can the soul be strengthened, ambition inspired, and success achieved"* (Helen Keller)
- *"I still find each day too short for all the thoughts I want to think, all the walks I want to take, all the books I want to read, and all the friends I want to see"* (John Burroughs)

Discussion

A road can serve as a rich metaphor for the path or journey we take through life. The narrow road, like the journey through life, may have sharp curves, steep hills to climb, danger, accidents, and misfortune. Mistakes can be costly and unforgiving. Like life itself, it can be risky and we may not reach our destination.

The road, however, can also serve as a symbol for the kind of journey we take. If we barrel ahead recklessly, ignore signs of danger, are unable to put on the brakes in time, we may risk harm to self and others. If we show no respect for the obstacles we face, we may be ill prepared to handle adversities when confronted by them. Rushing through life, pursuing project after project, material gain, occupational prominence, or whatever ambition may drive us, causes us hardly to notice a significant proportion of the beauty we pass by each day. We may go through life entrapped by our consumer tastes and desires, adopting a narrow view in pursuit of single-minded drives and ambitions, rarely enjoying the journey along the way. When such folks finally pause from their busy and consuming pursuits, they may be shocked that twenty years have passed and that not a single minute can be recaptured.

Nicky's drawing and story and the ensuing dialogue highlight how central the issue of loss and attachment is to him. He is a long way from home, even though he has traveled a great distance already. Even though he has negotiated and faced difficult challenges (sharp curves and steep hills), he is not sure he will make it back home, because he still has far to go. He is disturbed by the people he encounters who are more concerned about being "cool" than being respectful of the road and its surrounding environment (bullies who taunt and disrespect him) and who drive monster trucks and leave a trail of smelly gas that disrupts a nest of young rabbits.

The rabbits had to move somewhere else. Nicky too has found transitions to be difficult. Even transitions from one grade to the next at the end of the school year caused significant anxiety in his early years, and he met them by increased, aggressive acting-out. Nicky has learned a lot along the way. He no longer acts out aggressively and impulsively, he has learned to exercise care and pay attention along his road, but he is well aware that many curves and hills lie ahead and that he still has a long way to go.

Children who faced depriving conditions in the early months of life are not likely to develop secure attachments. It is more likely that they will develop anxious/insecure attachments, such as in Nicky's case or, in even worse scenarios, disorganized attachments that are usually associated with less favorable prognoses. In spite of the secure, loving environment provided by his adoptive family, he is still not sure he will make it home. "Making it back home" may symbolically represent a yearning to be reunited with birth parents, or simply to recapture the secure beginning in early life that he missed out on, leaving him in this persistent state of unrest, anxiety, and uncertainty about what lies ahead around the next sharp curve. John O'Donohue (2004a) refers to the home of our longing as "a shelter for the soul." If this crucial shelter, protection, and nurture are missing in the early months of life, it represents a profound loss. Such a devastating loss may compel a person to search for this elusive refuge that was vitally missing when he or she was most vulnerable and needed it the most.

Nicky has disdain for the businessman with his suitcase who makes a lot of money but doesn't care about the flowers and beauty along the road and doesn't even seem to notice them. Likewise, he shows contempt for those who are in pursuit of "being cool" but are highly disrespectful of others. These strong feelings may relate to the "riches" with which he perceives those who are securely attached have been endowed but that have been sorely lacking for him. Those "cool" folks in monster trucks, so disrespectful of others, I think most likely represent those who have teased and taunted him in school and socially rejected him. Nicky has been socially isolated, except by one youngster several years younger than he. Partly, this is the result of his earlier impulsivity and aggressivity, but it is also due to his anxiety and insecurity, which lead him to want to control and dominate in his social interactions with peers, which alienates would-be friends.

This story pulls us strongly to consider not only where the road can take us, our destination, but also how we wish to travel. What is the meaning and purpose of our journey? Where did we get on this road? Where do we want to get off? How will we know when we have gone far enough? How will we know if we are on the wrong road or have made the wrong turn?

Positive psychology (Seligman, 2002) posits that there are three distinct orientations to life: the pursuit of pleasure, the pursuit of engagement, and the pursuit of meaning. The pursuit of pleasure is focused not only on hedonistic gratifications but also on the wish that our children will enjoy life with zest, free from worry and at peace with the choices they make in life. The pursuit of engagement, as described in positive psychology, is involvement and invest-ment in activities for children at school, at play, and later in work, in which children can find so absorbing that they lose themselves. Finally, the pursuit of meaning, as viewed by positive psychology, is the connection with causes and purposes larger than the self, including the embracing of social responsibility. "We want our children to make a life that matters to the world and creates a difference for the better" (Commission on Positive Youth Development, 2005, p. 508). In Nicky's story his social concerns and conscience are evident. Nicky was concerned about the spill of gas on the environment and the way it dis-turbed the nest of rabbits and was disdainful of those who carelessly ignore the impact of their actions on the environment.

WHO AM I?

Evocative Projective Drawing and Storytelling:
"Fourteen Going on Twenty" (Adolescents)

   The Story.   Michele, fourteen years old, a pretty girl and a good student in ninth grade, is being pressured by her boyfriend to engage in sexual relations. She was conflicted because some of her young friends had confided in her that they were already "doing it" and teased her about being "late to the party." At the same time, early teen sex violated her religious beliefs and her family's moral values. Michelle knew that her parents would insist that she stop seeing Pete if they knew that he was pressuring her to consent to sex. The fear of pregnancy weighed heavily on her mind and was the scariest of all the possibilities. Michelle was not on birth control pills, nor would her parents have approved of that. She did not dare broach the issue with her mother; when she hinted to her older sister Karen, who just turned eighteen, that she might be tempted to have sex with Peter, Karen said, "Michelle, you better not be having sex with Pete, or I'll kill both of you!" That was the end of that discussion.

   Peter promised to use condoms, and both were quite aware that safe sex was an imperative. Michelle was really crazy about Peter and it was her first ex-perience, of feeling this way about any boy, even though she had attracted the attention of a number of boys, because she was not only pretty but socially en-gaging.

   Michelle gave into Pete's pressure, because she feared that she would lose him as her boyfriend. One week later Michelle approached Peter, who was one month away from turning seventeen, at his locker in school. She was taken back by how cool and distant he was. "What's wrong?" she asked. Pete said, "I don't think this is going to work for me. Can we be just friends?" Michelle was speechless. She walked away in shock and entered the girls' bathroom, where she collapsed in tears.

Drawing Directives.   "Please try to picture Michelle in your mind. Where is she? Is she with her family? Her friends? Pete? When you have a clear picture in your mind please draw it as best you can."

Follow-Up to the Drawing

1. *What is Michelle feeling in your picture?*
2. *Who do you think was hurt the most by this experience, Michelle or Pete?*
3. *What is the strongest feeling that Michelle is experiencing in your picture?*
4. *What other feelings do you think she might be experiencing in your picture?*
5. *Do you think that teens could be ready physically and hormonally for sex but emotionally unready?*
6. *What emotional risks might arise for young teens who are sexually active?*
7. *If early teen pregnancies are terminated, what emotional impact do you think that would have on the girl and the boy involved?*
8. *What do you feel are the emotional consequences of feeling used sexually?*
9. *If you had a chance to give Michelle advice what would you tell her?*
10. *If you had a chance to give Pete advice, what would you tell him?*

Storytelling Directives.   *Please continue the story of Michelle that left off with her crying in the girls' bathroom. Please continue the story of Michelle from that point. Who does she turn to help her? What are the consequences to Michelle of Pete dumping her? How do things work out for Michelle in the long run? What happens to Pete? Does the experience have any long-range consequences for him?*

Follow-Up to the Story

1. *How would the consequences for Michelle have differed if she had not partici- pated in sexual relations prior to Pete's dumping her?*
2. *Do you think it would have differed for Pete?*
3. *What are the lessons that can be learned from your story?*
4. *Have you known anyone who was sexually misused the way Michelle was?*
5. *Do you think guys are held accountable for early sexual activities in the same way that girls are?*
6. *What about the impact on girls versus guys with respect to early pregnancy?*
7. *Do you think that harm can result from early casual sexual relations even if no pressure is involved?*

Clinical Illustration: Nicole (Age Thirteen)

Nicole drew a picture of Michelle crying in the school bathroom with girl-friends.

Therapist: What is Michelle feeling in your picture?

Nicole: Sad, really sad. She is crying.

Therapist: Who do you think was hurt the most, Michelle or Pete?

Nicole: Michelle.

Therapist: Can you tell me more about why you think that?

Nicole: Pete didn't seem like he cared.

Therapist: What other feelings do you think Michelle may be experiencing?

Nicole: Mad, confused.

Therapist: Do you think that teens may be physically and hormonally ready for sex but emotionally unprepared?

Nicole: Sure.

Therapist: What emotional risks do you think teens may be unprepared for?

Nicole: Pregnancy, AIDS, herpes.

Therapist: What else can you think of that would be an emotional risk?

Nicole: Well, if the girl gets pregnant her life would be changed; there would be no chance to complete her education or to get a good job.

Therapist: If an early teen pregnancy is terminated what emotional impact do you think that would have on the girl and boy?

Nicole: Scared, nervous, and worried.

Therapist: What are the emotional consequences of feeling used sexually?

Nicole: Mad, really furious.

Therapist: Like a betrayal?

Nicole: Big time!

Therapist: If you had a chance to give advice to Michelle, what would you tell her?

Nicole: Get to know a guy a lot better first. Don't rush things. You are young; you have plenty of time.

Therapist: How about Pete, if you could give him advice, what would you say to him?

Nicole: You shouldn't have a girlfriend. You don't deserve one, because you don't know how to treat girls with respect.

Nicole's Story

"Her friends calmed her down. At lunch they wouldn't talk to Pete and yelled at him. No one could trust Pete again. Michelle didn't want people to feel bad for her. But she felt she had been tricked and taken advantage of. In a couple of years she got a new boyfriend and this guy treated her right. Pete could not find anyone; he would go from girl to girl but wasn't able to stay with anyone very long."

Therapist: What title would you give to your story?

Nicole: "Take Your Time and Wait"

Therapist: What do you think would have been different for Michelle emotionally if she had not given into Pete's pressure to have sex before he dumped her?

Nicole: She would have not been so sad, less angry, less confused, because he really pressured her.

Therapist: Do you think it would have been different for Pete if they had not had sexual intercourse?

Nicole: No, he was going to dump her anyway.

Therapist: What can be learned from your story?

Nicole: Wait till you find somebody that you know is right for you; don't be pressured. Wait before you make the decision.

Alternatives or Modifications

Evocative Scenario: "The Mark of a True Friend"

Directives.   Please consider what you would look for as signs that someone is a true friend. Please describe as many features as you can that you would look for to decide if the person meets your definition of a genuine friend.

Clinical Illustration: Mike (Age Fourteen).   "I would go by the following: one, someone who listens; two, who respects your secrets; three, someone who stands by you in times of trouble; and four, who is fun.

Variations on this Theme: What would you look for, what signs would tell you if a boy [girl] was trying to take advantage of you, to use you?

Discussion

Children appear to be growing up faster than ever—or could it be that children are being pressured to grow up faster than ever? The age of innocence, a protected period of childhood, seems more condensed than ever. Are children ready to face the potentially hazardous choices about sexual, drug, and alcohol experimentation that many kids are confronted with upon reaching puberty? Not only are adolescents faced with changes in their body that require altering body image, but they also must handle the responses of peers and family to their maturing bodies (Graber, Brooks-Gunn, and Archibald, 2005). The timing of onset of puberty has major implications for the adjustment of adolescents; being either earlier or later than is typical of peers is associated with poor adjustment (Stoff and Susman, 2005; Susman and Rogol, 2004). Earlier timing is associated with both internalizing and externalizing problems in girls (Graber, Seeley, Brooks-Gunn, and Lewinsohn, 2004). These same researchers report that early-maturing girls are at higher risk for both depression and conduct-related disorders. Early maturation in boys has been associated with an increase in depressive symptoms, alcohol use and abuse, and delinquent and externalizing behaviors (Ge, Conger, and Elder, 2001; Wichstrom, 2001, [cited in Graber, Brooks-Gunn and Archibald, 2005]). Late-maturing males are at higher risk for conduct problems and substance use (Graber, Brooks-Gunn, and Archibald, 2005).

The incongruous developmental pressures are sometimes reflected in the young adolescent's behavior. A thirteen-year-old girl, for example is sexually active with her boyfriend and drinking at parties but can only go to sleep with her night light on and her stuffed animals arranged in a particular formation on her bed. Such incongruity reflects the confusion that young adolescents experience as they undergo major hormonal shifts and restructuring of brain organization during the teen years (Siegel, 2005), not to mention confusion about cultural and moral expectations. Teens observe that their parents are just as bewildered as they are. A recent study revealed that timing of sexual intimacy is a key issue in preventing teen pregnancy. Teen girls who engage in sexual intercourse at earlier ages are at greater risk for premarital pregnancy than those who do so at older ages (Aseltine and Doucet, 2003).

In the quest for identity, seeking acceptance and approval from peers, in attempts to stake out their autonomy from parental/authority figures, in efforts to counteract boredom, feelings of emptiness, social anxiety or withdrawal, rejection, or perhaps due to a genetic predisposition, some adolescents are drawn to high-risk behavior. Many adolescents will experiment with alcohol or marijuana use, and explore their sexuality, but some become more engaged in risky sexual behavior, problematic alcohol use (including binge drinking), illicit drug use involving a range of potentially harmful drugs, and other high-risk behaviors, such as driving at dangerous speeds or while drunk.

When such behavior is undertaken to combat low self-esteem, gain acceptance of peers, or self-medicate a mood disorder, it may constitute "a risk behavior syndrome," in the sense that teens who experiment with substance use also tend to engage in other risky problem behaviors (Commission on Adolescent Substance and Alcohol Abuse, 2005; DuRant, 1995; DuRant, Getts, Cadenhead, Emans, and Woods, 1995; Jessor and Jessor, 1977; Jessor, 1991). Three risk factors are the strongest predictors of marijuana use from experimental to habitual use; those factors are peer or own involvement with substances, delinquency, and school problems (van den Bree and Pickworth, 2005). Longitudinal studies of adolescent alcohol use reveal the following progression: abstainer → normative drinker → high-risk drinker → problem-drinker (Power, Stewart, Hughes, and Arbona, 2005). These investigators found that paternal attitudes toward adolescent drinking and peer involvement in antisocial behavior predict movement into normative drinking. Social activity with peers predicts movement into high-risk drinking, and emotional distress predicts transition into problem drinking.

High levels of parental monitoring and parental support were protective factors against alcohol use and abuse in a Native American community (Rodgers and Fleming, 2003). These researchers found that among Native American teens who used alcohol, those who believed an adult in their community would monitor their behavior were three times less likely to report drunkenness in the past month than those who believed community members would not monitor them.

Depression is commonly observed in adolescents, and suicide is the third-leading cause of death among fifteen-to-nineteen-year-olds (Halifors, Waller, Ford, Halpern, Brodish, and Iritani, 2004). Both depression and suicide have been associated with drug use and early sexual intercourse. In a nationally representative sample, these investigators found that adolescents who engaged in risk behaviors such as drinking, smoking, and/or early sexual activity faced significantly increased odds of depression, suicidal ideation, and suicide attempts. The risk was highest among teens who engaged in illegal drug use. While these researchers stress that a causal link has not been established, involvement in early sexual activity or drug use should be a clinical indication for mental health screening for girls; both boys and girls who use marijuana or other illegal drugs should be screened.

Alcoholism is a factor in about 30 percent of all completed suicides, and an estimated 7 percent of those with alcohol dependence will die by suicide (Pompili, Mancinelli, Girardi, and Tatarelli, 2004). These same investigators note that about 50 percent of all people who commit suicide are intoxicated at the time. In addition lower minimum-age drinking laws have been correlated with higher youth suicides (Markowitz, Chatterji, and Kaestner, 2003).

In summary, high-risk behaviors in adolescents often lead to a cluster of problem behaviors, some with potential devastating consequences. The strategy above is intended to open the communication and dialogue with adolescents who are usually reluctant to talk to adults about these sensitive issues and about the vitally important choices that teens are faced with, often earlier than they are prepared to deal with them.

EVOCATIVE PROJECTIVE DRAWING AND STORYTELLING STRATEGY: "KIDS TAUGHT TO HATE THEIR OWN BODIES" (PRE-TEENS AND ADOLESCENTS)

The Story

Sarah was very attractive but thin to a degree that was unhealthy. Barely thirteen, she obsessed about the foods she ate or didn't eat, the calories she consumed, the readings on the bathroom scales at least once a day, and how she looked to herself in the mirror in her chosen clothes. If she decided she did not look good in the mirror she reacted strongly; her day was ruined. No matter how reassuring others—including her mother, her sisters, and her friends would be—for that day at least she hated the way she looked. Often she would cry on those days, sometimes hysterically. Other days when she was upset with how she looked in the mirror, she would get angry and throw a major tantrum. "I am not going to school looking like this!" she screamed at her mother, "and you can't make me!"

On the days she felt good about the way she looked; she would still need reassurance from her mother, sisters, and her friends, but on those days she would accept their reassurances. "Looking fat" in her eyes was almost always the reason for not looking good. Nothing that anyone could say to Sarah could relieve the torment she experienced on those bad days.

Drawing Directives

Now try to picture Sarah in your mind in whatever way makes sense to you. Do you picture her on a good day or a bad day? Is she alone or is she with others? If so, who is there with her? Where is she in your picture? Is she at school? Home? When you have a clear picture in your mind, draw it as best you can.

Follow-Up to the Drawing

1. *What feeling is Sarah feeling the most strongly in your picture?*
2. *What other feelings do you imagine she is feeling in your picture?*
3. *What is it in our culture that makes young people and even adults uncomfortable with their bodies?*
4. *If you were Sarah's best friend what advice would you give her?*
5. *Why do you think girls tend to suffer more torment about their bodies than boys?*

Storytelling Directives

Now make up a story about the next five years of Sarah's life through her high school years. Tell in your story whether or not she grows to be more comfortable and at peace with her body. Or does she continue to suffer the torment of thinking she is fat, when in reality she is quite thin? Is she able to make peace with her body? What is the turning point for her that enables her to let go of her harsh criticisms of her body? Tell in your story what you believe Sarah's life will be like at age eighteen. Will she able to be happy at that point?

Follow-Up to the Story

1. *What can be learned from your story?*
2. *If Sarah overcame her obsession with thinness, what or who helped her to do this?*
3. *If she was still tormented by these worries, what will it take for Sarah to be a happy person?*
4. *Have you ever known of anyone who suffered the ways Sarah did because of excessive self-criticism of his or her body? If so, what helped that person to be able to overcome these obsessive worries?*
5. *What ideas do you have for changing the cultural expectations with its overemphasis on youth, physical beauty, and excessive thinness?*
6. *Do you think that even the models on the covers of the teen magazines have some imperfections pertaining to their bodies?*
7. *If you had a chance to talk to the executives of the media industry who frequently promote the ideal of super-thinness, what would you like to say to them?*
8. *Is there anything else you would like to say about this issue?*
9. *Is there anything that you think adults just don't seem to understand about this issue?*

Alternatives or Modifications

Evocative Writing Assignment: "Self-Estrangement"   Please write about what you consider to be the unhealthy pressures that make some teens hate their bodies.

Evocative Role-Play: "Dialogue with Best Friend"   The therapist can take the role of the teen with the eating disorder and the adolescent can take the role of "best friend" and try to reason with and express concern for his or her friend's preoccupation with excessive thinness.

Evocative Quote: "I'd Rather Lose My Right Arm"   It has been widely reported that in surveys among teenage girls it is not uncommon to hear, "I would rather lose an arm than be fat." Please discuss or write about your feelings and thoughts about such a statement.

Evocative Scenario: "The Many Camouflages of Pain"   Teens try to hide and numb the pain they feel in their hearts and souls in many different ways that, sadly, create still more pain. Some drive too fast or recklessly, others drink too much or too often, some get high, some abuse hard drugs, while others cut or burn themselves, and some hurt themselves in other ways, such as starving themselves or making suicide attempts.

Directives

Please share your ideas about the sources of pain in the lives of some teens that lead them to engage in various forms of dangerous, high-risk, or self-harming behavior. Also, please discuss or write about what you think would be healthier choices that teens can make to cope with emotional pain. Finally, please share your ideas about what you think adults don't understand about teens today and what you think adults, including parents, teachers, and therapists, could do that would be more helpful.

Clinical Illustration: Larry (Age Fourteen)

First I would tell kids that emotional pain can come from breaking up with a boy or a girlfriend, losing someone in your family, failing a class, not getting to go to college, getting fired from a teenage job, getting beat up, or having been abused, especially sexually abused. Healthier choices for dealing with the pain would include talking to a school counselor, your friends, a therapist, or your parents. If you are being abused at home, you should tell someone who could help. You will feel calmer if you can find some way to get your mind off of it, but the most important thing is to get help. I would say to adults that adults sometimes just yell at kids. They don't try to understand or find out what is wrong and what is causing their hurt. Adults treat little kids better than they treat teenagers. The advice I would give to adults is to try to understand kids or get them to someone who can help. Take time to talk to them, to listen to them, to laugh with them, have fun with them. Those things could really help.

Discussion

It is sad that our culture all too often teaches young girls and, less frequently, boys to hate their own bodies. Our bodies are our homes in this life, the vessels that carry us through our lives. "If only I could be thinner, taller, better looking, more muscled, if only my nose weren't so big, or if only I could be blonde, or have darker features," are familiar refrains. Making friends with our bodies, since we are part and parcel of our bodies, is essential to living harmoniously with our self, and with life. Making friends with our bodies includes exercising reasonable care of them. The cultural images of what represents "body beautiful" are subject to fads, but one thing that typically does not change is that the "ideal" is something that most of us are not.

These pressures are experienced earlier in children's lives today and are keenly felt, especially by girls from middle school on, if not earlier. Studies have shown that early maturation, along with dating, can result in increasing eating problems for young adolescent girls (Graber, Brooks-Gunn, and Archibald, 2005). Of course, the complex pathways that lead to eating disorders include (in addition to biological, genetic influences) social, contextual, and cultural factors in interaction with one another. Sometimes the cultural messages that kids are bombarded with by the media lead children to feel estranged from their own bodies.

Many studies have been conducted to identify risk factors for eating disorders. They have consistently shown that girls are more concerned about dieting and more preoccupied with their body weight and pursuit of thinness than are boys. Among the risk factors identified are personality characteristics such as perfectionism, obsessionality, high degrees of self-criticalness, and low self-esteem. Of course, eating disorders are multidetermined and can be influenced by frequency of dieting or dissatisfaction with one's body. The adoption of an ideal of "slimness" puts adolescents, especially girls, at risk for eating disorders. In addition anxious/insecure attachment with parents, as well as biological and genetic factors, can play a role in the etiology of eating disorders (Cohen and Petrie, 2005; Commission on Adolescent Eating Disorders, 2005; Granillo, Jones-Rodriquez, and Carvajal, 2005; McGee, Hewitt, Sherry, Parkin, and Flett, 2005; Steinberg, Phares, and Thompson, 2004; Tylka and Hill, 2004).

EVOCATIVE PROJECTIVE DRAWING AND STORYTELLING STRATEGY: "NEVER GOOD ENOUGH" (ADOLESCENTS)

Some people spend significant portions of their lives trying to please folks who are impossible to please. These are the children who bring home a report card that has four As and one B+ and the parent says, "How come the B+?" These are children who try to help out at home but the parent points to the spot they missed when dusting the furniture. When these children are grown, some still seek the approval that the parent doesn't know how to give, probably because they never received it themselves from their parents. I wonder when I see this pattern how many generations back it goes. Generation after generation seeks to gain the approval of the previous generation, who also missed out on this acknowledgment. I have sadly cautioned adults headed home for the holidays not to expect what they have always been seeking from their parents, who simply can't give it. My warnings frequently fall on deaf ears, and the longing for that approval, that validation, and the persistent hope that this time will be different leads yet again to bitter disappointment.

The Story

Rebecca is an attractive and pleasant girl but not the prettiest or most popular in her tenth-grade class. She just turned sixteen and excels in academics. Her parents proudly discuss her accomplishments with their friends, but never did Rebecca hear these admiring words. What Rebecca heard was that she should be well rounded, play sports, and be a cheerleader. Neither of these activities appealed to Rebecca. She played the flute skillfully in the high school band, she was a high honor-roll student, and took several advanced-placement classes, but both of her parents had been athletes in high school, and her mother had been captain of the cheerleading squad. They urged Rebecca to try one sport or another, but she was simply not interested.

When she received a B in her advanced-placement chemistry course, her parents couldn't understand what was wrong with her. Her Dad repeatedly reminded Rebecca that her older brother John had also made the honor roll but that he was also a star of the high school basketball team and football team. Her mother reminded her often that her cousin Amy was a good student but that she also had broken the school record in the hundred-yard dash. Rebecca cringed at the familiar refrain, "Why can't you be like your cousin Amy?"

Drawing Directives

Now try to picture Rebecca in your mind. Is she with her family, or friends, or alone? What is she doing? Where do you picture her? Home? School? Another place? When you have a clear picture in your mind, please draw it as best you can.

Follow-Up to the Drawing

1. *Tell me about your drawing.*
2. *What would be a good title for your picture?*
3. *What is Rebecca doing in your drawing?*
4. *If others are included in your drawing, who are they and what are they doing?*
5. *If you could talk to Rebecca what advice would you give her?*
6. *How does Rebecca feel in your picture?*
7. *Do you think Rebecca can do anything that will please her parents?*
8. *Why do you think Rebecca's parents are so critical of her?*
9. *Have you ever known of anyone who faced a similar situation to Rebecca's?*
10. *What are some of Rebecca's strengths and good qualities?*

Storytelling Directives

Now I want you to think about a time when you tried your best and someone was not pleased. Tell the story of that experience, including what happened and as many details as you can remember, including what it was like for you and how it turned out.

Follow-Up to the Story

1. *What would be a good title to your story?*
2. *What did you feel when you did your best and someone was not pleased?*

3. *Can you think of other times when you experienced this same reaction? If so, which one was most upsetting to you?*
4. *What can be learned from your story?*
5. *Do you believe that some people are so critical that no matter what you do, you can't please them?*
6. *What are the best ways to cope with such people?*
7. *Is there anyone in your life that can't do anything right in your eyes?*
8. *If so, why do you think you are so hard on that person?*

Alternatives or Modifications

   Evocative Writing Assignments: "Impossible to Please"   Please discuss or write about a time when you were frustrated because you could not please someone whose expectations were simply too high, impossible to meet. Please discuss or write about why it is that though even professional athletes, who are paid enormous sums for their exceptional talents, are not able to achieve perfection, so many in our culture hold themselves to that impossible demand.

Discussion

Perfectionism has been associated with a wide variety of symptoms, including depression and anxiety (Frost, Heimberg, Holt, Mattia, and Neubauer, 1993; Hewitt and Flett, 1991; Joiner and Schmidt, 1995; McCreary, Joiner, Schmidt, and Ialongo, 2004), and also eating disorders (Ashby, Kottman, and Schoen, 1998; Bulik, Tozzi, Anderson, Mazzeo, Aggen, and Sullivan, 2003; Goldner, Cockell, and Srikameswaran, 2002; Joiner, Heatherton, Rudd, and Schmidt, 1997).
   Recent research has supported a multidimensional concept of perfectionism, with positive striving regarded as adaptive while overconcern with the expectations of others (inordinate desire to please) and excessive demands and criticalness of self seen as maladaptive. Depression and anxiety are correlated with the maladaptive forms of perfectionism but not with positive striving for high standards. In a study of perfectionism in African American children, it was found that a strong sense of community connectedness allows children to strive to do their best without viewing themselves as failures if their performance is less than perfect (McCreary, Joiner, Schmidt, and Ialongo, 2004). In contrast, European American children, who often lack a strong sense of community connectedness but are pressured to pursue individual achievements, tend to be more vulnerable to self-criticism for failing when striving for perfection.
   My own view is that striving for excellence and high standards can be healthy and adaptive but that any form of striving for perfection, except in such

discrete tasks as getting a 100 on a math test, is a futile, unrealistic goal. This can be easily demonstrated by considering the performance of outstanding, legendary athletes. I frequently use these sports metaphors in work with kids to help them establish realistic goals. Michael Jordan, who arguably was the greatest pro basketball player ever, did not hit his peak performance every game. Some games he was unstoppable, but other games were "off days" for him. I happened to watch one NBA game on TV when Jordan, as dominating as he was, missed seventeen shots in a row. It was his overall average, however, that was outstanding, that makes him perhaps the best of all time. Another example that I frequently use with kids is that while Babe Ruth was for a long time known as "the home run king," it is less well known that he also was the "strikeout king." So even the best athletes of all time were far from perfect; seeking perfection except in limited tasks is self-defeating.

EVOCATIVE SCENARIO: "MOVING OUT" (ADOLESCENTS)

"Teens and even younger kids get angry with their parents and say things like, 'I can't wait until I am old enough to move out.' Sometimes parents and siblings get so frustrated with their teen sons or daughters or siblings that they say, 'I can't wait either until you move out!' Yet moving out, leaving home, is a big step. Usually young people have mixed feelings about leaving home when the time comes. Describe what those mixed feelings might be. How will you know when you are ready to move out and leave home? What are the signs that you would look for that would tell you that you are ready emotionally to make it on your own?"

Directives

Do you think it is necessary to completely cut the ties with your family in order to prove you can make it on your own? Consider the following scenario.

Keith is nearly eighteen, a senior who will be graduating from high school in one month. For the past two months, ever since Keith received his acceptance letter to college he has been picking fights with his parents, his younger brothers, and his sister. His parents are puzzled by Keith's change in behavior. The college Keith wanted to attend had accepted him. His family thought he would be happy. What do you think is going on in this family? What could explain Keith's change in attitude and behavior?

Can you think of a time when you picked a fight with someone, perhaps a brother or a sister who was getting ready to go away to college or military service, or a close friend who was getting ready to move away?

Looking back on that experience now, do you think it was easier to part with your sibling or friend by getting mad at him or her than going through the pain of saying good-bye? What can be learned from your experience?

Clinical Example: Alexia (Age Seventeen)

Therapist: Let's pretend that today is the day you are moving out to go to college. What would your feelings be?

Alexia: I would be worried about making it on my own. I would be worried that maybe I didn't save enough money. If my family goes on vacation while I am away, I probably would feel left out because I wouldn't be invited if I were in college. I would also be happy to get away. I would be excited at first—the negative feelings will most likely come later. Maybe I would feel lonely once I moved out.

Discussion

The time for moving out is rapidly approaching for Alexia, and she does a good job of articulating the mixed, conflicting, and ambivalent feelings of young people as they approach the time of leaving home. It is not unusual for them to become defiant and rebellious in the months prior to leaving, thereby in a certain way making leaving easier. It is a way of saying, "I don't really need you anymore," which is an exaggerated statement of autonomy, since they have doubts about their true sense of emancipation.

EVOCATIVE IMAGERY AND FANTASY:
"TAKING THAT NEXT STEP" (ADOLESCENTS)

Graduations, marriage, birth of a child, and promotions are all examples of steps forward in life. Mostly these are happy and proud occasions, but they can also be scary. Troubling questions may emerge, such as "Will I be able to handle my new responsibilities?" "Am I ready to be a husband or wife or parent?" "Will people expect more of me now than I can deliver?" Growing up is marked by progressions as well as setbacks. Positive changes, although welcome, usher in new anxiety because of the greater challenges associated with one's advancement. It is common for young people to long for the simpler life when they were younger and had less responsibility.

Directives

I would like you to think about some of your important goals. I expect that you will be able to describe easily what the positive consequences will be of achieving those goals, but

I also want you to describe what might be unwelcome or scary about taking these big steps in life.

If the teen needs more structuring, the therapist could say, *Let's take graduation from high school or college, for example. What will be the best part of completing high school or college for you? Now, what would not be so great about finding yourself finished with high school or college? What would be scary about it? Think about the things you would worry about if that time were right now. How about getting married? What would you like about that? What would you not like about that? What about becoming a parent? What would you like, and what would you be worried about?*

Discussion

The struggle for autonomy begins early, at eighteen months, a time of moving away from the primary caregiver, usually the mother, to explore the wider world. When children leave the nest to go off to school, that is another important milestone toward greater independence from the parents. Graduation from high school and college are other major milestones in this emancipation process.

While our culture pushes hard the idea of separation and breaking of the bonds with parents, the children, even adult children, need to retain emotional ties and connections with parents and siblings. The relationships certainly need to be restructured as the children get older and more independent, but there is no need to think the ties have to be severed. There is undue pressure on both parents and kids to magically be all grown up and independent by eighteen, with boys often feeling this implicit demand especially.

Olga Silverstein (1995), in a workshop at the Ackerman Institute for the Family, stated, "American culture is so dedicated to individuality, with independence being the highest achievement of maturation." She noted that cutting off from the family became important by virtue of the Industrial Revolution. Silverstein observes that contrary to these cultural expectations, the more the family therapist can open up and expand the connections with other family members, the more benefit for the family. She states, "The more connections, the richer your life." She adds, "Making connections is the art of therapy—including connecting with self. Our culture has deprived us of what makes life endurable, which is a connection to others—community is important."

The conflict about growing up is universal. Opening up dialogue with teens about this issue may avoid major family misunderstandings that cause unnecessary heartbreak. If the conflict between moving ahead and the desire to remain in the relatively secure and sheltered, at least familiar, position of the present is recognized for what it is, it may avoid other more blaming or pathological interpretations. This is a developmentally expected conflict as teens approach adult life, and it may re-emerge throughout adult life as new advancements take place, but the conflict is usually most intense at the point of leaving home.

EVOCATIVE CHILD STATEMENTS AND EMPATHIC TRANSLATIONS: "WHAT ARE CHILDREN REALLY SAYING?"

> I don't like to forget about the inner life of the child.
>
> Daniel A. Hughes (2005)

If we are truly to understand children, we have to learn to translate the real meaning underlying their highly emotionally charged statements. An absolutely essential task of child and adolescent clinicians is to help parents and teachers learn to translate these statements. When we respond in literal or, even worse, in personal ways to provocative statements they make, we miss opportunities to understand them in a more meaningful and in-depth way. Obviously, the translations below will apply to the statements of many children in moments of great emotional distress but not to every child or every situation. They are offered as examples of some of the more common emotional underpinnings of such statements, but therapists in consultation with parents and teachers will be in the best position to translate for a particular child in a specific situation.

It needs to be stated explicitly that any statement by a child threatening harm to self or others needs to be carefully evaluated; the possible interpretations of such statements proposed here would not substitute for evaluation by a mental health professional. I would enjoy hearing from readers (www .rhinebeckcfc.com) regarding other possible translations of the statements below, as well as any additional emotional statements that are typical of children in crisis situations.

The child says: "I don't care!"

Translation: "I once cared a lot, but it hurts too much to care anymore," or "Please tell me that you care—that you haven't given up on me!"

The child says: "Nobody listens to me anymore!"

Translation: "There is something I need to tell you, are you ready to hear it?"

The child says: "You just don't get it."

Translation: "You think you really understand me, but you don't."

The child says: "How many times have I tried to tell you this?"
Translation: "If you really understood, I wouldn't have to keep saying it."

The child says: "I hate you!"
Translation: "Please tell me that you care about me, or at least that you don't hate me."

The child says: "I'm going to run away!"
Translation: "Please tell me you want me to stay," or "I hope you will stop me."

The child says: "I hate you, I wish you were dead!"
Translation: "The connection between you and me has been broken; it feels like you are no longer here. Please tell me you are still here for me."

The child says: "Stop saying how great I am!"
Translation: "I can't possibly live up to your inflated perceptions of me."

The child says: "Don't tell me you love me."
Translation: "It feels more comfortable to believe you don't love me; then I can keep you at a safe distance." [This is especially true of children with attachment difficulties.]

The child says: "I want to kill you!"
Translation: "I don't know what to do with my anger! It is scary to me. Please help me!"

The child says: "I am bad."
Translation: "I really believe that, please tell me it is not so."

The child says: "I don't feel anything."
Translation: "I have given up all feelings, because the shame, terror, humiliation, and rage are more than I can endure."

The child says: "I don't care if I live or die."
Translation: "Please tell me that I matter to you!" or "Does it matter to you if I live or die?"

The child says: "My birthday party was no fun!"
Translation: "I can only tolerate small doses of joy and excitement." [This is especially true of children with disorganized attachment (Hughes, 1998).]

The child says: "I don't like to be hugged."
Translation: "I don't know how to accept comfort, and affection makes me anxious."

The child says: "I just want to go out to play" [when parent(s) are trying to have a serious talk about a problem].
Translation: "I need to play, because the shame I feel when we talk about this problem is more than I can handle."

The child says: "I won't pick up my clothes, you can't make me!"
Translation: "I need you to know I had a bad day," or "I need a hug."

The child says: "I want to be a NBA basketball player."
Translation: "Please don't shoot down my dreams, no matter how far-fetched."

The child says: "I'll hang out with the kids that I want to!"
Translation: "Don't you understand that these are the only kids who accept me, no matter how much you disapprove?"

The child says (in the middle of an amusement park): "I want to go home, this is boring."
Translation: "I don't know how to regulate positive emotions; when I get excited I get anxious." [This is particularly true of traumatized children and attachment-disordered kids (Hughes, 1998).]

The child says: "I am a complete failure."
Translation: "Please tell me there is hope."

The child says: "I don't know if I can take anymore."
Translation: "Please tell me it won't always be this way."

Themes of Courage and Determination

Courage is resistance to fear, mastery of fear—not absence of fear.

Mark Twain

*J*udith Jordan in a presentation (2003) at the Stone Center defined courage "as the capacity to act meaningfully and with integrity in the face of acknowledged vulnerability. Courage does not involve denial of vulnerability. It takes courage to connect particularly if you have experienced trauma and violation in relationships, it takes enormous courage."

EVOCATIVE STORY:
"A STORY OF COURAGE AND DETERMINATION"

At age twenty-six, Mary Joyce started out on December 22, 1935, on a dogsled from Juneau, Alaska, with the goal of reaching Fairbanks, Alaska, a distance of a thousand miles (Pardes, 2004). The journey required traveling through deep snow, enduring temperatures that sometimes dropped to sixty degrees below zero, along with strong winds and blowing snow. Along the way she stopped to get tools and materials and with them build an entirely new sled, one that the dogs could pull more efficiently. On March 26, 1936, three months after starting her journey, she and her five dogs arrived in Fairbanks. The original sled and the one she built along her journey are on display in a rustic lodge that she once operated as a hunting and fishing retreat outside Juneau. In keeping with the obstacles and challenges this brave and determined woman faced and mastered, the lodge is located in a remote rustic area on the Taku River that can only be reached by a floatplane or boat. No roads go in and out of the lodge, and black and brown bears are frequently observed on the property.

Directives to the Child

Now I am going to give you a chance to tell a story. It doesn't have to be a true story. You can be creative and use your imagination to make up a story that shows courage and determination in facing a difficult situation.

Follow-Up to the Story

1. *What can be learned from your story?*
2. *Does your story remind you of any real person you have known or heard about?*
3. *Can you think of a time when you showed courage and determination to do what you believed was the right thing to do?*
4. *If not, can you think of a family member or have you heard family stories about anyone in your family, perhaps a great grandparent or uncle or aunt, who went against the crowd in order to do what he or she believed was the right thing to do?*
5. *Sometimes when people dare to do what they think is right, it can be a very lonely decision. Was this true in the story you created, or in the story about your own courage and determination, or the family story of courage and determination?*
6. *Sometimes there are stories in families about courage and determination of family pets. Are there any favorite stories in your family about pets who showed great courage or determination?*

Alternatives or Modifications

Evocative Quote: "Courage and Vision" (Pre-teen or Adolescents)   Please talk about or write about one or more of the following quotes.

- *"Do not go where the path may lead, go instead where there is no path and leave a trail" (Ralph Waldo Emerson)*
- *"Do the thing you are afraid to do and the death of fear is certain" (Emerson)*
- *"A person who's happy will make others happy; a person who has courage and faith will never die in misery!" (Anne Frank, diary entry, March 7, 1944, cited in Frank and Pressler, 1995, p. 210)*

Evocative Writing: "Defining Courage" (Pre-teens and Adolescents)   Write about your own definition of courage and give examples.

Evocative Story: "An Act of Bravery"   Please tell a story about an act of courage that you or someone you know performed. Give as many details as possible in your story and describe how you felt at the time.

Follow-Up

1. *There are many unsung heroes in the world who never get recognized or honored but heroes all the same. Can you name some that you know or have heard about?*
2. *Is there some way that you could be considered a courageous and unsung hero or heroine?*
3. *Is there a member of your family or a friend or someone that you know well that could be considered an unsung hero or heroine?*
4. *What can we learn from these everyday acts of courage?*

Discussion

Stories of courage and determination can be inspiring, but it is important that kids be helped to recognize that courage and determination can take many forms. Alongside the tales of heroic courage that have made some people famous, there are everyday acts of courage and perseverance that should be recognized and honored. Even getting out of bed in the morning can be an act of courage for a school-phobic child or an extremely depressed kid. Boyd and Ross (1994) have described their "courage tapes," videotaped interviews with children. The tapes are about thirty minutes long and are structured around questions requiring the client to describe how she/he had used courage to overcome problems and what advice he/she would have for others coping with similar problems. This approach offers great potential for highlighting the courage and determination of kids. They can be given a copy of the tape to keep.

Usually these small acts of courage and determination would "fly under the radar" of both the child and the family, but it is crucial that they do not escape the notice of the child or family therapist. The therapist can make a valuable contribution by alerting the family and child to look for and honor these everyday acts of courage and fighting spirit.

EVOCATIVE PROJECTIVE DRAWING AND
STORYTELLING STRATEGY: "THE COURAGE TO FACE
THE TRUTH" (PRE-TEENS AND ADOLESCENTS)

The Story

Marilyn is a tenth grader who is a hardworking, conscientious student. Her grade average is in the low 90s, and she aspires to go to a good college. Her only significant area of academic weakness is in math. If she goes to college she will be the first member of her African American working-class family to do so. Her family is supportive and shares the dream that she will go to college. During this school year, however, Marilyn is stressed because she is struggling in her algebra course. Her test scores have recently dropped steadily from the high 80s to the mid-70s. She is worried about the impact on her overall average and how this will affect her college plans. She worries about disappointing her family and her teachers. Lately she has slept poorly. She stays after school for tutoring in math, and that has helped, but she still feels lost. She approached the teacher, Mrs. Carson, who has been sympathetic and helpful, but none of these efforts have resulted in improvement on her test scores; in fact, they have continued to decline. Marilyn isn't the only one struggling in algebra. Several of her friends have also been worried about the approaching finals; some are even in danger of failing. One day when hanging out with some friends after school, her friend James disclosed to her and two other friends that he had a copy of the final exam. Marilyn was shocked as James told them the story of how their teacher had been called out of the room one day to the office; James had seen the final exam on top of her file cabinet. He took it and went down to the library to copy it and returned it to its rightful place at the end of class when their teacher was talking to some other students.

Marilyn went through a mix of powerful emotions. James was willing to share his copy of the final exam with the three girls, including Marilyn. She had never cheated before. If she was caught, the consequences could be severe. Besides, it wasn't fair to the other students, and more importantly, she knew it was just wrong. James argued that nobody would ever find out and that it could make the difference between failing and passing for him; Marilyn thought it could be the difference between getting into a good college or not for her. Her two girlfriends didn't seem to have a big problem with it. They began to chide Marilyn when she expressed her objections, saying, "Come on Marilyn, you are so uptight about everything. Loosen up a little, will you?" Finally, Marilyn reluctantly agreed to accept a copy of the exam from James. She didn't eat or sleep well for the next few days leading up to the exam. On the day of the exam she was pacing in her room before school, she broke out in a cold sweat and a state of panic. She was going against her better judgment, she was frightened, but it was too late to back out now. She took the exam and waited anxiously to find out the results. When she went to the math room to find out her scores, there was a note on the door saying that all students in the algebra class were to make appointments to meet with Mrs. Carson individually. As soon as Marilyn read the notice, her heart started pounding in her chest. She felt lightheaded and dizzy. Her breathing was rapid and shallow. She knew that the scheme had blown up in their faces.

Marilyn met with Mrs. Carson, who told her, "Marilyn, you are a hard-working, dedicated student, but you have struggled all year in my class. It has been a difficult class for you, and your grades have actually declined during the latter half of the year. On the final you got a 96. How do you explain that?" Marilyn didn't know what to say. Finally, she said, "I don't know." Mrs. Carson said, "Marilyn several students who have not done well in my class all year got high 90s and one got a 100 on the final. I can't help but view this as highly irregular and suspicious. Unless someone comes forward and explains this situation to me, I have no choice but to fail everyone in the class on the final."

Marilyn was speechless. She had not anticipated the calamity that would result from this one wrong turn in her academic career. Now everything she had worked for was in jeopardy, and even worse, students who did nothing wrong were going to suffer consequences for her wrong actions. She sought out her co-conspirators, James, Liz, and Kelly, who hadn't heard that Mrs. Carson was on to them. All three were absolutely opposed to coming clean. James said, "She is just bluffing. There is no way she is going to fail everybody. She can't prove that we didn't study out of fear that we were going to fail and as a result we did a whole lot better on the final. We can even say we studied together, and that will explain how we all came out about the same."

Marilyn could see that she was going to get nowhere trying to convince the group to do the right thing. She went home but again, she didn't eat. Her parents were concerned. They had noticed for more than a week now that Marilyn just didn't seem right. Something was wrong, and they had kept asking, but she couldn't tell them. She didn't sleep at all that night. The next morning, her eyes bleary, she went to Mrs. Carson and told her that she had copied the exam and that she and she alone was responsible. Mrs. Carson said, "I appreciate your honesty, Marilyn but I don't believe you were the only one involved. Do you really want to take the whole blame on yourself?" Marilyn said, "Yes, I do. It is simply not fair to the other students who had nothing to do with this, and I should have known better. I have done nothing like this before, and I am ashamed that I did this." "Well, Marilyn," said Mrs. Carson, "I am very sorry that you went against your better judgment, it's an awful price for you to have to pay. It took a lot of courage for you to come and tell me this, and I admire you for that. I hope it will be a valuable learning experience for you."

Drawing Directives

Please try to picture Marilyn in whatever way makes sense to you. She could be talking with her friends, talking to Mrs. Carson, taking the final exam, at home or in some other place. When you have a picture of Marilyn in mind please draw it as best you can.

Follow-Up to the Drawing

1. *Tell me about your drawing.*
2. *What title would you choose for your drawing?*
3. *What do you think of Marilyn's decision to take the blame for what happened?*
4. *What are some of the reasons that you think even good students like Marilyn are tempted to cheat?*
5. *What do you think Mrs. Carson will decide as to the consequences for Marilyn's actions?*
6. *Do you think she was right to take the whole blame for what happened?*
7. *What do you think the reactions of her friends who were involved in the cheating will be to Marilyn taking the blame?*
8. *How do you think Marilyn's parents will react when they are told?*
9. *If you could talk to Marilyn, what advice would you give her?*
10. *If you could talk to Mrs. Carson before she decides on what consequences to give to Marilyn, what advice would you give her?*
11. *If you could talk to Marilyn's friends, James, Liz, and Kelly, what would you advise them to do?*
12. *If you could talk to Marilyn's parents before they talk to her, what advice would you give them?*

Storytelling Directives

Please think about a time when you or someone you know showed the same kind of courage that Marilyn did in admitting that she was wrong. Even if you don't agree with her decision to take the whole blame, she still did something quite courageous. Any time that we admit that we were wrong and accept responsibility for our actions, it a true act of courage. Tell a story about a time when you or someone you know admitted wrongdoing and accepted the consequences.

Follow-Up to the Story

1. *What title do you choose for your story?*
2. *How is your story similar and how is it different from Marilyn's story?*
3. *What can be learned from your story?*
4. *Are there different lessons to be learned as compared to Marilyn's story?*
5. *Do you think it takes courage to be imperfect—in other words, to admit that we all have weaknesses as well as strengths and that we all make mistakes?*
6. *Why do you think it is so hard for us to admit when we are wrong and accept responsibility for our actions?*
7. *Do you think we learn more from our successes or our mistakes?*

Discussion

There are several important embedded features of this drawing and storytelling strategy. First of all, it frames facing the truth and admitting wrongdoing as an act of courage. Shame often makes it extremely difficult for children (or adults) to face the truth about their misdeeds. The story also normalizes mistakes and plants the seed of the idea that it takes courage to accept imperfections in ourselves. It also raises a thorny issue in terms of how far to go in accepting blame. It could be argued that Marilyn went too far in protecting her friends, even though her motivation was honorable, in that she did not want her classmates who were not involved to suffer the consequences. She knew that her friends who were involved in the cheating were not going to come forward, so, she felt, the only way she could protect her other classmates was for her to accept the whole blame. This issue can be the subject of intense debate, and kids will likely express strong feelings one way or the other. The strategy also elicits teens' capacity for empathy, particularly in the follow-up to the drawing when they are asked what advice they would give to Mrs. Carson prior to deciding on a punishment, to Marilyn's friends who were co-conspirators, and to her parents prior to confronting Marilyn. The degree to which they can identify and empathize with Marilyn will be of interest to the clinicians working with these youngsters.

The strategy also may open up a dialogue about the pressures that students feel in today's competitive world to qualify for the best colleges so as not to disappoint themselves, but in many cases their parents, especially, and perhaps their teachers as well. Sadly, as Walter Bonime (1986) pointed out, far too many children are groomed for the greater glorification of their parents while their genuine needs or interests may go unattended.

EVOCATIVE STORY:
"THE MARK OF A TRUE FRIEND" (ADOLESCENTS)

The Story

Melissa, fifteen years old, hardly spoke a word to other kids on the bus ride home after school. It was Friday, and she would have the whole weekend to try to make sense of what had happened that day at school. Her emotions gyrated between shock and panic. Her best friend, Cathy, had sworn Melissa to absolute secrecy after eighth period and then told her that she had been cutting herself on her arms and legs. Melissa could not believe what she had heard. Not in a million years would she have expected her best friend to be carving up her arms and legs with a razor blade. Melissa was speechless but finally had been able to ask Cathy if her parents or anyone else knew. Cathy said, "No, and you promised me you won't tell anyone either. Melissa, if you tell anyone I will never speak to you again." Melissa couldn't imagine anyone, let alone her best friend Cathy, inflicting wounds to her own arms and legs. She was confused. "Does this mean that Cathy intends to kill herself? Does this mean that Cathy is a really troubled kid and somehow I didn't pick up the signs? What am I going to do? I can't tell anyone, because Cathy will never speak to me again. She has been my best friend since sixth grade, but I don't like the fact that I am the only one who knows, and I don't know how to help her." These were some of the thoughts swirling through her head as she walked off the bus into her house. Melissa spent much of the weekend in her room, agitated, worried, and scared. She didn't sleep well, and she didn't eat much. By Sunday night her mother was worried.

When Melissa refused to come to dinner, her mother went into her room and insisted that Melissa tell her what was wrong. Finally, Melissa started sobbing and told her mother what happened. Her mother listened patiently and held her daughter tightly when her tears made it hard for her to talk. Melissa said, "Mom, I don't know what to do." Her mother said, "I think you do know what to do, and I trust you to do the right thing."

The next morning Melissa's mom dropped her off at school early. She went to her guidance counselor and told her about her worries about her friend Cathy. Her guidance counselor praised Melissa for her courage and her caring for her friend.

Follow-Up

1. *Do you think Melissa did the right thing? Why or why not?*
2. *Why do you think her guidance counselor was impressed with Melissa's courage?*
3. *If a friend is in trouble, whether it is due to cutting, threats of suicide, heavy drinking, or drug use, do you think a true friend will try to notify an appropriate adult so that his or her friend can get help? If so, why do you believe this?*
4. *If you disagree, what do you believe a true friend would do in this situation?*
5. *Have you ever been faced with a situation where a good friend needed help?*
6. *If so, what did you decide to do? What lessons did you learn from your own experience?*
7. *Do you think Melissa's mother was right not to tell her daughter what to do about the problem?*
8. *If you had a chance to talk with Melissa what advice would you have given her?*

9. *What advice would you give to her friend Cathy?*
10. *Do you think Cathy will forgive Melissa for telling the guidance counselor?*

Alternatives or Modifications

Evocative Role Playing: "A Little Help from My Friends" The teen is asked to role-play one of Melissa's other friends, who tries to help her decide what to do. These roles can then be reversed, which offers opportunities for the therapist to model various approaches to helping Melissa with her dilemma.

Evocative Writing Assignment: "Cutting to Numb the Pain" *Please discuss or write about the problem of self-mutilation among teens. Discuss what you think is the goal of self-harming behaviors and what feelings these teens are trying to communicate through such behavior.*

Evocative Dramatic Skits: "Exploring What Friends Can Do" In a group session, one teen could take the role of the guidance counselor or some other key adult at school, a trusted teacher or coach, whom a group of teens approach separately or as a group to express their concerns about a friend. Alternatively, the dramatization might entail a group of teens approaching the teen engaging in self-harming behaviors and trying to talk to him or her about getting help.

Evocative Imagery and Fantasy Techniques: "When Cutting Is No Longer a Problem" Teens presently engaging in self-harming behavior are instructed to imagine a time in the future when the problem of cutting will be resolved. They are asked to imagine what their lives will be like when cutting is no longer a problem. They are instructed to describe in as much detail as they can what changes they foresee in their lives when this problem has been put behind them.

Evocative Drawing: "Artistic Depiction of the Future without Cutting" Some teens may prefer to draw a picture of their lives in the future when cutting is no longer an issue. They can be asked to include others in the picture that they would like to have in their lives at that point in the future.

EVOCATIVE PROJECTIVE DRAWING AND STORYTELLING STRATEGY: "AN EVERYDAY HERO"

Directives to the Child

It would be nice if we all could play in the NFL and score the game-winning touchdown, or play in the NBA and hit the game-winning jump shot just at the buzzer, or play baseball in the major leagues and hit the walk-off home run in the bottom of the ninth inning in front of a stadium filled with people cheering and applauding. It is nice to fantasize about such heroics. It would be wonderful if we all could rescue or save the life of someone, like those heroic rescuers after the horrendous and devastating hurricane Katrina who were dropped by rope from helicopters and fetched people off rooftops and to safety. How special it would be if we could all bravely rescue someone from a burning building like our courageous firefighters do, or apprehend a dangerous criminal like our brave police officers do, or defend our country like our heroic military personnel do. These acts of bravery and heroism are often what kids fantasize about, because in each of us there burns a desire to do something heroic. While we may never have the opportunity to perform the kind of heroic acts just described, we may still be heroes or heroines as a result of everyday acts of courage. Do you remember the first time you jumped off the high diving board? Do you remember when you were learning to ride a bike and you told your parent to let go and you were on your own? Do you remember standing up to a bully? Do you remember helping a little kid who was being picked on by a bigger kid? Do you remember standing up for something you believed in or doing what you thought was right even though it was not popular? These were everyday acts of courage and heroism.

Evocative Drawing: "A Picture of an Everyday Hero or Heroine"

Now I want you to think about a time when you showed this kind of everyday courage and heroism. Maybe you didn't think about it that way at the time, nor did you receive a medal or any recognition of your heroism, but it was something that was hard to do, something that took courage, but you did it. When you have in mind such an act of courage or determination, please draw it as best you can.

Follow-Up to the Drawing

1. *Tell me about your picture.*
2. *What title would you choose for your picture?*
3. *Did anyone else witness your act of courage?*
4. *Were you or others surprised by your heroic act?*
5. *Did you receive any kind of recognition for what you did?*
6. *Did you recognize it as an act of courage at the time?*

Storytelling Directives

Please tell the story about your courageous and heroic actions. Tell about the hardest part of what you did. Talk about the feelings that came up for you at the time and afterward and the feelings of others who were there at the time. Tell about how it all turned out in the end.

Follow-Up to the Story

1. *What can be learned from your story?*
2. *What title would you choose for your story?*
3. *Are there other times that you showed this kind of courage and determination to do something that was difficult, but you did it?*
4. *Can you think of a time that you did something that you didn't think you could do?*
5. *Can you think of a time that you did something that you knew you could do but others didn't think you would be able to do it?*
6. *Is there an accomplishment that you are especially proud of?*

Clinical Illustration (Melissa, Age Eleven)

"The first time when I went off the diving board I was really scared. The same was true the first time I rode a horse but I can't remember that too well. I was at my friend's house and the diving board didn't bounce too much. I had been working up to doing this for a long time and finally I just took a run to the end of the board and jumped. When I jumped I felt like I was jumping out of an airplane. It hurt when I hit the water but I was glad I did it. I did it about thirty more times after that first one."

Therapist: What can be learned from your story?

Melissa: The first time is the hardest, after that it is no big deal.

Therapist: What title would you give your story?

Melissa: "Bombs Away"—when I finally decided to do it, I just ran to the edge and jumped.

Therapist: Can you think of any other time when you showed great courage and determination?

Melissa: The day I went into the hospital room to see my mother when I thought she was going to die. That was the scariest and hardest thing I have ever done. After that I didn't want to see her because it was too scary seeing her look that sick with all the tubes and everything. I was afraid to go back.

Therapist: You are right, Melissa; that took enormous courage. That was I'm sure a hard thing to do, and it clearly was upsetting to you, but somehow you managed to do it. Are you glad you did it now?

Melissa: Yes, but I hope to never again have to do anything that scary again.

Therapist: But even that you somehow managed to do. Have you ever done something that you didn't think you could do—when you surprised even yourself?

Melissa: When I drove a quad.

Therapist: Was that a good feeling when you realized you could do something that you didn't think you could do?

Melissa: It sure was, and I'll never let my brother forget it.

Therapist: Have you done something that other people didn't think you could do?

Melissa: I got an A+ in social studies.

Therapist: That must have felt good. Is there an accomplishment that made you especially proud?

Melissa: Getting an A+ in math.

Therapist: I am impressed.

Themes of Inner Strength and Interpersonal Resources

$\mathcal{F}$alse praise can be harmful; praise overdone can pressure the child. The art of building genuine self-esteem in children is to identify, locate, highlight, and reinforce authentic talents, interests, and personal qualities in children so that they become not dependent on the reassurance of the adult but come to increasingly trust their own resources.

IDENTIFYING STRENGTHS IN SELF

Evocative Imagery and Fantasy Techniques: "Hidden Gems in the Attic"

Directives.   Pretend that you are looking for something in the attic of your house, something that you misplaced and haven't seen for a long time. Perhaps it was a video, a favorite book, a CD, or a video game. As you look through boxes stored in the attic, imagine that you are frustrated because you are not finding the item. In the box you are now looking through, however, you discover something even more important. It is something that reminds you of some feature of your self that is of great value. It is like finding a hidden gem in the attic.

Think about what this surprise discovery could be. It could be a picture of you that reminds you of something you did that fills you with pride and a sense of accomplishment. When you look at the picture you are reminded, "Hey, I really did that!"

It could be a letter that someone sent you that you had forgotten about that describes some of your special qualities, perhaps from a former teacher or a grandparent. Maybe it is a picture of you receiving a big hug from someone who loves you and thinks you are terrific. Think about "the gem" you have discovered in the attic. Then please describe your discovery.

Alternatives or Modifications

Should the child draw a complete blank, the therapist can structure the project further by stating, *Let's suppose it is a letter that you find. A letter that when you read it, makes you feel "like a million bucks." It says things about you that make you feel just terrific about yourself. Who is the letter from? What does the letter say?*

Alternatively, the therapist can suggest, *You find a photograph of yourself. When you look at the picture, you smile and you feel good inside. Describe the picture. What are you doing? Are there others in the picture? If so, who are they? What is it about this picture that makes you feel so good inside?*

Clinical Illustration: Jesus (Age Twelve)

"I found a baseball in the attic that was given to me (the game ball) that was used in the game that got us into the championships. I threw out a base runner who was trying to steal third, and I also hit a home run in the game. It was the only time I hit a home run in a game. All the players signed the ball, and it was the best game I ever played."

Evocative Drawing Strategy: "A Mountain of Strengths and Talents"

Directives. Draw an outline of a mountain on a 8.5-by-11-inch or larger sheet of paper. The interior of the mountain is left as white space. Each session, starting from the first, ask the child to add at least one talent or strength to the mountain. Start filling in from the bottom of the mountain and climb to the top. When the child reaches the top of the mountain by filling in the whole mountain with his/her talents and strengths, the child and therapist take turns summarizing the child's mountain of strengths, talents, and good qualities. The family can be invited to this session if the child is comfortable with it, and the family can be encouraged to go out and celebrate in his or her honor the mountain of talents and strengths.

Alternatives or Modifications

If the child blocks and is unable to state a talent, strength, or good quality, urge him or her to pick at least one from the menu below:

Talents	Personal Qualities
Math	Nice smile
Science	Sense of humor
Reading	Good-looking
Music	Funny

Talents	Personal Qualities
Singing	Witty
Social studies	Smart
Languages	Well spoken
Artistic	Kind
Creative	Sensitive
Leader	Caring
Baseball	Generous
Football	Helpful
Tennis	Polite
Drama	Hardworking
Soccer	Good manners
Gymnastic	Leader
Skiing	Good listener
Crew	Friendly
Track	Likeable
Cross-country	Gentle
Other sport (specify)	Energetic

Evocative Drawing Strategy: "Someone I Admire"

Directives to the Child.   Draw a picture of someone that you admire, someone you look up to and respect. This could be someone that you admire so much that you wish to be like that person.

Alternatives or Modifications

If a child prefers, he or she can bring in a photograph of the person or simply tell about the person. Obviously, if the child wants to include more than one person, this only enhances the effect of this strategy. Some children may wish to make a collage that depicts the qualities they admire in such a special person.

Follow-Up
1. *What are the qualities you admire in this person?*
2. *What qualities or talents that you admire in this person do you see in yourself?*
3. *Has anyone ever surprised you by pointing out talents or good qualities that you didn't know you had?*

Evocative Drawing: "A Badge of Ability" (Hardy and Laszloffy, 2005)

Directives.   Make a badge like a policeman or fireman's badge and write on the badge three abilities or talents that make you proud. If you wish, you can wear your badge and take it home with you.

Evocative Writing Assignment: "Cumulative Strengths List" (Mordock, 2004)

Directives. My longtime colleague John Mordock (2004) suggested this technique to me. Each session the child is invited and encouraged to add to a cumulative list of strengths. If the child has a hard time getting started, the therapist can offer a menu of strengths and invite the child to pick from the list the ones that apply to him or her. In subsequent sessions the child would be encouraged to add a new strength to the list.

Alternatives or Modifications

Children who resist the above approach are invited to use pictures from magazines to depict their strengths. Children are asked to add to their collage each session by cutting out a picture that would depict an additional strength. Another option is to invite kids to draw a picture that shows something they do well and make a cumulative collection of such drawings.

Evocative Dramatic Skit: "Honored Guest"

Directives to the Therapist. The child is asked to be an honored guest on Dr. Dave's [the therapist] talk show. The child takes the part of the honored guest, and other guests and family members are invited to the show to talk about the nice things about the child that led to an award about to be given. Finally, the child is interviewed. The therapist should be sure the traits or good deeds being honored are genuine. Perhaps the best way to do this is to ask the child to pick one from his or her three top abilities that were displayed on the "Badge of Ability."

Evocative Drawing Strategy: "My Team"

Directives to the Child. *There are nine players on a baseball team on the field. They work together and back each other up. In basketball, there are five players on the court who try to work as a team. Pick either a baseball or a basketball team. Draw the nine players on a baseball team or the five players on a basketball team, whichever you choose. On the players' jerseys write the names of the people on your team, people who love and care about you, who support and help you. They could be family members, teachers, friends, coaches or others who support you in your community, such as scout leaders, church or synagogue leaders, anyone who is on your team.*

If you choose a baseball team and come up with more than nine members for your team the others can be on the bench, ready to come in and pinch-hit whenever they are needed. If you choose a basketball team and you have more than five members for your team, they can be bench players too, ready to come into the game when you need them. Add as many as you want, it's your team!

Alternatives or Modifications

Another option for a child who doesn't like to draw is to do a collage, cutting pictures of basketball players on the same team from sports magazines and writing the names of the players on the child's team on the jerseys. This may add impact if the child uses players from his favorite basketball or baseball team to add the names of his own "teammates." For kids who are football fans, the same exercise can be done with the eleven players on a football team who are on the field at any one time.

Evocative Imagery: "The Mystery Gift Auction"

Let's have fun pretending that you are bidding in an auction along with other folks for a mystery gift. The gift is beautifully wrapped in a rectangular box with gold ribbon, but neither you nor the other bidders have any idea of what is in the box. The bidding is very intense, but in the end you win the auction with a twenty-five-dollar bid. The auctioneer hands you the beautiful box with gold ribbon and wrapping, and all eyes are on you as you go off to the side to open your mystery gift. When you open the box what you find is a gift card in a beautiful handwriting that says, "These are the three things about me, about my life that I would like to keep into the future."

What are those three things about you or your life as it is now that is so valuable you would not want it to change; you would want to hold onto and continue to keep into the future?

Clinical Illustration: Sherry (Age Thirteen)

"The things I would like to hold onto into the future are one, to be thin; two to be smart; and three, to be athletic."

EVOCATIVE WRITING ASSIGNMENT: "HUMOR, AN INNER RESOURCE TO BE TREASURED AND HONORED" (PRE-TEENS AND ADOLESCENTS)

Directives

I would like you to think about a time when you were really upset, angry, sad, scared, or worried about something, and someone said or did something that made you laugh, something really funny, and this made you feel better. Write about that experience and any other situations like this when humor helped you to cope with a difficult situation.

Alternatives or Modifications

A child may prefer to draw a picture of the humorous situation or make a collage to depict the humorous situations that helped him or her to cope with adversity.

Evocative Quote: "The Gift of Humor"   Please discuss or write about the meaning of the following quote: "Laughter is the sun that drives winter from the human face" (Victor Hugo).

Discussion.   I have always marveled at children who have experienced so much suffering and deprivation in their lives who can still manage a good sense of humor. What a treasure, what a valuable resource to sustain you through life it is when you can see the comical and absurd side of life and have a good belly laugh once in a while.

Kate Rutherford (1994) described the therapeutic value of humor in psychotherapy. She noted that humor enhances the therapeutic relationship. Utilizing an Adlerian framework, Rutherford suggested that humor could increase social interest, reduce feelings of inferiority, and increase the courage of our clients to be imperfect and take themselves less seriously.

Evocative Writing Assignment: "The Qualities That Make Me a Good Person"

"The continual desire to regard the self as good is a unique feature of *Homo sapiens*. What is biologically special about our species is a constant attention to what is good and beautiful and a dislike of all that is bad and ugly" Jerome Kagan (1998, pp. 190–91).

Directives.   Write about your qualities that reveal your "goodness" as a person. If you have a hard time coming up with your good qualities as a person, think about what your best friend would say about you, if asked about your good qualities. Good qualities include kindness, generosity, caring about others, politeness, friendliness, helpfulness, to name just a few. Perhaps, you could write about a time when you were helpful, unselfish, giving, kind, or caring to others.

Alternatives or Modifications

Some children may prefer to simply tell a story that illustrates their good qualities; others may choose to draw a picture depicting one or more of these qualities; and still others may wish to make a collage that displays pictorially one or more of these qualities.

Evocative Quote: "Seeking Virtue" (Pre-teen or Adolescent).   *Please discuss or write about the meaning of the following quote: "Virtue is its own reward" (Marcus Tullius Cicero).*

Evocative Use of Symbols: "Symbolization of Virtue"   The child is asked to pick from a collection of miniatures those that would best symbolize her/his good qualities.

Discussion.   Kagan (1998) states, "Humans are selfish and generous, aloof and empathic, hateful and loving, dishonest and honest, disloyal and loyal, cruel and kind, arrogant and humble; but most feel a little guilt over an excessive display of the first member of these seven pairs" (p. 191). Kagan notes that there is universal human knowledge that maliciousness is wrong, that all human societies have rules and laws forbidding certain behaviors. A subjective sense of virtue is adaptive and is sought by every child. Such a feeling about oneself contributes to a sense of health and life satisfaction.

Evocative Writing Assignment "Helping Others"

> Not what we give, but what we share—
> For the gift without the giver is bare;
> Who gives himself with his alms feeds three—
> Himself, his hungering neighbor, and me.

> cited by Camp, 1990

Directives

I would like you to write about one or more times when you did something that was helpful to others that gave you a feeling of satisfaction. It might have been a time when you helped a younger child, a brother or sister, or a friend. Maybe it was a time when you helped an elderly person or a disabled child or someone who was being picked on.

Alternatives or Modifications

Some children may prefer to simply tell a story about helping others or draw a picture to depict the experience(s). Making a collage of such experiences is another option that some children may choose. Still another alternative is to ask the child to picture in his or her mind such an experience then either tell about it or draw it.

Discussion

Opportunities for developing a sense of virtue, to have validated one's capacity to give in a beneficial way to others, are more available to the privileged than to the severely economically oppressed members of human society. One of the most helpful interventions with children of wounded spirit is simply validating their capacity to give to others. It may be as simple as a teacher asking a child to take a message to the front office, or a parent asking the child for help in the house; even that validates her/his ability to be helpful. When exercised and reinforced, this capacity to help others has been a key feature in children who are identified as resilient in overcoming adversity in their lives. Yet it is so simple we may overlook it.

IDENTIFYING AND TAPPING INTERPERSONAL RESOURCES

It is important to also recognize and draw on resources within the family and community. Resilience research (Benson, 1997; Bronfenbrenner and Ceci, 1994; Werner, 1995) has consistently noted the importance of family and social support systems to buffer against adversity. Even the presence of one person close enough for the youngster to confide in protects against depression (Rutter, 1990).

Evocative Projective Drawing and Storytelling Strategy: "A Dog Named Teddy"

Newfoundlands are big dogs, the size of a St. Bernard, and are best known for their incredible swimming ability, due to their webbed feet. They were often used on sailing ships as rescue dogs. If a sailor fell overboard into the icy waters off the coast of Newfoundland, this magnificent breed of dogs would immediately jump in, happily rescue the sailor, and pull him back to the ship. The thick coat of the Newfoundland protects them from the icy water and subzero temperatures. Newfoundlands have been known to rescue family members while swimming even when they didn't need rescuing, because they heartily enjoy their heroic role as protector and rescuer.

The Story.   Teddy, a beautiful black Newfoundland dog that weighed over 160 pounds, was a much-loved member of the Meadows family. The Meadows family will always remember him as their special dog. Newfoundlands are wonderful family dogs. Of all Teddy's special and loveable traits, the one that the Meadows treasured the most was his temperament. Teddy adored the Meadows' daughters, Lee and Elizabeth. Lee was almost three years old when the Meadows brought Teddy home, just eight weeks old. Elizabeth was only one year old. Teddy grew up with the girls and soon considered himself the overseer of the children; if he thought the girls' parents were not exercising proper supervision, he would step in to correct the situation. The girls in turn, along with all the children in the neighborhood, loved Teddy.

In the wintertime, when the girls would go down the hill on their sleds, he would delight in grabbing the rope of the sled by his teeth and pulling them back up the hill. Of course, he was also quite mischievous, and to the Meadows girls' great annoyance he would at times pull their gloves off with his teeth and romp around with them, forcing Lee and Elizabeth to chase after him. He thought it was great fun!

Teddy was so gentle that even though he outweighed the girls by many times, he would allow them when they were only five and three years old to lead him around on his leash for a walk around the Meadows' large yard. He loved long walks with the girls and their parents along the country road they lived on, but an amazing thing would happen on these walks. Teddy would always position his body between the girls and the road, and if he thought they were getting a little too far out in the road he would use his hips to gently nudge them over. Even though Teddy was friendly to everyone, he was extremely protective of "his children," including the other children in the neighborhood.

Sadly, the Meadows only had Teddy for four years before he died, but he will always be remembered as a special part of their family. What a wonderful thing it would be if every child could have someone in his or her life like Teddy, even for a short time. It could be a pet, or a loving grandparent, or a special aunt, uncle, or cousin—someone who loved and protected the child and made him or her feel special. Since parents are only human, they make mistakes and can't always be there in just the way the child needs. This special pet or person helps give to the child what parents alone can't always give as much as they might want to.

Drawing Directives. *Please think about someone in your life who has been special to you. It might be a special pet or person, a teacher or a coach, a friend, a grandparent, an uncle or aunt, a brother or sister, or cousin. Think of someone, besides your parents, who was there for you when you were younger or is right now in some special way. Take your time, but when you are ready please draw that special person or pet.*

Follow-Up to the Drawing
1. *Tell me about your picture.*
2. *[If there are others in the picture] Please describe the other people or animals in the picture.*
3. *How old are you at the time of this picture?*
4. *What feeling does this picture bring up for you?*
5. *What title would you give your picture?*

Storytelling Directives

Now I want you to tell a favorite story or describe a favorite memory you have of that special person or pet that has played an important role in your life. Take as much time as you need to think about your special person or pet and to come up with one of your favorite memories or stories about that special person or pet.

Follow-Up to the Story

1. *Are there other things you remember or other stories you would like to share about this special person or family pet?*
2. [If it is not clear from previous statements] *Is that pet or person still in the child's life?*
3. *If not, can you tell me what happened to the person or pet?*
4. *Can you go farther and describe what the loss* [if applicable] *meant for you and the family?*
5. *Who in the family was most affected by the loss?*
6. *Who else can you turn to for help and support?*
7. *Have you helped someone else in a way that was meaningful to you?*

Alternatives or Modifications

Some children may prefer to do either the drawing or story but not both. It is important to honor the ways in which children can most comfortably communicate their feelings and ideas.

Evocative Writing Assignment: "Someone Who Made a Difference"   Write about a person or a pet that has had a major impact on your life. Write about how the presence of this special person or pet has helped you in your life.

Evocative Use of Symbol: "A Symbol of a Helping Person or Pet"   Ask the child to pick from a collection of miniatures a symbol that would best represent that special, helpful person or pet in her/his life.

Discussion

While this exercise can be powerful and reinforce the child's awareness of interpersonal resources, the risk, of course, is that the child will not be able to think of anyone who has played a special role in her/his life. In that case, it is crucial that the therapist "scale down" to help find something positive in the child's life. Help the children to think about someone who has influenced them in a positive way. Ask them to think about someone they look up to, someone who has been kind to them. Or if no one individual stands out, try to focus the child on a time when a grandparent, uncle or aunt, brother or sister did something that they considered especially kind and helpful. If they are unable to identify such an occurrence in the family, as might be the case with some angry or aggressive children, pursue such an experience with a Sunday school teacher, Boy or Girl Scout leader, coach or any other person outside of the family who in some way was helpful to them or touched their hearts.

I use the language "touched their hearts" in the sentence above quite deliberately, because in my judgment, to address the invisible wounds of these children (Hardy and Laszloffy, 2005; Crenshaw and Mordock, 2005a, 2005b) we have to use the language of the soul. Andrew Fussner has stated, "Aggressive children have too many tears inside" (Fussner, 1998). Unless we connect with kids in a heartfelt way we will not be able to effect meaningful change. Many of the evocative strategies in this volume are designed with this purpose in mind.

The question as to whether the child can remember a time when he or she has done something to help someone else is often overlooked in clinical work. In formulating a treatment philosophy in residential treatment (Crenshaw, 1990b), I have argued that we gain far more leverage for change in children when we highlight strengths rather than "pouncing on pathology" or "documenting damage" in kids. We also need to focus on "what is right" with them. Does a child or family need deficits pointed out or documented yet again? If change and healing is our purpose, we gain far more leverage by delineating strengths and assets in the child and family and then building on them.

> Nature, in giving tears to man, confessed that he
> had a tender heart: this is our noblest quality."
>
> Juvenal, *Satires*, c. A.D. 100
> (cited by Camp, 1990).

Evocative Imagery: "A Gesture of Generosity"

Think about a time when your heart was touched by a totally unexpected act of kindness. Try to picture in your mind the unexpected act of kindness, even if it was just a small gesture of kindness or generosity that meant a lot to you.

Drawing Directives. When you have a clear picture in your mind of such a time, please draw it as best you can. Or if you prefer you can picture a time when you did something that was kind, thoughtful, or helpful that touched the heart of another person. Then please draw a picture of that time.

Follow-Up to the Drawing

1. *Tell me about your picture.*
2. *How old are you at the time of your picture?*
3. *What feelings does your picture bring up for you?*
4. *What title would you like to give to your picture?*
5. *Are the others in the picture still in your life?*

Storytelling Directives

Now, when you are relaxed and ready to do it, I would like you to tell me a story of a time when someone did something that you did not expect, an act of kindness that touched your heart or perhaps a time when you surprised someone by doing something kind or helpful.

Follow-Up to the Story

1. Do you believe there is more evil or goodness in the world?
2. Why do you believe the above?
3. What changes do you hope to see in the world during your lifetime?
4. In yourself, do you see more good or evil?
5. How does it make you feel when you do something kind for someone else?
6. How does it feel when someone does something kind for you?
7. Between someone doing a kind thing for you or you doing something kind for someone else, which feels better to you?
8. Is there a change you would like to make in yourself that would make you feel better about yourself?

Alternatives or Modifications

Some children may prefer just to tell the story. Or other creative children may want to create a collage depicting these acts of unexpected kindness.

Evocative Quote: "A Bonus"   Please write about or discuss the meaning of the following quote: "It is one of the most beautiful compensations of this life that no man can try to sincerely help another without helping himself" (Ralph Waldo Emerson).

Evocative Story and Imagery: "The Sled Dogs of Denali"

The Story.   If you visit the vast and beautiful state of Alaska, you will not want to miss the sled dog demonstration at Denali National Park. Among the hazards faced by these working dogs and the park rangers called "mushiers," whom they pull behind them, are temperatures that can drop to forty degrees below zero or even colder, high winds that causes drifting snow that completely covers trails, or enraged moose who don't want to move off the trail to let the dogsled team pass (Fortier, 2002). The rangers have used dogs since 1921 to patrol the park, deliver essential items to park wildlife researchers, and break trails.

Karen Fortier (2002), the kennel manager at Denali, states, "The rewards of traveling by dog team can only be achieved if there is mutual respect between the dogs and the mushier. Each relies on the other, and over time, a deep level of trust and companionship is reached" (p. 3).

One of the thrills of visiting the dogsled demonstration at Denali is the opportunity to meet the dogs. They are unusually friendly; they love the attention they receive from the visitors. What is unforgettable, however, is the actual demonstration, when five of the dogs are harnessed to a sled pulling one of the rangers. One striking feature of this demonstration is how much these working dogs love to run and do their jobs. As soon as the harnesses and sled come out, all the dogs jump on top of their doghouses and begin to howl excitedly. They hope they will be picked to do the run. As soon as the harnesses are attached and the mushier releases the brake and gives the signal, the dogs take off with great enthusiasm.

The dogs work as a team, but each of the dogs knows its specific job. The two dogs in front, selected for their leadership traits, are the "lead dogs." They follow the commands of the mushier to turn to the left or right. The dog in the middle is called the "swing dog" and has the important role of maintaining balance, since a turn too sharp could cause the sled to turn over. The two dogs in the back are called the "wheel dogs." These dogs are usually larger and stronger than the others, and they do the heavy pulling. The adult dogs teach and mentor the pups and play an important role in preparing them to become part of the team.

Directives   Please think about your safety team. Think about all the people and perhaps family pets that work as a team to make you feel safe. The list might include

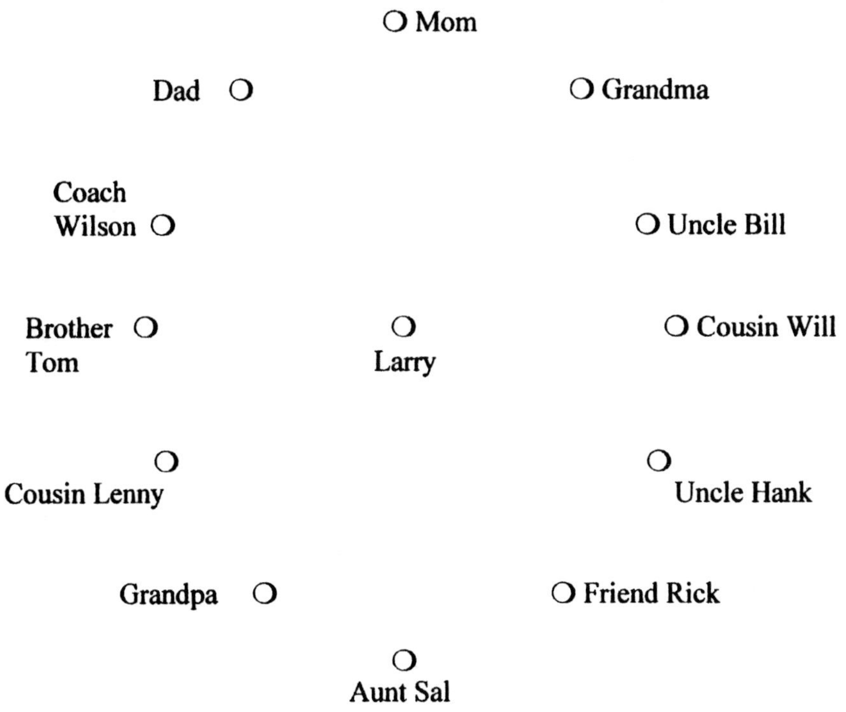

O **Mom**

Dad O   O **Grandma**

**Coach
Wilson** O   O **Uncle Bill**

Brother O   O   O **Cousin Will**
Tom   **Larry**

O   O
Cousin Lenny   **Uncle Hank**

Grandpa O   O **Friend Rick**

O
Aunt Sal

Figure 11.1.   Circle of Safety

your parents, grandparents, older brothers and sisters, godparents, aunts, uncles, cousins, family pets, teachers, coaches, and friends, and anyone else you can think of who helps you feel safe. Make a small circle in the center of the page and write your name under that circle. Then make a large outer circle made up of small circles, and next to each of those outer circles write the names of the members of your safety team. Make the circle as wide as possible to include all the members of your team who look out for you and protect you. This is your "Circle of Safety."

Discussion

This exercise makes explicit by means of a diagram the family and interpersonal resources available to the child, so essential to resilient functioning in life. Sadly, some people who have solid support systems of family and friends do not, because of pride or shame, make adequate use of those crucial resources. Others who would be receptive to such support simply do not have that circle of safety to turn to. Still others in moments of crisis or psyche anguish lose sight of both internal and interpersonal resources. This particular strategy will be of value for these kids especially, in emphasizing their available family and social/community support systems.

12

Themes of Empathy for Self and Others

EVOCATIVE IMAGERY AND FANTASY:
"TO FORGIVE OR NOT?" (ADOLESCENTS)

Directives

I would like you to think about the wrongs that have been done to you by others whom you have not been able to forgive. Forgiveness can be at least as helpful, if not more, to the forgiver as to the forgiven. By letting go of a wrong done to you in the past, you may lighten your load. Holding onto a grudge requires energy and determination that might be put to a use that would be more helpful to you. If you are holding onto resentments toward another person even to a slight degree, would you be ready to let go of one or more of them?

If not, ask, "Will it serve me best to hold onto these grudges or would I benefit by letting this one or even more than one go?" If you still believe it is best for you to hold onto these resentments, then you are not ready to let them go. Try to get an image in your mind of putting the resentments and grudges you hold in a backpack. Some of these resentments and grudges you carry are heavier than others. The stronger the resentment, the more intense the grudge, the heavier the weight.

Try to visualize that backpack. How heavy is the weight of that bundle of resentments and grudges you carry now?

Is that backpack of resentments and grudges light and easy to carry, maybe about ten pounds? Or is it getting heavy, perhaps twenty-five pounds? Or maybe it is already too heavy a load; could it be as much as fifty pounds, or even a hundred? If so, that is a lot of weight to be carrying around. Can you picture in your mind a time in the future when you will be able to lighten the load you carry by letting one or more of those resentments or grudges go? If so how much will the backpack weigh then?

If you are ready to let go of some of those resentments, think about the ones you are willing to let go. Who are the people you are willing to forgive at this point? You don't have to tell me about those wrongs or hurts that you are willing to let go or the people you are now willing to forgive, if you wish to keep it private.

Clinical Illustration: Rob (Age Fourteen)

Therapist: Rob do you feel there are some resentments, some grudges, that you have been carrying like a weight on your back for a long time?

Rob: Yeah, I guess so.

Therapist: How much is that weight in your backpack that you carry with you wherever you go?

Rob: I don't know.

Therapist: Is it fairly light, say five or ten pounds, or more substantial, maybe twenty-five pounds, or quite heavy, say fifty pounds?

Rob: I would say maybe thirty pounds.

Therapist: That's a pretty heavy load. Are there any of those grudges or resentments you are ready to let go of, that might lighten your load?

Rob: I'd have to think about that one.

Therapist: Sure, take all the time you need, and you don't have to give me an answer today if you want to think about it for a while. I want you to be sure you are ready to let go of a grudge or some hurt that has wounded you along the way.

Rob: I think I could forgive John.

Therapist: Is this a hurt that you are able to talk about with me, or do you consider it too private?

Rob: John was my closest friend until sixth grade. We did everything together. When his family went on trips they would invite me; when my family went on vacation they would invite John. Sometimes one or the other would not be able to go because of some reason, but we were always invited. We did sleepovers at his house and my house, we went on camping trips, we played sports together, we played countless hours of video games together, we were more like brothers, closer than just friends.

Then in sixth grade, John just started pulling away from me. Whenever I would call to invite him over he was always busy or something. I finally got the message. John had new friends, he had moved on and made friends with "cooler kids." He was never mean to me, but he just didn't have time for me. I am still trying to get over it.

Therapist: That must have hurt you deeply, and you still are trying to recover.

Rob: I felt stabbed in the back. I just couldn't believe that he turned his back on me that way. We spent so much time together and had so much fun.

We were part of each other's family. I still miss spending time with his family; they were like a second family to me. Both his mom and dad were great; I even liked his kid sister, even though she was a pain sometimes.

Therapist: So you lost not only your best friend, who was more like a brother, but also your second family. No wonder this has been hard for you to accept. But you feel that you are ready to forgive John, you no longer want to hold a grudge?

Rob: My resenting him just makes everything worse. John might be friendlier to me if I didn't resent him so much. He just stays away from me at this point. I think he feels bad.

Therapist: So you don't think John intended to hurt you? He just changed as he got older and was drawn to different kids as friends?

Rob: Yeah, but it still hurts.

Therapist: I am sure it does, regardless of how you explain it. But does it make it any easier to forgive him if you believe that he did not intentionally want to hurt you?

Rob: I do believe that. I would like to forgive him.

Therapist: Have you been thinking about this for a long time, since this seems like a big step?

Rob: Yes, I have wanted to do this for a long time but just haven't been able to do it. I talked with my minister, Reverend Perry, about it, but I just couldn't do it.

Therapist: What tells you that you are ready now?

Rob: I am sick of the way this eats at me. I am tired of being hurt and angry. I want to move on. I have new friends now, none as close as John and I were, but they're good friends.

Therapist: Since this is such a big step, would you like to think about it between now and next week, in case you want to change your mind?

Rob: No, I want to do it.

Therapist: By forgiving John and letting go of that grudge, how much weight are you removing from your back?

Rob: I would say about twenty-five pounds?

Therapist: That's what I call lightening the load!

Discussion

There is an intricate and close tie between empathy and forgiveness. It is nearly impossible to forgive if you lack empathy for the other or yourself. Rob is a bright and articulate fourteen-year-old and is able to beautifully express through words as well as metaphor the heavy weight that holding a grudge entails. One of the reasons that John and Rob went separate ways in sixth grade is that their interests diverged. Rob was a top student, while John was average at best. John was passionate about sports, while Rob had a wide range of intellectual interests and hobbies, and although interested in sports he was not the outstanding athlete that John was. Rob's ability to finally view the drifting apart in a less personal way was a major step toward letting go of the grudge. Since I knew this had been a major source of hurt and resentment for Rob, I attempted to slow down and restrain the change to test his resolve to take this step. Rob won the battle of initiative, as he should have, and convinced me that he was determined to do this.

The motivation for letting go of the hurt is the best possible for therapeutic change: "I am sick of the way this eats at me. I am tired of being hurt and angry. I want to move on." Bonime (1988) points out that the best possible therapeutic motivation is when a person reaches the point that they are "sick and tired of being a certain way and want to change it." This is the point that Rob reached, and yet I was amazed that he felt by taking this step that he would remove 83 percent of the weight he was carrying on his back.

Evocative Rituals: "Forgiveness of Others"

Repeat after Me.   Now I want you to think about the process of letting go and forgiveness. You can say the following words out loud or silently to yourself if you wish: "I am ready to let go and forgive you [say the name(s)] for what you did to me [name the hurts and wrongs done to you] so that I can lighten my load and move forward with my life." How much weight do you feel you dumped by letting go of these particular resentments or grudges? How heavy is that bundle of resentments and grudges now?

Clinical Illustration

Therapist: Rob, are you sure you are ready to take this step?
Rob: I want to do it. I wish I could have done it a long time ago.
Therapist: Okay repeat, after me [see the directives above].
Rob: I, Rob, am ready to let go and forgive you, John, for moving away from me, even though it hurt me more than anything else so far in my life, so that I can lighten my load and move forward with my life. I know you did not do this deliberately to hurt me. I now forgive you.
Therapist: How much weight are you carrying on your back now?
Rob: Not much, I would stick with about five pounds.

Additional Steps or Modifications

Communicating Forgiveness.   Are there any other steps that you would like to take in the letting go of these particular hurts, resentments, or grudges? Would you for example, want to tell the person or persons that you have forgiven them?

Clinical Illustration of Communicating Forgiveness

Rob: Yes, I think I would like to tell John. I think we would both feel better if I did. I don't know how I would do that just yet. It won't be easy.

Therapist: I agree with you. It will take a lot of courage to approach it directly with him, but I think you are right that it will probably help both of you. And courage is something you have a lot of. I don't know either how you will do it, but I am confident you will find a way.

Postscript

Rob is an inspiring kid, and two weeks later he worked up the nerve to call John at his home. He told me later it was one of the hardest things he has ever done. He told me that John's mom answered the phone and that he had the impulse to hang up the phone, because it was so awkward he was afraid he would not be able to summon his voice, but he did. When he identified himself, his mother was very cordial and immediately thereafter put John on the phone. Rob asked if John would meet him at the local pizza place tomorrow after football practice. John agreed, and they met the following day at Mickey's Pizza Parlor.

Rob was able to tell John that he has resented him the past two years because he moved away from him as a friend and that had hurt terribly but that he was now ready to forgive him. John was relieved and told him that he has felt very guilty that his interests had taken him in a different direction but that there were many times when he would have liked to spend time with Rob but he had known that Rob was so hurt and angry that he didn't know how to approach him. John also told him he pulled away further because seeing how hurt Rob was had made him feel so guilty that he just wanted to avoid him. John told Rob that he knew that was wrong and that he was very sorry that he did not have the courage to approach Rob. They agreed to talk more and get together once in a while, recognizing that the closeness they enjoyed in the past was no longer possible because they each had moved on at this point and each has a new group of friends.

EVOCATIVE WRITING: "LETTERS OF FORGIVENESS" (PRE-TEENS OR ADOLESCENTS)

Directives

Would you want to write a letter to the one or more persons you have forgiven? You do not have to send it to anyone. Would you like to write such a letter and not send it? If you don't send it, you will be free to express whatever feelings remain inside without fear of consequences. You may later want to write a letter that you would actually send.

Discussion

The option to write a letter that is not sent may be helpful to pre-teens or adolescents who have not been able to completely get past their hurt or anger. It may be a helpful intermediate step prior to actually sending a letter to a person they are ready to forgive, making that letter more truly a letter of forgiveness.

Clinical Illustration: Carrie Ann (Age Seventeen)

Dear Dad:

I have tried for a long time to forgive you, but it is not easy. How could you move to Boston and just forget about me? Do you know how much I worried about you when you left mom? I worried that you wouldn't have enough to eat. I was worried sick about you. I wondered if you were lonely. I would lay awake at night worrying about if you got sick, would anyone know? Would anyone take care of you? I worried about how much you were drinking? Did you ever worry about me? You remembered my birthday twice after you left. But I can't tell you how crushed I felt that on my ninth birthday you didn't come to see me, you didn't send a present, you didn't call, you didn't send a card; you just forgot about me! How could you do that? Don't you know how much I loved you and missed you? You need not answer those questions, because I know the answer to them all. Soon after my ninth birthday I found out about Beth. You were all wrapped up with Beth, and I was no longer on your mind. You couldn't even remember my birthday. That hurt like you will never understand. After that I saw you less and less, and I tried to make you unimportant to me. I even tried to hate you! I did hate you for a while. But it just made me more miserable. And as hard as I tried to pretend otherwise, you still are important to me. You will always be my Daddy.

Love,

Carrie Ann

Discussion

Carrie Ann was seventeen when she wrote the above letter, which she did not send. Her father had left when she was seven. Even though her father was a heavy drinker and had treated her mother badly, she had been his special little girl, their only child. His visits with Carrie Ann were sporadic and inconsistent, perhaps because seeing her and being reminded of his loss was too painful for him and led him to drink more.

Whatever the reason the lack of follow-through was devastating to Carrie Ann. Her ninth birthday marked the turning point, when he completely forgot Carrie Ann's birthday and his relationship with a woman, Beth, whom he eventually married, became known to Carrie Ann. The fact that another woman had taken the special place in her father's heart that had once belonged to her was extremely hard for her to forgive, and you can see in the above letter she is still struggling with intensely ambivalent feelings toward her father. A year later she wrote the following letter, which she did send to him.

Dear Dad:
　I hope you still remember me. I am your daughter Carrie Ann. I am eighteen now. It has been eight years since I have seen you. I think I would recognize you but I am not sure. I don't think you would recognize me if you saw me on the street. I will be graduating from high school in June. I am proud of the person I have become but I have had to work very hard to get here. If you knew me I think you would be very proud of me too. It breaks my heart that I am writing to my father as if I were talking to a stranger but that is what you have become to me. As much as I want to I am not ready to forgive you because I still hurt too much, but I would like to invite you to my graduation. I have cleared it with mom and she is okay with it. I do not wish to meet Beth, however, at least not yet. I feel we have to get reacquainted first. I am sorry but I just can't handle getting to know her when I feel I don't even know you anymore. I would like to have a relationship with you because you are still my father, and you are in spite of my anger and hurt, still important to me. I hope you will come to my graduation. Let me know as soon as you can.
　Love,
　Carrie Ann

Sadly, Carrie Ann never received a response to her letter, nor did her father come to her graduation. Prior to Carrie Ann sending the letter we talked about the possibility that she would not get the response she was hoping for. We discussed the possibility that she would be hurt still more. Carrie Ann said she understood that, and yet she needed to make this overture to her Dad, for herself. She did not want her own feelings to be the barrier that blocked possible reconciliation with her father. Carrie Ann was courageous in taking the risk that her invitation would be rejected or even worse ignored, as it turned out to be. Carrie Ann decided that she would be able to live with the loss better if she was convinced that she had done what she could from her end to bridge the divide with her father. My heart broke for her when day after day, week after week, leading up to the graduation she went to the mailbox and there was no answer to her letter. Yet she still insisted that she was glad that she went to her graduation knowing that it was not because she did not invite him that her father was absent. Carrie Ann, indeed, had many reasons to feel proud of the person she had worked hard to become, and the way she handled this issue was another one.

Evocative Ritual: "List of Wrongs"

Would you like to write down the hurts or wrongs that you are willing to forgive and then tear it up to symbolize that it is over? These steps are sometimes called rituals or forgiveness. Do you think such a step would be helpful to you in symbolizing that you are ready to let go and move on?

Evocative Role-Playing Strategy: "Empty-Chair Technique"

One other step that might be helpful is called the "empty-chair technique." You could pretend that the person or persons you are forgiving are sitting in one or more of these empty chairs; you can talk to them right now and tell them you forgive them. Do you think you would like to try that? If not, can you think of any other steps or rituals that might be useful to you as you try to forgive others?

The Unforgivable

You don't have to tell me about it if you prefer to keep it private or if you prefer you can tell me at a later time, a time that would be more comfortable for you, but has anyone hurt you or wronged you in a way that you consider unforgivable? If so, I am truly sorry that something so terrible happened to you. Can you picture or imagine any conditions or changes that would allow you to forgive what you now consider unforgivable? You may answer this question in your mind and keep it private, or you may tell me if you wish to share.

EVOCATIVE IMAGERY AND FANTASY: "FORGIVENESS OF SELF"

In order to have empathy for others we must have empathy for self. Empathy is the ability to understand, appreciate what another feels, and show this understanding and appreciation to the other. Likewise, in order to forgive another, we must be willing to forgive ourselves.

Directives

I want you to think about that bundle of resentments and grudges that you carry in the pretend backpack. Part of the weight in that backpack is the things you have not been able to forgive within your self. How heavy is that load right now? Is it getting lighter, heavier, or about the same?

Can you think of anything you have done—again, you can keep it private if you wish—that you would be willing to forgive yourself for? Perhaps it was something you did that really hurt someone. Maybe you did something foolish; something that embarrassed you. Possibly you feel humiliated by what you did, or didn't do, when you look back on it. If so, welcome to the human family. As far as I can tell, no one is perfect, we are all human.

Are there some things you have done or not done that you are willing to forgive and let go? Are you willing to accept your imperfections, your humanness? If not, what would it take for you to be ready to forgive yourself for one or more of the misdeeds you have committed?

Evocative Rituals: "Forgiveness of Self"

Repeat after Me. *If you are ready to do this, please say silently to yourself or out loud if you wish to share, "I forgive myself for* [name the wrongs you are willing to forgive]. *I accept my humanness and my imperfections and am willing to join the human club. I will do my best to learn from my mistakes, but I realize I will make other mistakes, because I am only human. I hope I will forgive those mistakes as well and learn all I can from them."*

"List of Misdeeds" *Do you think any of the rituals we used with forgiveness of others could be helpful to you in your efforts to be forgiving of yourself? Would you like, for example, to write down on a piece of paper the things that you are willing to forgive? Then you can decide what to do with it. You could tear it up into little pieces and let them scatter in the wind, or bury them, or dispose of them in some other way that would be meaningful to you.*

Evocative Writing: "Letters of Forgiveness of Self" *You could write a letter of forgiveness to yourself specifically naming the things you are willing to forgive. You could, if you wish, file the letter in a folder marked "Forgiven."*

Directive Evocative Strategy: Empty Chair "I-Me" Dialogue. *Another ritual of forgiveness consists of using the empty chair for an "I-Me" dialogue. Either the "I" or the "Me" could represent the forgiving part of yourself, and the other part could argue that you are not worthy or deserving of forgiveness. The forgiving part of self would need to convince the unforgiving part that you are worthy.*

Evocative Role-Playing: "I and Me Debate" Another option would be for the child to assign the role of "I" or "Me" to the therapist, with the child taking the opposite side, and the two engaging in a lively debate, with each arguing his or her respective positions and then switching roles. If the therapist is assigned the negative, critical position, the therapist should titrate the strength of his or her argument so the child is not overwhelmed. No such constraints pertain when the therapist is articulating the positive, accepting side of self.

Evocative Writing: "I" and "Me" Written Dialogue. You could also write out this debate between "I" and "Me" by drawing a line down the center of an 8.5-by-11-inch sheet of paper. On one side of the page write the arguments "deserving" or "not deserving" made by either "I" or "Me"; on the other side of the sheet write the opposite.

Evocative Drawing: "Tower of Misdeeds and Mistakes"   Another exercise that is useful for developing perspective taking skills is to use a scaling technique. The child is asked to draw a tower that would visually show by its height how big the misdeeds and mistakes are in "the eyes of the child." Right next to the tower "in my eyes," the child is asked to draw a tower to show how high it would be "in the eyes of the world."

The child should be asked, "Do you have other ideas that might help you to be more forgiving of yourself?" Remember, children are often more creative and imaginative than we are and frequently come up with helpful ideas.

Discussion

One of the most helpful tools available to the child therapist is empathy expressed in the therapeutic relationship. The therapist's attempts to understand through sensitive and attentive listening to the child—what is said and not said, the way it is said, the degree of feeling behind the words, or if not said, implied by nonverbal communication or embedded in symbolism—leads to what Daniel Stern (2004) and Daniel Siegel (2005) refer to as "transformative moments" in therapy. At these moments, as explained by Siegel (2005), changes are occurring in the brain, including the forming of new synaptic connections and new neural firing patterns that reflect the neurobiological correlates of the child's experience of "being seen," "being heard," and "being understood."

For children who grow up in environments that are toxic, this experience partly derives its transformative power from its uniqueness. These moments of intense connection can contribute to a process of meaningful change in the child. It is through the therapist's acceptance of the child that the child gradually learns to accept his or her self. It is through the experience of the therapist's compassion for the child that the child learns to have compassion for self and others. As a result of the understanding shown by the therapist toward the child, the child comes gradually to an understanding of self. And it is through empathy shown to the child by the therapist that the child can learn empathy for self and others.

As Meyers (2000) notes, empathy for self lays the groundwork for empathy with others, so the powerful, healthy, growth forces set in motion by the child's experience of empathy from the therapist can lead not only to changes in brain organization and functioning but to major changes in the child's internal as well as interpersonal world. This ripple effect, which is not easily captured in psychotherapy efficacy studies, may most truly reflect the value of child and family therapy.

EVOCATIVE PROJECTIVE DRAWING AND STORYTELLING STRATEGY: "THE FIGHT THAT NO ONE CAN WIN" (PRE-TEENS AND ADOLESCENTS)

Olga Silverstein (1995), now retired from the faculty of the Ackerman Institute for the Family, stated in a presentation at the institute that when a family fight is over the issue of who is right and each person is determined to be right, no empathy is possible. Walter Bonime (1987) in psychoanalytic supervision made the point that if the drive is to prevail over the other, to win no matter what, there is no peace in the family, and, on the scale of nations, there will be no peace in our world. Empathy is essential to understanding and respecting the feelings of others; insistence on being right no matter what the cost destroys the capacity for empathy.

The Story

Millie's father was a teacher with very strong opinions. Her mother was no "shrinking violet" herself; in other words, Millie's mother also voiced her opinions strongly. Millie liked a good fight herself. She argued frequently with her teachers as well as her parents, sometimes because she too had strong opinions, but other times she argued just for the sake of argument.

You can probably imagine what happened when the family gathered around the dinner table. Sooner or later someone would say something that provoked a strong reaction, and the family would engage in their favorite sport of heated argument. In the end everyone was frustrated, because no one could ever win the argument.

Once Millie had a friend, Carol, who was thirteen, the same age as Millie, for an overnight visit. Carol could not believe what happened at dinner. She thought she was watching a ping-pong match as the heated exchanges went back and forth. Carol did not say a word, nor did she eat much, because her stomach was all churned up from the tension in the room.

Drawing Directives

I would you like to please think about Millie's family and picture them in your mind. Are they at the dinner table, in the living room? What are they doing? You can include

Millie's friend Carol if you wish. It is your picture, so draw it any way you wish. When you are ready, please draw it as best you can.

Follow-Up to the Drawing

1. *Tell me about your drawing.*
2. *What is the strongest feeling you experience when you look at your picture?*
3. *How do you think Millie is feeling in your picture? Are there other feelings that she is experiencing?*
4. *If you included Millie's friend Carol in the picture what do you think she is feeling? Are there other feelings she is experiencing?*
5. *If you didn't include Carol in your picture, what do you think she was feeling when she was unable to say a single word?*
6. *Why do you think my story is titled, "The Fight That No One Can Win?"*
7. *Why did it seem to Carol that she was watching a ping-pong match?*
8. *If you had been invited to sit at the table as Millie's friend, how would you have felt?*

Storytelling Directives

I would like you to make up a story about how things turned out in the long run for Millie and her family. Pretend that you were invited by Millie five years later to come to dinner with her family. Make up a story about what that experience would be like. Millie is now eighteen. Do they argue the same, less, or more than they did when Millie was thirteen? Do you feel as uncomfortable during dinner as Millie's friend Carol did five years ago, or has something changed in the family? Pretend you are at Millie's home for dinner and make up the most interesting story you can about that experience.

Follow-Up to the Story

1. *Has anything changed in Millie's family?*
2. *Is so what are the changes that you notice?*
3. *If nothing has changed, how do you explain that?*
4. *What would have to happen for the family members to give up their need to argue so much?*
5. *Millie is approaching the age when she soon will leave home to go to college or find a job. If the frequent arguing has not stopped, how do you think she will feel about leaving home?*
6. *Have you ever known of a family that argued as often as Millie's family did?*
7. *If you had a chance to give Millie some advice, what would you tell her that might help her to cope with her difficult family situation?*

13

Themes of Healing,
Transformation, and Hope

Don't part with your illusions. When they are gone you may still
exist, but you have ceased to live.

Mark Twain

EVOCATIVE FANTASY: "THE MAGIC STONES"

This evocative strategy is intended to engage children in meaningful dialogue
around the three critical domains of their interpersonal world—family, school,
and friends—and concluding with a focus on their relationship to self. The age
range that this strategy will appeal to is wider than might be expected, since
teens as well as younger children are fascinated with magic and mystery. Of
course, the sophistication and depth of the response will be influenced by developmental capacity.

Directives

*I want you to pretend that you visit an interesting gift shop and you notice three small,
beautifully designed wooden boxes. You decide to open the three boxes and find that each
contains a magic stone. In the first box, underneath the stone is a note that says, "When
you hold this magic stone in your hand, you can change anything you wish about your
family." In the second box under the magic stone the note states, "When held in your
hand this magic stone permits you to change anything you wish about your school." In
the third box under the magic stone is a note that says, "This magic stone when held in
your hand makes it possible for you to change whatever you wish about your friends."
Now, which magic stone do you wish to hold in your hand first?*

211

The stones I use are quite colorful and beautiful; they were purchased in various gift shops and are readily available. If the therapist does not have a collection of stones, fancy buttons of different designs and shapes will do fine. To add to the suspense and drama for the kids I enclose each of the stones in Viatka straw-inlaid boxes. These beautiful and unique boxes come from the city of Viatka, in the Kirov area of central Russia;. this traditional folk-art item is now available outside of Russia. These strikingly pretty Viatka boxes are handmade of European linden or birch. Then the straw is cut into small pieces, dried, and hand-glued or inlaid to make the intricate geometric designs. The last step is to lacquer the box to fix the design. Children are fascinated with the beauty of both the stones and the boxes that contain them; they lend an air of distinction and importance to this fantasy strategy. The Viatka boxes can be ordered from the Russian American Company at (800) 742-6228, website www .russianamericancompany.com.

Follow-Up Sample Questions

1. *What made you decide to pick that magic stone first?*
2. *Tell me what you would like to change about your* [family, school, and friends]?
3. *Which of the stones do you choose second? What would you have wanted to change about your* [family, school, and friends]?
4. *How about the third magic stone? What would you want to change about your* [family, school, and friends]?
5. *Now, there is a fourth box, and the magic stone in this box allows you to change anything you wish about yourself. What would you like to change about your self?*

Follow-Up Questions

1. *How would your life be different if you could make these changes in your family, school, in your friends, and yourself?*
2. *Are there some things about your family that you would like to keep just the way they are and see them continue into the future?*
3. *Are there things about your school that you would not want to change, not now or in the future?*
4. *Are there things about your friends that you would want to keep the same both for now and into the future?*
5. *Finally, are there things about yourself that you don't want to change, not now or even into the future?*

Clinical Illustration (Lynn, Age Thirteen)

Lynn, oppositional and strong-willed, picked the box containing the magic stone that would allow her to change her school first. Lynn said that what she would change about school is that "there would be no more finals or midterm exams, no Spanish." She also added, "The teachers wouldn't be so uptight." She also shared her concerns about the drug problem in her school: "The teachers don't really know what is going on in terms of drugs. I wish we had our old principal back—he was really cool." When asked why she had picked this magic stone (school) first, she said, "That's where I have the most problems."

Lynn next picked the box that contained the magic stone that would allow her to change her family. When she held the magic stone in her hand, she said, "I wish my parents were back together but not fight." Lynn than took the "magic stone" from the third box (Friends) and said, "I wish my friends didn't turn their backs on me. Kids who I considered to be my best friends don't even speak to me anymore. It stinks, it hurts a lot." When Lynn took the "magic stone" from the fourth box (Self), she said, "I would like to be more books smart and a little taller. Reading a book takes a long time. I can't concentrate very well."

Lynn's responses in all probability were more revealing and led to richer dialogues than if I had just asked the questions directly. She had been strongly opposed to participation in therapy but through this face-saving device she was able to engage in a meaningful way. Her responses suggest that she is experiencing a significant degree of pain in all three social domains of family, friends, and school, and that she also is not happy in her relation to self.

Clinical Illustration: Jenny (Age Thirteen)

"I would pick the magic stone that allows me to change school first. I would make the school larger, about twice the amount of kids. I would change the amount of homework I get; it is too much. I would like my Dad to come and pick me up at school more often and be more involved with school.

"Then I would pick the magic stone that allows me to change some things about my friends. I would like to have three old friends who have moved away back at school with me. I really miss them. I still see them once is a while but not very often.

"The magic stone that would allow me to change things in my family I chose last because this is the hardest one for me. I would change the fact that I don't get to spend enough time with my Dad. I would reverse the divorce and go back to when there was no anger or tension between my parents. I would have to go back to when I was four or five. I would change where my Dad lives so he wouldn't be so far away. I would like him to be more involved in lots of things in my life but now he is not."

Alternatives or Modifications

Evocative Quote: "Hopes and Dreams" (Pre-teens or Adolescents).   Please discuss or write about the meaning of one or more of the following quotes.

- "Go confidently in the direction of your dreams! Live the life you've imagined" (Henry David Thoreau)
- "It's difficult in times like these: ideals, dreams and cherished hopes rise within us, only to be crushed by grim reality. It's a wonder I haven't abandoned all my ideals, they seem so absurd and impractical. Yet I cling to them because I still believe, in spite of everything, that people are truly good at heart" (Anne Frank, diary entry, July 15, 1944, in Frank and Pressler, 1995, p. 332).

Evocative Writing Assignment: "Obstacles to Living Our Dreams" (Pre-teens or Adolescents).   Please describe, or write about some of the barriers that prevent people from pursuing their dreams and living the life they imagine.

Evocative Fantasy and Drawing Strategy: "A Picture of the Life of Your Dreams" (Pre-teens or Adolescents).   Please picture a life for yourself in the future, the life of your dreams. When you are able to picture it, please describe and/or draw it as best as you can.

Evocative Quote: "Optimism and Hope" (Pre-teens or Adolescents).   Please discuss or write about the meaning of one or more of the following quotes.

- "Keep your face to the sunshine, and you cannot see the shadows" (Helen Keller)
- "It is never too late to be what you might have been" (George Eliot).

Evocative Imagery and Fantasy: "Turning the Clock Back"
If you could turn the clock back to an earlier time, what age would you choose and why? Describe what your life was like at that age.
Clinical Illustration: Kristin (Age Twelve)
"I would turn the clock back to when I was two. I was going to nursery school in upstate New York, and my parents were still together. I hate the city. I loved living in the country and I had a lot of friends that I left behind when we moved to the city when I was nine."

EVOCATIVE SCENARIO: "TURNING POINTS"

Floyd Patterson, a former heavyweight boxing champion of the world, tells the story of a teacher who took a special interest in him and went out of her way to help him. He credits that teacher with helping him to turn his life around when he was headed in the wrong direction (Van Ornum and Mordock, 1988).

Directives

Please think about some kind of difficulty you have faced or obstacles that you have overcome. What was the turning point for you in facing and surmounting this challenge in your life? Was there a particular event or a situation that was a turning point for you? Was there a particular person who played a key role in helping you get through such a difficult time? What did you learn from that experience that you would be willing to share?

Clinical Illustration: Richard (Age Thirteen)

"Last year at school when other kids were getting on my case and wouldn't let up, my parents, the assistant principal, and you [therapist] were helpful in getting me through it. The kids are only slightly better in the way they treat me but I am handling it a lot better. I learned that sometimes a molehill seems like a mountain but it isn't. I've learned to treat it like a molehill."

Discussion

The interpersonal world from infancy on is a primary shaper of who we become. This evocative strategy appeals to most kids and early adolescents; it engages them in discussion about the crucial connections within family, school, and the larger community of friends, and finally their relationship with self. Olga Silverstein (1995) stated in a presentation, "Therapy is all about making connections including connection with self." She also asserted, "Disconnection may be harder than death. It is a more confusing kind of loss." In clinical work, we encounter the pain of disconnection in many forms.

   Disconnection is the fertile ground where the seeds of symptoms are planted (Fussner, 1999). If we treat the symptoms but don't address the disconnection, we are "whistling into the wind." This evocative technique goes to the heart of the disconnections in the lives of kids in a playful context that sets the stage for kids to talk about those vital ruptures in their interpersonal world. Child-development research suggests that the best long-term predictor of healthy adjustment in adult life is adequate social functioning in childhood. James Garbarino (2006) in a lecture states, "Social rejection is like a psychological malignancy—in every culture the kids turn out badly, because social acceptance is one of the most basic needs of the human being." The work of Daniel Stern (1985) has determined that the interpersonal world of the infant is pivotal in getting a child off to a good start in life via empathic matching from the mother and/or father.

Hardy and Laszloffy (2005) make the case that among the different kinds of trauma, the most neglected in the mental health field is sociocultural trauma. They describe the crucial role of community in the lives of youth. Those who grow up in extreme poverty and those who experience devaluation due to race, gender, class, or sexual orientation may experience disruption in all facets of community. Hardy and Laszloffy (2005) divide community into three segments: primary, which includes family; secondary, which consists of the wider social network of friends from school, sports teams, scouts, and other social activities; and finally, the cultural community. The cultural community constantly sends messages to a given youth as to how he or she is perceived in the context of prevailing cultural norms, attitudes, and expectations. A child of color or growing up extremely poor, regardless of color, typically receives devaluing messages from an early age. Hardy and Laszloffy (2005) define devaluation as "being stripped of the essentials of one's humanity." They point out that if kids experience success in one domain of community, it helps to buffer them from the impact of disruption in the other two domains. "The Magic Stones" strategy will stimulate dialogue about these essential relations to the three community domains as well as relationship to self.

EVOCATIVE PROJECTIVE DRAWING AND STORYTELLING STRATEGY: "ELI AND ZUKO IN THE LAND OF ENDLESS HOPE"

The Story

Once there was a young zebra named Zuko who wandered away from his papa and mama zebra and became lost and confused. He wandered into unfamiliar territory and was frightened by the possibility of lions and tigers that would love to eat a zebra for dinner. Zuko was sad and scared. He was quickly losing hope that he would ever see his mama and papa again. Then he saw an elephant on a distant horizon. Zuko decided to approach the elephant, cautiously. Perhaps the elephant would be friendly and help Zuko find his papa and mama. As Zuko came closer to the huge elephant, many times larger than he,

Zuko began to shake in fear. Zuko stopped, frozen in terror as he looked at this mountain of an animal only a short distance ahead. Zuko called out in a quivering voice to the elephant, whose name was Eli, "Can you help me? I am lost." Eli asked, "Why are you shaking?" Zuko wanted to cry, but bravely he said, "I am scared. I don't know where I am, and I can't find my mama or papa."

The elephant said, "My name is Eli. What is your name?" "My name is Zuko. Can you help me?" Eli replied, "I don't know if I can help you to find your mama and papa, but I can show you the way to the Land of Endless Hope, where anything is possible. Follow me, and I will take you there."

Zuko was already tired when he started out following Eli, and he followed him for a long time. He was so weary he didn't think he could take another step when finally they arrived at the gate to the Land of Endless Hope. Eli passed through the gate first, followed by Zuko, whose legs were ready to give out. When Zuko passed through the gates, he looked up and couldn't believe what his eyes saw. His mama and papa were waiting for him in the Land of Endless Hope, where all things are possible.

Drawing Directives

Try to get a picture in your mind of Zuko and Eli. Where do you picture them? Are they just meeting or on the way to the Land of Endless Hope or passing through the gates where Zuko is reunited with his mama and papa? When you have your picture of Eli and Zuko clearly in mind, please draw them as best you can.

Follow-Up to the Drawing

1. *What is Zuko feeling in your picture?*
2. *Why do you think hope is so important?*
3. *Can you think of a time when hope was important to you or someone you know in getting through a difficult situation?*
4. *Do you think Zuko would have trusted Eli and made the long trip to the Land of Endless Hope if he didn't have hope?*
5. *What were some signs that Zuko saw that made him trust Eli?*
6. *What signs would have told Zuko not to trust Eli?*

Storytelling Directives

I want you to think about Zuko meeting Eli when he was about to lose hope. At just that point Eli showed him the way and accompanied Zuko to the Land of Endless Hope, where all things are possible. Pretend for a moment that you are Zuko. Have there been any Eli's that you have encountered in your life, someone who has shown you the way to a more hopeful place just when you needed it the most? It could be a parent, a grandparent, an uncle or aunt, a big brother or sister, a teacher, a coach, a minister, a priest, or rabbi. It could even be an Eli inside of you that always holds out hope that takes you to a better place when things are really tough. It could be your beliefs or spiritual faith that take you to a more hopeful place. Think about this for as long as you need to, and when you are ready to tell me your story of the Eli in your life, please do. If you can't think of someone who was there to show you the way when you really needed it, make up you own story about someone who could have been a big help to you when you faced a tough situation. When you are ready, tell me your story.

Follow-Up to the Story

1. *Is your story of your "Eli" real or pretend?*
2. *If pretend, who are the people in your life who give you the most hope?*
3. *If real, what would be one word that would best describe your "Eli?"*
4. *Have you been an "Eli" for someone else? If not would you like to be if the opportunity arose?*
5. *What can be learned from your story?*

Clinical Illustration: Follow-Up to Angela's Drawing (Age Eight)

> *Therapist:* What would be a good title for your drawing?
> *Angela:* "To the Land of Endless Hope"

Figure 13.1.   Zuko and Eli on the road to the "Land of Endless Hope"

Therapist: What is Zuko feeling in your picture?

Angela: He is feeling very scared. He can't move very fast because he is shaking so much and he is afraid he might get lost again because the elephant is way ahead of him. But he is also excited because Eli is taking him to the Land of Endless Hope.

Therapist: Why do you think hope is so important?

Angela: If you believe in it, it is more likely that you will find what you want or your wish will come true. If you just believe in yourself and have hope it will happen.

Therapist: Can you think of a time when hope was important to you or someone you know in getting through a hard time?

Angela: I don't know. One time I was lost in a hotel. They had a big birdcage in the hotel. I got separated from my mother. I was about three years old. I was able to finally find her, but I was very scared.

Therapist: Do you think Zuko would have followed Eli if he didn't have hope?

Angela: No. He had to have hope. If he didn't follow Eli he might have just stayed there. He would have been easy prey for lions or tigers.

Therapist: What signs do you think Zuko was looking for that told him to trust Eli?

Angela: Eli was really big; he could protect him. He knew his way all around the land.

Therapist: What signs would have told Zuko not to trust Eli?

Angela: If Eli's face was like really mad, like he didn't like zebras or something. By the tone of his voice and the way he looked at him.

Evocative Writing Assignment:
"Someone Who Led the Way" (Pre-teens and Adolescents)

Write about a time when someone "showed you the way." Perhaps you were feeling lost or without direction and someone you turned to was helpful in getting you back on the right path. If you prefer, instead of writing, you can simply tell me the story.

Discussion

Hope is a vital ingredient that keeps people going when faced with a serious illness or a desperate financial situation that oppresses them. Hope is often the essential bridge from present unbearable conditions to the possibility of better days ahead. Without hope of something better the child or family might stop trying and resign themselves to endure the pain of their present situation. Hope can fuel the determination of people to weather hard times.

EVOCATIVE CHILD-CENTERED THERAPEUTIC PLAY:
"HEALING THE WOUNDED AND SICK"

In the beginning phases of therapy, typically the child is the doctor who heals the puppet characters or the play animals that are brought in with various injuries and illnesses. The child's identification with the healer and the healing process is a hopeful prognostic sign. The therapist can track the severity of the injuries, wounds, and illnesses of the puppet and animal figures brought to the healer. It is noteworthy as well whether the wounded recover or worsen, perhaps even die. One hypothesis to be checked against other data in the form of redundant themes and patterns within the symbolic play is whether the degree of woundedness of the animals reflects their own perceived damage; it is also possible that the animal's response to treatment is a barometer of their own hope of healing.

Another variable to track is the degree of compassion and empathy shown by the child in his or her role as doctor and how consistent these qualities are. This facet of the symbolic play may yield clues not only to the child's life experience but also the degree of trust or mistrust in the therapist as a potential healer. It is important within the framework of a collaborative approach to therapy to view these as tentative hypotheses, some of which will be confirmed and others discarded as more data is gathered as therapy proceeds.

Clinical Illustration: (Lucy, age Seven)

Lucy had a history of exposure to chronic domestic violence. She was drawn to the doctor's kit early on in therapy. She asked the therapist to bring the animal puppets to her office to be examined and treated. Most of the animals had serious wounds, and she was very kind and attentive to them.

Lucy: What animal have you brought to me today?

Therapist: I want you to take a look at my golden retriever; he is not acting right. Can you help him, Dr. Lucy?

Lucy: Let me take a look at him. I'll check his pulse, his blood pressure, and listen to his heart.

Therapist: Do you think there is something wrong with his heart?

Lucy: I don't know but I want to check it. Poor fellow, he is such a nice dog.

Therapist: He is a wonderful dog; I hope it is nothing serious, Dr. Lucy.

Lucy: It is too early to tell. Now please be quiet—I am trying to concentrate.

Therapist: Sorry, Dr. Lucy, I am just worried about him.

Lucy [after using the stethoscope]: I am afraid it is his heart.
Therapist: What? What is wrong, Dr. Lucy, with his heart?
Lucy: I don't know, we have to run more tests, but I am afraid it is serious.
Therapist: Dr. Lucy, do you think he has a broken heart?
Lucy: I am afraid so.
Therapist: Will we be able to help him through this? Will he recover and get well again?
Lucy: We are going to do everything we can. It is too early to tell. I don't know.
Therapist: Is there any cure for a broken heart?
Lucy: I can't say: I just don't know yet.

Discussion

Even though this therapeutic dialogue is offered as an example of child-centered symbolic play, notice that the therapist, through the metaphor, introduces the tentative hypothesis that the dog is suffering from "a broken heart." If "Dr. Lucy" had rejected that notion, I would have followed the path she chose instead, but she embraced the possibility as worthy of further investigation. It is fascinating that neurobiologists have identified a neural network around the heart that appears to be particularly attuned to the state of our relationships (Siegel, 2005). "Heartbreak" is not simply a romantic or poetic metaphor.

Almost certainly a child-centered therapist who is a purist would strongly object to my collaborative interpretative activity within the metaphor—that is, my suggestion that the dog might be suffering from "a broken heart." I would argue that I was being "child responsive." As noted, if "Dr. Lucy" had rejected the tentative suggestion that the dog's condition was a broken heart, I would have followed the path she chose instead; "Dr. Lucy" not only did not dismiss out of hand the tentative diagnosis of a "broken heart" but thought it was worthy of further investigation. I would maintain that such collaborative interpretative activity embedded in the symbolic play enriches the therapeutic process and leads to potentially healing therapeutic dialogue.

Lucy's ambivalence about trusting the therapist and risking the possibility of further hurt should he prove not to be reliable was reflected in the unpredictable shifts that took place in her playing the role of the doctor. Usually she was responsive to the needs of her patients, but other times she would be surly and impatient. Most of the times she made herself available, but other times would not answer the phone or would even hang up when I called for an appointment. "Dr. Lucy" would sometimes go on vacations and close the office without prior notice to her patients.

These mood shifts and unpredictable changes were likely a result not only of her tense and sometimes violent family life but also a reflection of her fears that I would not be there for her at a critical time, that I might let her down or even abandon her if she were to let her guard down. In my role as the one bringing animals for treatment, I reflected the feelings that I thought she was struggling to master.

Therapist: I can't believe Dr. Lucy went off on vacation without telling us in advance. Who can you trust? Who can you rely on? Even those you think are going to help you, can really let you down. It is so confusing. Dr. Lucy was so kind and helpful. We really trusted her. Now she doesn't answer my calls, and even hung up on me. I don't know what to make of it. I am hurt and angry. Yet she has been so good to us in the past.

Lucy: Well, I am back. I will see your animals. Bring them to my office and I will take care of them.

Discussion

In response to my reflecting the feelings of being betrayed and abandoned by Dr. Lucy, she suddenly reappears and shifts back to being a kind, compassionate healer. The play drama can be understood as Lucy's attempt to communicate her unpredictable, shifting world, which has often left her feeling crushed. Because of the instability that has been the hallmark of her life, she wrestles with whether to chance trusting her therapist; will he too suddenly shift in his attitude toward her, adding further hurt and disappointment to her already barely tolerable pain? "Dr. Lucy" returning and resuming her kind, healing role gives clues as to which way she is leaning in trying to resolve this conflict.

Obviously, in the intolerable situation at home that Lucy faced, simply working with her issues of invisible wounds and consequent lack of trust without addressing the toxic family situation would offer little benefit. Her parents reluctantly agreed to work with another therapist to address their own issues and to make the home a safer and more predictable place for Lucy and her brother Andy. Andy was older and had more friends and interests, which took him out of the home more often than Lucy, so he was spared some of the emotional injuries that Lucy suffered.

Toward the middle and ending phases of the year-long therapy with Lucy, she became trusting enough to allow me to play the role of the doctor, and she would bring the sick and wounded to me to care for. When she played the doctor in the later phases there were no more dramatic shifts. "Dr. Lucy" faithfully took care of her patients in a reliable manner that reflected her greater trust and the improved stability at home. During the ending phase she even allowed herself to be sufficiently vulnerable to be "the patient" herself and to be treated by Dr. Dave.

My door will remain open to Lucy and her family through the remainder of her developmental years, because she made it clear through the redundant themes of her play that being able to call on a healer when really needed is essential. I "heard" the message, and she has been in a few times since we ended the first course of therapy, when brief crises have arisen. Her parents, to their credit, continue working with a marriage and family therapist.

Evocative Drawing and Imagery: "A Healing Place"

Drawing Directives. Please try to picture "a healing place" for you. It is a place where you feel at peace, free of worries, and totally safe and relaxed. During the time you are there you don't have any concerns or troubles, and when you leave your place of healing you have new energy and ability to face your worries and troubles. Use your imagination to create a place of healing for you. When you are ready, please draw it as best you can.

Follow-Up to the Drawing
1. *Tell me about your picture of a healing place for you.*
2. *Is this a place that you have gone to or a place that you have created in your mind?*
3. *When you go there in your mind, do you picture yourself alone or with someone?*
4. *If with someone, describe why you picked that person or persons to be with you in your place of healing.*

Storytelling Directives. Please think about a time when you really needed a place of healing. It may have been a time when you were upset, worried, angry, or sad. Perhaps it was a time when you felt that nobody could understand how you felt? When you have such a time in mind, please tell me the story.

Alternative Directions and Modifications

If the child blocks and is unable to create a story, the therapist can "downshift" and emphasize that the child doesn't have to be extremely upset but also normalize that everyone gets upset at times. Everyone wishes at times that they could go to a place that is calm and peaceful for them, a place of safety, of refuge, a place where they can be alone or be with just a few people who they would want to be with them. If they are still unable to do it, perhaps they could try to think of the kind of situation that would make them want to go to a place of healing.

Another scaling-down alternative is to ask the child to think of someone he or she knows who went through an upsetting or hard time and could have used a place of healing. Again, it would be important to normalize the experience and explain that everyone has upsetting things that happen to them at times, though some experiences are more upsetting than others.

Follow-Up to the Story

1. *What title would you give to your story?*

2. *You probably did not call it a "healing place," but has there been for you somewhere along the way, a place that you would go, a hiding place, perhaps a secret place, a fort in the woods, or maybe a corner of a closet in your house, that you would go to when bothered or upset about something?*

3. *If so, you have already discovered the need that everyone has for what I call a "place of healing." Sometimes things happen that really hurt or wound us and we need a time and place to heal. We don't always need to be alone; we may want at those times to be around those we love and trust the most. That, however, may not always be possible. If a bully is picking on you in the schoolyard, you might want your big brother to be there with you but that may not be possible. But at times like that no one can stop you from going to "your healing place" that you have created in your mind. Now, I want you to close your eyes if you are comfortable doing so and go right now for a few minutes to your "place of healing." When you are ready you can open your eyes and refocus on this room in the present moment.*

4. *Please hold onto your "healing place" picture. You may think of other details you would like to add that would make it just right for you. The more real, colorful, and rich you can make it, the more useful it can be to you. It is important to practice going to your "healing place" each day, even if you don't have an upsetting experience. You can go there just to feel calm and relaxed. The more you practice going there in your mind, the easier it will be when you really need to go there. Picture in your mind just as you did in your drawing as many details as you can—sounds, sights, smells, and anything else that makes it seem like you are actually there in your place of healing.*

5. *You can make more than one picture and have more than one healing place. You may love both the ocean and the mountains. They could both be healing places for you, but at a certain time, you might feel more like going to the mountains than to the ocean. So, if you are able to come up with more than one healing place, it will give you a choice at a time when you are upset as to which place to go to in your mind. There is no right place, just the right place for you. Since this is your creation, you are in charge of it. No one can take it away*

from you. It is your healing place, where you can go in your mind whenever you feel bruised or hurt by something upsetting that happens.

EVOCATIVE ROLE PLAYING TECHNIQUES: "BEST FRIEND IN TROUBLE"

Let's pretend that your best friend is in trouble, facing a very stressful and difficult situation. He or she turns to you for advice and help. Let's role-play what you would say or do to try to help your friend. Which role do you want to take?

Discussion

Children, especially when stressed, can benefit from having a place of healing. For some children it might be a rainbow that appears in the sky after a storm. For other kids it might be the mountains, or a lake, a river, a waterfall or a peaceful spot in the woods. It might for some children be their church or synagogue or mosque. For another child it might be a tree house or a fort built with friends in the backyard.

Some cautions and drawbacks to this strategy need to be considered. A subset of children even with the modifications suggested above may not be able to use their imagination to create a place of refuge, safety, and healing, because in their world there has been no such thing. This may be an alien concept to a child growing up in a high-crime urban neighborhood with frequent exposure to community violence.

If an inner-city family at nighttime has to dive to the floor to escape stray bullets from a gunfight in the streets, the concept of "a healing place" may indeed seem far-fetched. In this case, it is important to validate their reality, to acknowledge that when violence comes right to their doorstep, when bullets penetrate the walls of their home, when they witness shootings in the neighborhood on the way to school, they are not going to find it easy to create in their mind "a healing place."

At a time of eminent danger, of course, it would be risky to go to a "healing place" in their mind even if it were possible, because of their need to react quickly to the threat. At the same time, I don't think we should assume or prejudge anything. Children in the inner cities, exposed to constant violence, often have the same hopes and dreams of other children, especially when they are young. Some of these hopes and dreams will be crushed as they get older and they encounter the unfavorable odds of overcoming the huge barriers of poverty, limited educational, vocational opportunities, and perhaps discrimination due to race, class, or gender. Like children anywhere, a number of these children are creative, artistic, imaginative, and may be able to create a "healing place" in their mind even if none exists in their reality. In that instance, it would be crucial to discuss issues of timing, when would it be helpful and when it would not be helpful, to go to their "healing place" in their mind.

EVOCATIVE PROJECTIVE DRAWING AND STORYTELLING STRATEGY: "THE MAGICAL BRIDGE THAT LEADS TO THE PLACE YOU WANT TO BE" (ADOLESCENTS)

Let's have some fun pretending that there is a magical bridge that crosses over a turbulent body of water; it can be somewhat scary crossing over the bridge, since the waters are raging below and the currents swift. It is a bridge that you would not want to fall from, because the waters below can be treacherous. It may be scary and difficult at times during the crossing, but because it is a magical bridge, when you reach the other side you find yourself in the place you always wanted to be—a special land or place that you can either make up in your imagination or a real place that you love and would like to go to.

Drawing Directives

When you are comfortable and relaxed try to picture that magical bridge and be sure to include yourself and anyone else you wish in the picture. When you are ready, draw your picture of the bridge and of you and any others you choose to accompany you, and write the word "Start" on one side of the bridge and "Finish" on the other side. Put yourself on the bridge according to how close or faraway you are now from the place you want to go.

Follow-Up to the Drawing

1. *What would you choose for the title of your picture?*
2. *Why did you decide to place yourself on the bridge at the point that you chose?*
3. *If you did not make it all the way across the bridge to the place that you want to go, what obstacles stand in the way of your completing your crossing of the bridge?*
4. *If others came with you, who are they, and why did you choose them to accompany you on the crossing?*
5. *If you have not made it across the bridge, how confident are you that you will make it to the other side to the place you want to go? Rate your confidence on a ten-point scale, with 10 being totally confident and 1 showing no confidence at all.*

6. *Is your bridge a strong, safe one or is there danger in crossing your bridge? Can you think of some ways to make it safer?*

Storytelling Directives

Please think about the place on the other side of the bridge that you want to reach. What is this place like? Describe what it looks like? What are the features of this place you like best? Is this a real place you have been to or is a make believe place that you invented in your imagination? Besides the people you chose to accompany you on the bridge, are there others that you would like to join you in this special place of your dreams? After you have reflected on these questions and feel ready, make up a story about the place that you reached when you crossed over the bridge.

Follow-Up to the Story

1. *What would be a good title for your story?*
2. *Of all the places you could have chosen to go, why did you choose this place?*
3. *How do you think the story will turn out in the long run? If you could be in this special place, would you want to stay there forever, or would you want to stay for a while and then move on to someplace different?*
4. *Is there anything you left out of your story of this special place that you would like to add or anything you wish to change?*

Discussion

According to J. C. Cooper (1978) in *An Illustrated Encyclopaedia of Traditional Symbols,* a bridge can symbolize communication between heaven and earth; one realm and another; or uniting man with the divinity. Cooper explains further, "In crossing the perilous bridge man proves he is a spirit and returns to the lost Paradise" (p. 25). Bridges, in addition to symbolizing the connection between this world and next, can symbolize rites of passage, conquering and mastering some difficult challenge, reaching an important milestone, or perhaps beginning a new chapter in life after confronting some painful aspect of one's past life. The last sentence of Thornton Wilder's (1927 [reprinted 1955]) Pulitzer Prize–winning novel *The Bridge of San Luis Rey* reads: "There is a land of the living and a land of the dead and the bridge is love, the only survival, the only meaning" (p. 148). Thus the rich symbolism of a bridge serves as an evocative symbol for the projective drawing and storytelling strategy described above.

Creating hope is a very delicate operation with timing a critical variable. Not only do we risk minimizing and trivializing the pain of our child and family clients if this is not done in a sensitive way, but we also can make the mistake of trying to move our child clients too quickly through their sense of hopelessness and despair. Children may need their feelings validated and worked through before they are truly able to adopt a more hopeful outlook. Creating hope is also in conflict with the survival orientation of many low-income families who may need to keep expectations low in order to survive the repeated disappointments they face (Hardy and Laszloffy, 2005). For these children and families hope can be dangerous, because it may set them up for crushing and intolerable further disillusionment.

EVOCATIVE STORY AND IMAGERY: "THE BEAUTY OF A SINGLE ROSE"

> The Rainbow comes and goes,
> And lovely is the Rose.
>
> William Wordsworth

The Story

There once was a man who was quite well known in his chosen field who loved gardening and beautiful flowers. He was stricken by polio in his youth, and late in life complications from his illness confined him to his bed. His daughter, knowing how much he enjoyed his garden and loved flowers, brought him a single rose from his garden each day. He studied each rose so carefully and intensely that, he reported, he was able to derive nearly the same degree of pleasure that he used to gain from tending the flowers in his garden.

Evocative Drawing: "A Single Red Rose"

Please try to picture a single rose or if you prefer another flower. What color is it? Is it red? Is it pink? Is it apricot or some other color? Can you smell your flower? What does it smell like? When you have a picture of your flower clearly in mind, please draw it and make it as beautiful as you can.

Evocative Imagery: "Intense Focusing on Beauty"

Please study closely and carefully your picture of your flower. Concentrate on it as hard as you can. Enjoy the beauty of your flower as fully as you can. Study it so that it will be etched clearly in your mind so that you will be able to call up your image of your flower anytime you wish. When an image that is scary or upsetting to you comes to

Figure 13.2.   Photograph of Single Rose
Photograph courtesy of Michael Gold/The Corporate Image

mind, replace it with your image of something incredibly beautiful, your picture of your flower. You will discover the beauty of a single flower can take you away from the image that is upsetting to you. Study your picture and the image in your mind of your beautiful flower, do it often, and you will be amazed how that one flower can overtake the disturbing thoughts and images that come into your mind.

Alternatives or Modifications

There is beauty in the world all around us that we don't always take time to notice. What are some other examples of beauty, images that you can use to replace any disturbing or scary images that come into your mind? Perhaps it is a rainbow, a sunset, a child smiling, or a grandmother hugging her grandchild, or a simple act of kindness. Please describe or feel free to draw or write about the other images of beauty that are special to you. It could be a mountain, a lake, the ocean, a waterfall, or a flower garden that reminds you of the beauty to be found in the world all around us.

You can make your images of beauty even more real, more powerful in your mind by spending a little time each day looking at the images of beauty you have drawn, or the ones you have pictured in your mind, or by studying new ones in the world around you. It could be a cardinal or bluebird in a tree that you usually notice but don't really focus on, or perhaps you don't even see it. Study these examples of beauty as if it were just you and that cardinal and nothing else. These are the images that you can develop into even stronger images to overtake the unpleasant and disturbing ones that sometimes trouble you. Have you thought of any other examples of beauty in the world?

Evocative Proverb: "Seeing the Beauty Surrounding Us"   "Everything has beauty, but not everyone sees it" (Confucius).

Discussion

Milton Erickson was the man who focused so intensely on the single rose that he was able to compensate for his inability to leave his bed. The story has always inspired me. I was also inspired and deeply moved by Victor Frankl's book *The Search for Meaning* (1946 [1967]) and by his struggle to retain a sense of humanity and dignity in the midst of the brutality of a concentration camp, where he was beaten and tortured and his family was killed. But his captors could not strip him of his sense of dignity and humanity. His determination to hold onto his humanity gave him a sense of purpose and meaning that enabled him to survive under the worst conditions imaginable. Frankl explained that we can't always choose the circumstances of our lives, but we can choose the attitude we take toward those conditions, and that is the ultimate human freedom.

14

A Tribute to the Fighting
Spirit of Children

If a man does not keep pace with his companions, perhaps it is because he hears a different drummer. Let him step to the music which he hears, however measured or far away.

Henry David Thoreau, *Walden,* chapter 1

In this chapter I will introduce you to Billy, Sally, and Sherry. These are children who exemplify the courage and fighting spirit of children. Each faced an entirely different set of challenges, but they have in common the resilient spirit, determination, and courage that has inspired me in my work with so many youngsters and their families. In the final three chapters I will recount the stories of Roy, Max, and Jerome, who overcame unbelievable obstacles and adversity in their lives. In all three of their stories evocative strategies played a key role in the clinical process. In Max's and Jerome's cases readers will recognize the strategies previously described in this volume. In Roy's case, readers will be introduced to an evocative strategy, "Peeling the Onion," that the author learned from Dr. Eliana Gil (1996). I was given permission to tell their stories in detail, although, of course, their names have been changed, along with details, to protect their identities; they (or their surviving families) are hopeful that sharing their courageous battles to overcome adversity will benefit child and family therapists in helping other kids facing similar harsh life circumstances. I am grateful to them for their generous wish to help others and for the unique and extraordinary experience of accompanying each of them a short distance on their journey to overcome unfathomable odds. They and many other children like them have taught me what true courage, determination, and hope is all about, and they will always occupy special places in my heart.

231

BILLY, AN EXAMPLE OF COURAGE AND PERSEVERANCE

In my work with children, I had to let go of certain biases and prejudices along the way. I decided, for example, a long time ago that while I was comfortable working with children who were suffering psychotic episodes in a multidisciplinary setting like the Astor Home for Children, I did not feel comfortable treating them as private patients in my office. I received a call, one day, however, from a child psychiatrist whom I greatly respect and with whom I had collaborated in the past. She was treating with a wide array of medications a child, thirteen years old, who was in the midst of an acute psychotic episode and recently had been psychiatrically hospitalized. Upon his discharge from the hospital she asked if I would be willing to do the outpatient psychotherapy with him and his family; she would handle his complex medication regiment. I agreed to do so, and it has turned out to be a most rewarding experience. The commitment of this youngster and his family to battle against this major psychiatric illness has been truly inspiring to me. Billy and his family live far from my office in Rhinebeck, New York, and bringing him every week was a major commitment for them, but they came without fail.

When Billy began therapy with me he was experiencing extreme mental suffering and anguish. He was tormented by visual and auditory hallucinations often, of a command nature, telling him to kill himself or his family. He frequently thought that people were coming to kill him and his family. He also had extremely disturbing dreams about his family being tortured—his mother raped, his little seven-year-old brother cannibalized, and his father being boiled alive in grease and oil.

In view of how frightening this material was to Billy, I worked with him to strengthen his hold on reality and on strategies to help him anchor himself safely in the present moment when he was swept up in the undertow of these powerful and frightening images, voices, and dreams. His parents kept him under close watch at all times. His father was a retired New York City fireman who had been involved in many emergency rescue situations, including mental health crises, so he was very competent to maintain this kind of vigil. Otherwise, it would not have been safe to proceed with outpatient therapy under these conditions. I, nevertheless, worried about Billy's safety and the safety of his family during this period.

In the family sessions we worked on self-calming and self-soothing techniques, ways to exercise control over and distract from the disturbing thoughts and images. As to his frightening dreams, I used drawing techniques to help desensitize him to the most potent and frightening images, a technique I have described in previous writing (Crenshaw, 2001). In addition I constantly searched for islands of health and strength in Billy that would counterbalance his view of self that he was a psychiatric disaster case. With the help of the medications (frequently adjusted by the child psychiatrist), the caring, support, and commitment of his family, and most of all his own determination and courage, Billy slowly and gradually made a heroic comeback from this devastating psychiatric condition. He experienced some significant setbacks along the way but was able to avoid further hospitalization and gradually began to stabilize. He was able to re-enter school, first on a limited schedule of two hours a day, three days a week, but gradually increasing until at present he is attending school full-time.

Billy's school system and teachers are unusually caring, cooperative, flexible, and helpful; they deserve enormous credit. I have pointed out frequently, however, to Billy that while he has had tremendous support from his team of family, school, and mental health professionals, it has been his own resolve to overcome the odds and to come back from the tortuous mental state he was suffering that has inspired everyone on the team to give their best. The lion's share of the credit, without question, belongs to him and his loving family. I am still seeing Billy as of this writing, and there may well be some rough road ahead, but Billy has taught me a lot about what real courage and strength is all about. To me, he is a true hero.

Postscript

Billy is now eighteen; he has weathered major setbacks, including an extremely difficult last school year, with the same courage and resolve described above. As a result of a period of relapse into psychotic symptoms, he missed a great deal of school and as of this writing will have to take a few more courses in the next school year. He continues, however, to be hopeful and is making plans for college. Billy has made a number of good friends since the earlier summer, and he had a group of eighteen boys and girls for a party at his house to celebrate his birthday.

THE STORY OF SALLY: "AMAZING DETERMINATION"

I was quite saddened when I asked Sally, a personable seven-year-old with a good sense of humor and a warm smile, to read a simple paragraph for me. She began to stumble and agonize as she tried to sound out each of the words. She had an expressive language disorder, and although determined, she was quite frustrated. Her parents were concerned; she was having more "meltdowns" at home, and they felt it was due to the pressure of not being able to read when most of the children in her class could.

When I asked Sally to draw the worst thing that ever happened to her, she drew "a book." Then she told me how each time she would read in class the other kids, at least some of them, would laugh. She told me her worries about going into second grade, that she was scared the kids would make fun of her, "because I don't read too well."

I asked Sally to draw a picture of her when she thought the problem was behind her and she no longer had a problem with reading. She drew a picture of a beautiful scene in the woods with lots of flowers and trees; in the midst of this peaceful scene she was reading a book. I asked, "How old are you in the picture?" Sally said, "I am eight." I said, "You will be eight next month." She said, "I know, it won't be at the beginning of the year, but it will happen when I am still eight."

Given her courage and determination I don't doubt for a minute that she will conquer her reading problem. Even if it does not happen in the next year, it will happen. I found it distressing to see a child this young in such pain and under this degree of pressure due to a learning disability that is no fault of her own. But I also marvel at her strength, her hope, and perseverance and I would not for a moment think of betting against Sally being successful in life.

Postscript

It has been approximately seven months since I wrote the above story of Sally. I met with Sally recently, and she told me that she is now reading more confidently in her small reading group. She drew me a picture of her reading in the future with confidence in front of a large group.

THE STORY OF SHERRY:
COURAGE AND A HEART BEYOND WORDS

The crucial healing element of "coming to voice" (Hardy, 1998) as part of the therapy of children oppressed by the scars of sexual violence was taught to me in a dramatic way by an eleven-year-old girl whom I will name "Sherry." The self-contempt and self-hatred that Sherry revealed was extremely painful for me to witness. A sweet, sensitive, and caring child, her spirit had been crushed by devastating repeated sexual exploitation by her uncle. On one occasion when her uncle was demanding that she perform fellatio she refused. In retaliation, he tied her hands, gagged, and blindfolded her, and threw her in the trunk of his car. He drove for what Sherry thought was hours; she was locked in the hot, dark, smelly trunk, terrified that she was going to die of suffocation. When he finally stopped he unbound and ungagged her, let her out of the trunk, and demanded again that she perform fellatio on him. This time she complied. She turned to me at this point of the story and shouted, "And I hated myself for it!"

She then sobbed inconsolably for a long time. This scene of such intense, searing pain in the soul of a child is etched in my mind and heart forever. In my judgment, no amount of cognitive disputation, logical questioning, or cognitive restructuring would have made a dent in these deeply held self-incriminating beliefs had she not been able "to find her voice" to lay open in a safe and mutually trusting therapeutic relationship the terrifying emotional experiences that were at the root of these faulty cognitive beliefs.

After Sherry was able to tell me about the horrifying experiences that formed the emotional foundation of her self-hatred and loathing, the cognitive techniques of disputation, logical questioning, and restructuring were more useful and effective. She worked hard, made good progress in therapy, and she started to make friends; her nightmares gradually ceased, and she made remarkable academic gains in school. Unfortunately, at about this time her father lost his job, and the family moved to a large city where the mother had extended family. In one of the saddest and most heartbreaking experiences of my career, I was notified three years later that Sherry had been raped and murdered leaving her high school after a nighttime rehearsal of a play in which she had the leading part. Her mother told me that she had spoken frequently of our work together and that her last three years had been the happiest years of her life. I will carry in my heart both the joy and pain of having known Sherry for the rest of my life. Some encounters in therapy are life-changing not only for the child but also for the therapist. I was outraged that Sherry had to die in a grotesque act of sexual violence, when she had worked so hard with incredible courage and determination to face and overcome the trauma of sexual exploitation as an even younger child. In spite of the heartbreaking ending, which I will never completely get over, I count it as a special privilege that I was able to be a part of Sherry and her family's lives for a brief time and that it had been so meaningful for her as well as for me. The fighting spirit and courage of children never ceases to amaze and inspire me.

Roy: A Story of a Child's Courage and Fighting Spirit in Facing Trauma

INTRODUCTION

$\mathcal{R}$oy's pediatrician referred him when he was eleven for symptoms of depression, including frequent suicidal ideation and occasional threats of killing himself. Roy was unusually contemptuous of self. His self-loathing was of a degree that I had rarely seen in a child his age. One possible determinant of Roy's dour mood was a slight family predisposition toward depression, with a maternal aunt and grandmother described as chronically depressed, although neither had been diagnosed or ever treated for major depression or dysthymia. Prior to my work with Roy he had been treated with a variety of SSRI medications without clear benefit; he had had some unpleasant side effects, including significant weight gain, which worsened his self-image problems.

Early on in treatment I used empathy practice exercises (see Crenshaw and Mordock, 2005a). Roy expressed empathy and understanding toward other kids in the practice exercises but was unable to show that same consideration toward self. His capacity for empathy was blocked specifically in relation to self.

EMPATHY FOR SELF AS A YOUNGER CHILD

When a child is unable to show empathy for self, that inability is often rooted in complex emotional factors. This is why I advocate an integrative approach to child psychotherapy. When a more straightforward approach, such as social skills training with emphasis on empathy, is not sufficient to produce change, the integrative therapist can adjust the therapeutic approach to focus on the

237

psychodynamic forces that may be blocking change. If the child is being seen in individual therapy, the approach can be changed to family or group therapy, in order to include more of the key persons in the therapy process. Or the circle may need to be enlarged even more, to include the influence of cultural, ethnic, racial, and socioeconomic influences; the interventions may need also to involve the larger systems that exert influence in the child's life, such as schools, courts, probation officers, religious leaders, close friends, and extended family.

A strategy that may be useful when therapy progress is thwarted by the child's lack of empathy for self is to use imagery and gestalt therapy techniques to assist the child in making an empathic connection to the child he or she had been before a disturbing or traumatic experience occurred.

I asked Roy to tell me about some of his earliest memories of upsetting experiences. Roy was able to remember a time when he got into trouble playing with a child around age four. He and the other child had been playing on a big dirt pile that his friend's father was going to use for a garden project in his backyard. At one point the two boys had started throwing dirt at each other in a playful manner, but things got out of hand and one of the clods caught the other child, Bobby, who was slightly younger, in the eye. When Bobby went running into his house crying, Roy was scared. He didn't know if he should go into Bobby's house to see if he was okay or wait for him to come back or just go home.

Roy's house was directly behind Bobby's house with just an alley separating the two houses. His dilemma was solved by the appearance of Bobby's father, a very tall man with dark hair, a moustache, and a loud, booming voice. Bobby's father said to Roy in a stern, loud, and intimidating voice, "Roy, I want you to go home now, and I don't want you playing with Bobby on that dirt pile ever again!"

Roy was confused and scared. Bobby's dad was really angry. Roy worried that he had hurt Bobby really badly. He didn't know whether Bobby's dad meant he couldn't play with Bobby again or just that they couldn't play together on the dirt pile. Roy was also scared that his parents were going to be upset with him. They were both teachers in the local school, and Bobby's dad was the school district's superintendent. Roy had managed to get their boss very riled up, and he was quite sure that he was in big trouble.

Roy remembered vividly walking up the hill to the back door of his home. When he reached the back porch, he could hear his mom talking to someone on the phone. Roy's heart began to pound, his pulse raced, he broke out in a cold sweat; he just knew that Bobby's father had called his mom and was reading her the riot act about her son and telling her that he was never to play with Bobby again. He timidly opened the back door and stepped into the kitchen and let the screen door slam behind him to announce his arrival. Roy remembers feeling incredible relief when he realized his mom was on the phone to a friend.

Bobby's father never called, and within a week Roy and Bobby were playing together, though never again on the ever-inviting dirt pile.

Therapist: Roy, tell me how you felt when Bobby's father was speaking sternly to you in anger.

Roy: I was scared, very scared. I was afraid that I really hurt Bobby and that his father might not let me play with him again. I also thought my parents were going to be really mad.

Therapist: So you can put yourself in Roy's shoes at four years old and appreciate how a little kid would feel when a huge man is glaring at him and speaking sternly and at the same time worried that he had hurt his friend and might not be allowed to play with him again. To make matters worse, both of your parents worked for this man. That's quite a scary situation and a lot of worries for a little kid. So you are able to show understanding and compassion toward the four-year-old Roy, but not toward the eleven-year-old Roy you are now. What else do you remember in the way of early upsetting experiences?

Note to Clinicians

It is interesting that although Roy was able to identify and empathize with the younger boy he was at age four, as well as some subsequent ones at ages five and six, all of these early memories of upsetting experiences were times when he got into trouble. This pattern of remembering vividly early experiences in which he had done something wrong yielded important clues as to the roots of Roy's inability to show empathy for self after a certain age, which was later determined to be around seven.

The experience he remembered just before his seventh birthday involved being duped by some older boys into a scheme that once again landed him in trouble with Bobby's father, much to the dismay of his parents. The older boys claimed that a lady who lived near the school, and who was known in the community as a rather strange person and a hermit, as well as ill tempered, especially toward children, was really a witch. The fourth-grade boys told Roy that this eccentric lady loved to catch and torture children. The older boys baited Roy and dared him to run up to her front porch and drop a brick on it and then run "like hell." The older boys shamed Roy, told him he was a chicken, a sissy. The older boys watched at a safe distance when Roy decided he would rather take his chances with the "witch" than to be labeled a "chicken" or a "coward."

What the older boys didn't tell Roy was that they had already pulled this stunt three times in the past week, so the angry lady was lying in wait for the next kid foolish enough to try it again. Roy, petrified and trembling with fear, walked ever so reluctantly up the sidewalk to the lady's front porch. The moment he let the brick drop, perhaps before it hit the porch floor, the lady sprang out the door and grabbed Roy, who was immobilized by terror. He had an image of being boiled alive in a pot. The lady said, "I've had enough of this, little boy; tell me your name." Roy complied instantly, because the alternative was even scarier.

The woman's house was right next to the school. She called the school superintendent, Bobby's father, and gave him the name of the culprit she had caught in her well-planned trap. Bobby's father called Roy's parents, and after dinner that night they took Roy to meet with the superintendent at his house. Roy was certain, due to the prior incident, that "his school days were over." His parents realized that Roy had been set up by the older boys and were aware of how terrified he was, so they were supportive of him, although firm in their insistence that he had been very wrong to drop the brick on the lady's porch under any circumstances. Bobby's father was stern, exacted a promise from Roy that he would not pull a stunt like this again, but he was not nearly as harsh as Roy expected.

The next day his father accompanied Roy to the lady's house, where Roy apologized to her and promised never to do it again. All in all, Roy felt he got off easy for this particular "crime." Roy was now able to express empathy for the young boy he had been, just short of seven, when this incident occurred. He could appreciate that he had been not only quite young but also gullible and easily manipulated by the older boys. He could also appreciate how scared he had been on the porch when he had been suddenly grabbed by this very strange lady, who he was convinced was a witch. He acknowledged that this incident was one of the most frightening things that ever happened to him, far scarier that facing Bobby's father for the second time.

After that incident Roy's capacity for empathy for self was lost and replaced with a harsh, condemning attitude. The experiences that Roy described after age seven retained the theme of doing something wrong; like the incidents recalled prior to that age, from an objective viewpoint they did not constitute "federal crimes," but he showed no empathy for self. In fact, he would refer to his stupidity, how much he hated himself, and how he deserved to die.

In my mind I grappled with the mystery of the lost capacity for self-empathy occurring after age seven. He could appreciate how scared, confused, gullible, and vulnerable he had been prior to that age, but not subsequently. What could account for this dramatic change?

PURSUING THE TURNING POINT

Therapist: Roy, you are able to appreciate how scared you were when the lady grabbed you on her porch. When you were in second grade, however, and got into trouble for being too rough on the playground, you referred to yourself as "stupid," an "idiot." I am curious about this change, because you were only slightly older but far harsher in your view of self. What do you think could explain such a change?

Roy: I don't know. I guess I just started doing a lot of dumb things and going bad.

Therapist: Roy, how bad? Have you really done anything so terrible that you believe is unforgivable? After all, at age eleven you are still just a kid.

Roy: It feels that way to me. It is hard to explain, I guess.

Therapist: Roy, I do understand that this is how you feel. It really feels to you that you are stupid, bad, and a rotten kid, but I just see no evidence to support that belief. I guess what we really need to focus on is how you came to believe such a thing. What could possibly have convinced you beginning in second grade that you are such a "stupid," "bad" kid, and why do you still buy it?

Note to Clinicians

My modest goal in this interchange was to establish that these ingrained, self-condemning views were simply beliefs that might not be true; they can be challenged and disputed ("and you still buy it?"). Roy was not ready, however, to critically examine the evidence supporting these beliefs ("I just feel that way; I can't explain it"). These beliefs were not ego-alien to him. At age eleven he had come to accept these self-castigating views as indisputable, ego-syntonic facts. If all Roy had needed was modeling by the therapist to challenge and effectively dispute these beliefs, the beliefs would have been ego-alien, and he would have been motivated to work on modifying these distorted cognitions.

Roy was not, however, in the throes of battle with these punitive self-concepts; quite to the contrary, he had totally embraced this habitual way of viewing self. It was clear that the cognitive-behavioral approach although helpful to many kids, would not "go the distance" in this case.

I met with Roy's parents with his consent and knowledge, and I advised them of my concern that Roy's punitive views of self, while consistent with early signs of mood disorder, were more complicated than that single determinant. I told them I had observed a sharp line of demarcation between Roy's ability to be empathic toward self for experiences before age seven and his harsh and self-condemning attitudes for experiences subsequent to that age. I asked the parents if they could think of anything that occurred to Roy or happened within the family around that time that could have dramatically altered his view of self. Immediately, Roy's father said, "We are not going to talk about that. It's behind us now. It doesn't have anything to do with Roy's problems now. We don't want to dredge all of that up again."

I had no idea what the father was referring to, but I did know that I had triggered a maelstrom of affect within the father and that almost certainly it had something to do with Roy's problems of viewing himself so harshly. Roy's mother was also skeptical of the father's immediate rejection and reflexive assumption that the family secret had no bearing on the family's problems. She said to her husband, "Wait a minute, John. How can you say that? It might have a lot to do with why Roy hates himself. We at least need to let Dr. Crenshaw know what happened. It is very painful; I would rather not talk about it either, but if there is a chance it will help Roy we have to talk about it." The parents proceeded to tell me what they knew about the story, and I've added in the account below further details supplied later by Roy in his sessions with me.

Roy had started taking piano lessons at age six from a man who was a retired music teacher and had moved to the community five years prior. The man was in his midsixties and lived alone; no one knew too much about him, except that he attended church regularly on Sundays. He was friendly and well mannered and was rumored to have been widowed, but no one knew for sure.

THE TRAUMA EVENTS

Shortly after Roy's seventh birthday he went to Mr. Hamilton's (fictitious name) house for his piano lesson, and his teacher fondled Roy's genitals while Roy was trying to play the piano. Mr. Hamilton firmly instructed Roy to continue practicing, both hands on the keys, while Mr. Hamilton gently rubbed his genitals. While Roy was scared, uncomfortable, he was also, to his great dismay, aroused. The gentle stroking of his private parts felt good, and he was sexually excited. At the end of the lesson, Mr. Hamilton gave Roy a candy bar and told him, "This needs to be our little secret, just between you and me. I know how to make little boys feel really good." "Promise me," Mr. Hamilton said, "that you will never tell anyone about our little secret, and I will teach you not only about playing the piano but also how to feel really good."

Roy promised he would not tell. The following week when Roy went for his piano lesson, his teacher told him to unzip his pants. This time while

Roy attempted to practice his assigned lesson, Mr. Hamilton fondled his penis underneath his clothes. Although Roy once again felt uneasy, uncomfortable, and quite guilty about these secret pleasures, Mr. Hamilton was right. He really knew how to make a boy feel good. Roy was even more excited and sexually aroused the second time. At the end of the lesson Mr. Hamilton gave him two candy bars and once again reminded him that this was their little secret and that nobody else should know, because they would not understand.

Sometimes Roy's mother would drop him off for his lesson and return in time to pick him up at the end of his lesson. On this particular occasion, however, Roy's mother was waiting the whole time in the next room. Roy found this disturbing; he knew that what was taking place in the lesson with Mr. Hamilton was wrong, but he was confused, scared, and didn't know what to do.

The following week Mr. Hamilton told Roy that he was going to introduce him to a whole new kind of pleasure. Before Roy sat down on the piano bench, Mr. Hamilton told Roy to drop his pants and underwear to his ankles. Meanwhile he told Roy to start playing his lesson while Mr. Hamilton crawled under the piano and performed fellatio on Roy. The pleasure was unlike anything Roy had experienced before and with his mother in the next room he began to feel extremely guilty.

When Roy went home he didn't feel like eating his dinner that night. His mother sensed something was terribly wrong. She went up to his room to talk with him about what was wrong. At first Roy insisted that he just didn't feel well, but his mom persisted, and he started crying. He finally told his mom what had been going on during his piano lessons. His mother became hysterical, and his father called the police. The police came to the home and talked to his parents first. Roy's father was extremely angry. Roy wasn't sure if he was angry with him, Mr. Hamilton, or both. His mom was just as upset but more sad than angry, and she was clearly worried about her son. She did her best to support and comfort him during this extremely disturbing and bewildering experience.

Roy was scared, very scared. He could hear his father's voice rising in anger while talking to the police. He thought he was in big trouble. He had promised Mr. Hamilton he would never tell, let alone turn him into the police. "What will Mr. Hamilton do?" he wondered. "Will he seek revenge? Will he call me a liar? Will he tell the police that Roy is a little boy with a wild imagination and that he made the whole thing up because he doesn't want to practice his piano lessons? Then will the police come back and arrest me?" These were just some of the disturbing questions sweeping through Roy's mind at this awful time.

Roy didn't tell his parents or the police about the pleasure he experienced from the incidents of molestation, but this was at the heart of his intractable self-condemnation and painful sense of shame, and it became the central focus in our therapeutic work.

The interview with the police was difficult for Roy. It was different from talking with his mom about what happened. The police officers, Sergeant Hooper and Detective Warwick, were interested in facts and details. They wanted to know when each of the incidents happened, specific dates, at what point during the lesson these things happened, exactly what Mr. Hamilton had said and done, what Roy had said and done in return, where Roy's mother had been when this was going on, and whether there had been anyone else in the house at the time. They wanted to know how Roy felt about Mr. Hamilton; if he liked his piano lessons; how he felt about practicing his piano lessons; and whether he was angry for any reason with Mr. Hamilton or had ever wanted to quit his piano lessons. Finally, the interview was over, and the police were on their way to Mr. Hamilton's house to talk to him.

Roy went to his room and cried and cried. His mother tried to comfort him as best she could, but he was beyond comforting. He was convinced that the police would be back soon and tell his parents, "Your son is a liar and we are going to have to take him down to the police station." But the police did not come back that night.

Roy's father spent a portion of the night pacing back and forth in an anguished way in the downstairs living room. When Roy saw him downstairs from the second floor landing on his way to the bathroom in the middle of the night, he was even more convinced that his father was furious and that he blamed Roy for all of this trouble to the family.

The next day was Saturday, so the sleep-deprived family did not have to get up early. At around 11:30 AM the doorbell rang. Roy looked out the window from his room and saw a police car parked in front of the house. He experienced utter panic, he wanted to run or hide, he was certain that they had come to arrest him, to take him away to a juvenile center for bad boys.

THE NIGHTMARE WORSENS

Roy tiptoed out of his room and from the second floor landing he saw that it was Detective Warwick and an officer he didn't know. Roy's parents thought that he had finally gone to sleep and was in his room snoozing away, but he wasn't. He was hiding behind the banister on the second-floor landing when his parents invited the officers to come into their living room. Roy could make out the conversation, even though they were speaking softly—a conversation that he was never supposed to hear. Detective Warwick told his parents that when they arrived at Mr. Hamilton's home last night they had informed him that they were there to discuss a matter concerning one of his piano students, Roy Atkinson (fictitious name).

Mr. Hamilton had told the police in what they described as a very calm, polite manner that he had no idea what this was about but he did not intend to pursue this any further without the presence of his attorney. The officers had agreed to meet with Mr. Hamilton and his attorney the following morning at the police station at 9:30. When neither Mr. Hamilton nor his attorney arrived by 10 AM and they could not reach them by phone, the officers had driven to Mr. Hamilton's home.

When Mr. Hamilton did not answer the doorbell, they had looked in the garage, to see that his car was parked inside. They had found the backdoor unlocked and entered the house. They had searched the downstairs and then the upstairs, and then they had gone to the basement. They had found Mr. Hamilton dead. He had hung himself. From all indications he had killed himself the night before, sometime after the police left. Roy was stunned. His mother said, "Oh my God, no!" "What will we tell Roy?" His father said adamantly, "We will tell him nothing. As far as he needs to know Mr. Hamilton got scared and left town. He doesn't need to know the gory details."

His mother asked the officers whether they would need to talk with Roy again. They told her, "Probably not. Unless something else turns up, we can close the books on this." Roy did know the gory details, however, and there was no way he could "close the books" on this sad, tragic, confusing, and disturbing set of events. He made his way quietly back to his bedroom and ever so carefully closed the door. When he closed the door he dropped to the floor, his back to the door, his face buried in his hands, and the thought vividly etched in his mind as dramatically as the neon-lit signs in Times Square: "I killed Mr. Hamilton. If I hadn't told like I promised, Mr. Hamilton wouldn't be dead."

There were two major disparities between the account of these events as offered by Roy's parents and what I learned from Roy as our work unfolded. First, the parents were not aware of the pleasurable aspects that Roy had experienced as part of the incidents of molestation. His unbearable shame and self-loathing regarding these secret pleasures, combined with breaking his promise never to tell, had left Roy in a state of hidden despair and self-hate. In his mind there was a direct link between his secret sexual pleasures, his betrayal by telling the secret, and the death of Mr. Hamilton. In his judgment, a boy capable of such deceit, evil, and forbidden pleasures did not deserve to live.

The other main discrepancy was that even at Roy's age of eleven, the parents did not believe that Roy knew anything about Mr. Hamilton's suicide. This was crucial, since part of the healing needed was centered on the damaged relationship between Roy and his dad. Roy could not confront his parents with his knowledge of the suicide for multiple reasons. Roy was convinced that his father was still angry and blamed him for the whole tragic set of events. Ever since that night when he told his mom what happened he had perceived a distance from his dad that had not been there before.

In addition, his sneaky manner of discovering the truth about what happened to Mr. Hamilton, hiding behind the banister and eavesdropping, was too reminiscent of the secret pleasures, broken promise, and betrayal of Mr. Hamilton. To acknowledge that he knew the facts was just too painful for Roy. It evoked the destructive sense of shame that had caused so much of his suffering.

Note to Clinicians

While a biochemical predisposition mediated by genetic factors may have contributed to this child's depression, self-contempt, and suicidal ideation, as well as faulty cognitions and beliefs, I don't believe that approaching the biological or cognitive factors or the combination of the two would have constituted adequate treatment, although such a combination has been demonstrated to be effective for many other children.

The Roots of his Devastating Shame-Based Beliefs

Adequate treatment for Roy required a comprehensive approach that involved pursuing the details of his trauma narrative and the emotional basis for his self-condemning views of self. A small sample of the therapeutic dialogue is reproduced below.

Therapist: Roy, since you have drawn a blank trying to explain how you went from showing understanding and compassion toward self to hatred of self after age seven, I asked your parents if they had any ideas. They told me about what happened with Mr. Hamilton [Roy looked shocked, because almost nothing had been mentioned about the whole tragic episode after his father told him that Mr. Hamilton had left town in a hurry after the police talked to him]. That whole experience must have been very disturbing to you.

Roy: I killed Mr. Hamilton.

Therapist: What do you mean?

Roy: I promised him I would never tell but I did and after the police talked to him, he killed himself.

Therapist: So as far as you're concerned, you killed him? Why do you think your parents believe that you don't know what really happened?

Roy: I was listening at the top of the stairs. I heard everything. I was so scared. I was afraid that I was in trouble, that the police had come back for me. I couldn't believe it when they said Mr. Hamilton had hung himself in the basement.

Therapist: No wonder you see yourself as such a "bad kid." That horrible night when the police arrived you thought they were coming to arrest you, and when you heard that Mr. Hamilton was dead, you have believed ever since that you are a murderer. Roy, what a huge burden you have carried and for such a long time.

Roy: I did kill him.

Therapist: Let me understand this, Roy. You somehow were able to sneak out of the house, a seven-year-old kid, and travel about twenty blocks across town, somehow get into Mr. Hamilton's house, subdue him, carry him on your back to the basement, put a rope around his neck and hoist him off the ground? You didn't kill him, Roy.

Roy: No, but I caused it to happen.

Therapist: Tell me why you believe that.

Roy: I broke my promise.

Therapist: That is not the same as killing someone.

Roy: If I hadn't broken my promise, he would still be alive.

Therapist: Roy, I want you to listen carefully. I know that you think that what happened with Mr. Hamilton, which has been a never-ending nightmare for you, is your fault, but you are wrong. Mr. Hamilton was a very sick man. An adult who initiates sexual acts with a young child is a deeply troubled person. He killed himself because he was a very sick man. You did the absolutely right thing by telling your mother.

Roy: No I didn't. How can you say that?

Therapist: Roy, after I talked with your parents, I talked with Detective Warwick. You are not the first child that Mr. Hamilton molested. In fact, he had been arrested three prior times for child molestation. He was what is known as a sexual predator, a man who was skilled in preying on young children by using piano lessons to gain access to children and then sexually violating them. He escaped the authorities by moving from community to community and state to state. There is no telling how many kids altogether were hurt as a result of his sick mind. Mr. Hamilton killed himself because he was sick and tormented and couldn't face the consequences of what he had done. None of that has anything to do with you. Roy, why did you think the police came back to the house to arrest you?

Roy: What I did was horrible. It was wrong and I knew it was wrong.

Therapist: And that is why you told your mom and that was the right thing to do. Whenever adults take advantage of children sexually, it is always the adult's responsibility, not the child's. Adults have far more experience in these matters than kids, and it is up to the adult to make sure that certain boundaries don't get crossed. It is never the responsibility of the child; they have little knowledge or experience in these matters.

Roy: But I didn't say anything until it happened three times.

Therapist: It took a lot of courage for you to tell, Roy, and I respect and admire you for doing the right thing. Mr. Hamilton was counting on the fact that you would never tell or at least not until he was long gone and had moved on to another place to prey on other little boys. That's why he got away with hurting so many kids for such a long time. He would target boys who he felt would be too scared or too guilty to tell. In your case, he miscalculated. He didn't realize what a gutsy kid you are.

Roy: But I didn't tell sooner [voice starts to crack] partly because it felt good.

Therapist: Of course, it felt good. Your body responds in a sensual, pleasurable way to being sexually stimulated, it is perfectly natural to feel pleasure and be aroused when sexually stimulated. This was all new to you, but Mr. Hamilton had lots of practice in ways to sexually arouse young kids.

Roy: But I knew it was wrong at the time but I didn't try to stop it because it felt good.

Therapist: I am sure it did feel good but it is never the child's responsibility to set the boundaries with an adult; it is always the adult's responsibility.

Roy: I enjoyed it. I went along with it.

Therapist: Roy, you are equating your body's pleasurable response to being sexually stimulated to being responsible, guilty, bad, deserving of punishment, and even deserving to die. Have you ever helped your mom or dad peel an onion? [I am extremely grateful to Dr. Eliana Gil (1996) for introducing me to this intervention in a presentation.]

Roy: Sure.

Therapist: What happens when you peel an onion?

Roy: You start to cry. Your eyes get all watery.

Therapist: Do you make the decision to tear up and make your eyes watery?

Roy: No, it just happens.

Therapist: This is exactly what happens when an adult sexually stimulates a child. It is not a decision you make. Your body just responds in a natural way. In the case of peeling an onion, your eyes get watery; in the case of sexual stimulation, you feel pleasure. It has nothing to do with being responsible for the abuse, nothing at all.

Roy: I never thought about it that way.

Therapist: When you go home tonight ask your mom if you can peel an onion. See if you can prevent your eyes from watering.

Roy did, and of course his eyes got watery, and he was deeply affected by the experience. By this direct experience he realized that the body just responds in its natural way to certain kinds of stimuli. If someone pretends they are going to punch us, we blink—it is automatic. The body can't help but respond in its natural defensive way.

This experiential exercise was more effective than most of the therapy dialogue addressing this issue. He had previously believed that his body's responding in a pleasurable way was compelling evidence of his "badness," and it was only through the bodily experience of tearing up while peeling the onion that he could be convinced otherwise. The belief was a somatic conviction and therefore it could only be uprooted through a somatic experience, which "hit home" when words alone made little impact.

Obviously, more work needed to be done, but this was a significant turning point. The cognitive disputation, logical questioning, and cognitive restructuring work gradually got easier. Family therapy sessions to restore the connections between Roy and his dad were another important aspect of the subsequent work, but again, that work moved faster and was more effective once we got over the hurdle of Roy being able to experience empathy once again toward self.

The night that Mr. Hamilton killed himself his torment and suffering ended, but Roy's was just beginning. The degree of anguish and suffering this boy had experienced in the ensuing five years drove him to the desperate point of chronic thoughts about suicide, the very way that Mr. Hamilton died, whom emotionally Roy believed he had killed. What a burden for any child.

His parents were shocked to find out that he had known all along about the suicide and had carried this silent burden ever since. They were deeply saddened to learn that all of these years he had felt responsible for the death. Opening up the communication in this family and ending the secrecy was also a very important breakthrough, because after all, the nightmare that had caused this family such unbelievable pain had been incubated in secrecy. Also, Roy had suffered secretly all of these years due to the well-intended efforts of the parents to protect him from the truth. The secret had made it impossible for communication to take place with the very people Roy needed to talk to most, his own parents. The healing process could not begin until the secrecy ended.

With these changes the healing process could move forward, and the now openly expressed empathy toward Roy from his parents further solidified and reinforced his growing empathy for self. This truly was one of my most heartbreaking, and also rewarding, clinical experiences, and Roy and his family will always occupy a special place in my heart.

16

Max: A Story of a Child's Fighting Spirit in Facing Unspeakable Loss

INTRODUCTION

*M*ax's mother, a single parent, and his grandfather brought him to treatment at age twelve because he was an angry boy and was becoming increasing oppositional and defiant at home. The three of them lived together in the grandfather's home. Max had been about four years old when his grandmother died and had few memories of her. The death of the grandmother had been quite devastating to both the mother and grandfather. Max's father had left his mother shortly after his birth. He had offered no financial support, and he had not seen Max since shortly after his birth. His mother did not know his whereabouts. Max, after some token resistance in the beginning, became gradually more invested in the therapy process and was particularly interested in the projective drawing and storytelling strategies. The projective drawing and storytelling strategy "Miguel's Endless Search" led to unusually meaningful and productive therapeutic dialogue. This strategy is described in detail in chapter 4.

THERAPEUTIC DIALOGUE FOCUSED ON "MIGUEL'S ENDLESS SEARCH"

Max's description of his drawing: "That's Miguel, and he is talking to a big guy, and he is asking him if he has seen what he was looking for."
    Therapist: What would be a good title for your drawing?
    Max: "The Lost Soul."
    Therapist: Tell me more. Why did you pick that title?

251

Figure 16.1.   Miguel talking to a stranger

Max: Because it seems that he has lost something that he can't get off his mind; he just keeps asking everyone he meets if they have seen what is missing, and he doesn't even know what it is. Other people think he is weird.

Therapist: Do you think he is weird?

Max: Yeah, kind of weird. But I like it. I like weird characters and weird stories. This is my kind of story.

Therapist: Who is the other person in the drawing?

Max: A stranger in the street.

Therapist: What do you think it is like for Max to go up to strangers and keep asking these same questions?

Max: I would say he is one sad and lonely guy. He has to feel desperate to make a fool of himself that way. No wonder he is so angry.

Therapist: Oh, that is very interesting. So, Max, you think there is a link to Miguel feeling so angry and his constant searching for the important thing missing in his life?

Max: I think that is what it is all about. Whatever he lost has ruined his life. He can't get over it. That's all he thinks about.

Therapist: That is so interesting, Max. So, it is like whatever he lost has wounded him, left him with a hole in his heart, an ache in his soul that won't go away.

Max: Like an arrow right through the heart.

Therapist: No wonder he hurts so deeply. So you think his anger is just a cover-up?

Max: Yeah, the kids make fun of him; his family thinks he is weird too, so he is furious. No one takes him seriously, but no one sees how much he hurts.

Therapist: Max, I am so impressed that you can see how much he hurts. So he is not a bad kid, or a weird kid either. He has a good reason to be angry, because he is hurting and no one sees it. The more desperate he feels to find what has been missing the more people think he is weird and the more lonely and sad he feels.

Max: This kid is in a very bad place.

Therapist: You really feel for him and understand his hurt.

Max: I think if someone doesn't help him soon, I don't know what he might do.

Therapist: What do you think he might do?

Max: I think he might kill himself.

Therapist: What worries you about Miguel killing himself?

Max: He seems so desperate. I don't know what he might do.

Therapist: Max, you are a sensitive kid; you really understand his pain, his loneliness, and anger. You realize he is not a "bad kid" but a confused, lonely, scared, and sad kid. Suppose you lived in his village and he came up to you. What would you do to try to help him?

Max: I need to think about that one for a minute.

Therapist: Take your time; I have all the time you need.

Max (after a long pause): I would say, "Look, Miguel. I will help you look for what is missing, but if we can't find it, you are just going to have to face up to it and deal with it. It would be crazy to just keep looking. Maybe what you are missing is not going to be found. You have to get on with it.

Therapist: Max, that sounds like the most helpful thing that anyone has said to Miguel so far. You would help him look for what is missing. Then Miguel is no longer alone in his search. He has someone to go with him and help him look. That comes from a very compassionate heart. You have a very kind and tender heart; I know this from your love of animals. But you also make clear to Miguel that at some point the search has to end; maybe what he is looking for can't be found and he has to grieve that loss. He has to face it and go through the anger, the sadness, the guilt, the fear, and all the other emotions he may have inside about his loss that he has never fully expressed. Then he will gradually be able to move on. Now, what if he says, "If I can't find it, I will kill myself"?

Max: Oh, man, I would tell him to make an appointment to see you.

Therapist: But I don't have an office in Spain [both laugh]. Seriously, you are not his therapist, and you are very right to point him in the direction of seeing a therapist who is qualified and trained to deal with someone feeling that desperate, but as a friend, what would you say to him?

Max: I would tell him that is a stupid thing to do. "What if you killed yourself and three months later the thing that was missing was found? No one really knows; it is crazy to kill yourself."

Therapist: Would there be anything else as his friend that you would want to say to him if he was talking about killing himself?

Max: I would tell him, "Look, I am your friend, if you kill yourself I am going to be really pissed at you!"

Therapist: You know if Miguel had a friend like you, Max, I don't think he would be thinking about killing himself. Does Miguel remind you of anyone you have known?

Max: A little bit.

Therapist: Whom does he remind you of "a little bit?"

Max: Myself.

Therapist: Really? In what way does Miguel remind you "a little bit" of yourself?

Max: I am a pretty angry guy myself.

Therapist: So you can identify with Miguel that way. You have been angry for a long time?

Max: Big time.

Therapist: Are there other ways that Miguel reminds you of yourself?

Max: I have thought about suicide before.

Therapist: How serious was it? Did you think about it once in a while, or did you think about it a lot?

Max: Not very often. I wouldn't really do it, but when I get really angry, when kids have been picking on me a lot, I think about it.

Therapist: How do you know you wouldn't really do it?

Max: I couldn't do that. I would be too scared to do it. It would hurt my mother and grandfather too much.

Therapist: It sounds like you have done some careful thinking about this. Have you thought about ways of doing it?

Max: I know where grandpa keeps his guns and ammunition. They don't think I know, but I do.

Therapist: It sounds like you would like me to give them a heads-up to get those guns out of harm's way.

Max: No way, I didn't say that!

Therapist: I think you did, in a certain way that was important for me to hear with the "third ear."

Max: Third ear! What the hell are you talking about?

Therapist: Sorry, that is psychology talk for listening with the mind and heart, not just the ears. I think you want me to know that you don't feel completely safe when you are feeling really down and entertaining thoughts of suicide, and you have access to your grandfather's guns, and neither your grandfather or mother know that you might be in danger or have access to the guns.

Max: You are not going to tell them, are you?

Therapist: I believe that your better judgment led you to tell me so that I would do something about it. If I just pretend that this is unimportant, I would be taking the attitude that you are not important and that what happens to you doesn't matter much. But you do matter, you are important to your mom, your grandfather, and you matter to me.

Max: You can't do that. I thought everything I tell you is confidential!

Therapist: It is, but there are a few exceptions to that rule, and one of them is that when you tell me something that leaves me feeling that you are unsafe, I am going to do something about it. I will not treat that as an unimportant, because what happens to you is important to me. You can be angry, and it is okay for you to be angry with me, but I will not treat your safety as a trivial matter.

Max: If you tell, I will never trust you again.

Therapist: If I didn't tell, if I did not do something to respond to your communication that you sometimes have suicidal thoughts that go as far as thinking how you would kill yourself and that you have access to guns and ammunition that the adults in your life are unaware of, then I would strongly advise you to never trust me again. If you wish, you can tell them; we will sit together with your mom and grandfather and explain that the guns and ammunition need to be secured so that you can't have access to them because sometimes you have these thoughts of harming yourself and you don't feel safe knowing that you could get to the guns easily.

Max: Okay, I would rather do it that way. Let's get it over with.

Therapist: Okay, please invite your mom and grandfather to come in and join us.

Note to Clinicians

The dialogue above validates the power of these evocative drawing and story-telling techniques to create meaningful dialogue between the child and thera-pist. In this case it opened up the dialogue between Max and his therapist, and more importantly his family, about suicidal thoughts and urges that were plac-ing him at risk. The identification with Miguel in the story led Max to dis-close his own sense of hopelessness and periodic suicidal ruminations, which had reached a point of specificity as to method and means of carrying out the suicide. Whether this material would have been disclosed at some point in the therapy without the facilitation of the projective drawing and storytelling strat-egy is a matter of speculation. In all likelihood it would not have surfaced as quickly as it did in response to the story of Miguel's pervasive sense of loss and despair.

Max was then asked to tell a story about Miguel. (See directions to the strategy in chapter 4.)

MAX'S STORY

"When Miguel was about four years old, he found out that his grandmother was missing and he has been going around asking if anyone knew what he was looking for. All he can remember is that he saw his grandmother on a bridge. She had lost her husband and was very depressed and thinking about jumping off the bridge or maybe she wandered off into the woods close by and never was found."

Therapist: Why did you pick his grandmother for what was missing in his life?

Max: It was the first thing that came to my mind.

Therapist: How do you think it would affect him if he didn't find what was missing?

Max: He would not be asking the same question over and over if this wasn't really important to him and if he didn't have a lot of feelings about it. If he didn't find her, he would be very upset.

Therapist: Do you think he will eventually find her?

Max: He probably will find her.

Therapist: Why do you think so?

Max: He won't give up until he does.

Therapist: That is a good point. He has been searching a long time and he has been teased and shunned by other kids because they think he is weird, but he just keeps looking. This guy just doesn't give up, does he? He is very determined. Does he remind you of anyone else in that way, someone who just keeps on going even when things are really tough?

Max: No, I don't think so. I can't think of anybody.

Therapist: It reminds me of you.

Max: How do you figure that?

Therapist: Because you don't give up either.

Max: Why do you say that?

Therapist: You have told me that there are times when you have felt just as bad as Miguel. There are times when you think about suicide. You have even thought about how to do it and how you would get the means to carry it out. But you didn't do it. When you sensed there was danger that you might do it, you told me in your own way about it, and together we talked about it with your mom and grandfather, and now the guns are stored away where you can't get them—because you are determined to live, determined, no matter how hard it gets, not to give up. You told me after I said I was going to do something about the danger you were in that you would never trust me again. But here we are, the very next session, and you are working as hard as ever to understand Miguel and, more importantly, yourself. That's what I call determination.

Max: I guess I am no quitter.

Therapist: You can say that again.

Max: I guess I am no quitter.

Therapist: Okay, wise guy, may I ask you a few more questions about your story?

Max: Sure, go ahead.

Therapist: You said Miguel, because he was no quitter, would eventually find his grandmother?

Max: Yeah, he won't stop until he finds her.

Therapist: When he finds her will she be alive or dead?

Max: Dead.

Therapist: How do you think Miguel will handle that bad news?

Max: A lot better than anyone would think. Because at least now he knows; before, it was driving him crazy not knowing what happened to her, and nobody had answers for him, and everyone thought he was weird and crazy.

Therapist: Max, I think you may be right about that. I have always believed that kids can deal with just about anything if they know the truth and are prepared for what they must face. What drives kids crazy is when adults are not truthful with them and kids don't know what to believe or who to trust. Adults do this because they think they need to protect the kids from the harsh reality, but they are mistaken, because what kids imagine is far worse usually than the reality, no matter how grim.

Max: Yeah, adults have that all wrong.

Therapist: Max, in your story, does Miguel find out how his grandmother died?

Max: Yeah, he found out.

Therapist: What did he find out?

Max: He found out that she committed suicide.

Therapist: Did anyone else in the family know?

Max: They all knew except Miguel. They didn't think he could handle it. They said he was too young, so they kept the secret all those years. It drove him crazy.

Therapist: That is very sad. So a big part of what was missing for Miguel was his inability to trust even his own family. He knew there was a secret, a mystery, and he couldn't rest until he found the missing pieces. He spent most of his childhood in this endless pursuit of what was not being said, the mystery, and the secret, what was being withheld from him. When he finally discovered what it was, it sounds like from your story that it was almost a relief, like a weight had been lifted off of him.

Max: That's exactly how he felt.

Therapist: Does your story remind you of anything or anyone who had a similar experience of secrets that were later found out?

Max: I don't know, I will have to think about that one.

SESSION FIFTEEN: THREE MONTHS LATER,
NO LONGER PRIMARILY WITHIN THE METAPHOR

Therapist: I have been thinking a lot lately about you and your situation, Max, and Miguel in that story we did early on, about his constantly searching for something that was missing in his life. I have a strong sense that your anger relates to something missing for you. It's just a hunch, but I wanted to throw that out so we could talk about it directly.

Max: Well, I don't go around asking everybody if they have seen what I have been looking for.

Therapist: No, you don't, you hide it much better than Miguel did. I think that partly you hide it behind your anger.

Max: I don't get it. What do you mean?

Therapist: When you bark and growl at people, or like I explained about how some kids put on a gorilla suit to keep people at a distance, then people do not get close enough to see that you are not a "bad kid" but rather a hurting kid. You don't want them to see the hurting part of you underneath the gorilla suit, because that would make you feel too vulnerable. You would be afraid that people would take advantage and hurt you again.

Max: I still am not following you.

Therapist: I think it is happening right now. I think you feel that I am getting very close to understanding something very important about you and that all of a sudden your brain is shutting down and you aren't able to process it, because it is scary to know that someone is getting so close. But I won't hurt you, I won't judge you, I won't criticize you, I just want us both to be able to understand you better.

Max: Now I am completely lost. Could we talk about something else?

Therapist: If you need to, but we will come back to this at another time when you are able to stay with it and focus on it. It seems too upsetting for you now. We will come back to it at a time that is more comfortable for you. I am glad you can tell me when you need me to give you some space.

Note to Clinicians

Clearly, this youngster, who had a high-functioning brain and intellect, was unable to process the interpretation of the painful, vulnerable core self "beneath the gorilla suit," and he demonstrated this by suddenly becoming inarticulate and unable to think. It is crucial in therapy with resistant children to assume that when they call on their defenses, even primitive ones, it is because they need them in order to manage the anxiety that the therapy provokes ("Could we talk about something else?") and that it is important to honor these defenses ("I am glad you can tell me when you need me to give you some space"). At the same time, it is equally imperative that we plant firmly the expectation that we will revisit the "hard stuff" ("We will come back to it at a time that is more comfortable for you"). Most kids will not initiate discussion about the really painful things in their lives; the therapist has to actively facilitate and structure such moments in therapy.

Children will prefer to avoid the painful therapeutic exploration of their visible and invisible wounds. Yet unless therapy is intended just to provide "balm for the wounds" and not address the complex emotional process that underlies acting-out or symptomatic behavior, the therapist must create the trusting context, must structure and facilitate the therapeutic communication that leads to gradually revealing and addressing the wounds, especially the invisible wounds: insults to the child's dignity, scars to the child's soul, or the crushing of the child's spirit. It will be difficult and emotionally taxing work for both child and therapist, and it is not for the timid at heart. In order to accomplish this emotionally focused work of therapy, the therapist must have a conviction that it is helpful and beneficial for the child to experience the split-off emotions that were too powerful to be integrated at the time of the original experiences. Healing also requires integration of the split-off, fragmented memories.

Neuroscience (Siegel, 1999) has discovered that traumatic memories are stored in a different part of the brain than are non-traumatic memories. Until the traumatic memories are integrated and stored in explicit (autobiographical) memory the implicit memories (traumatic memories) are susceptible to being triggered by various internal and external stimuli that are reminders of traumatic experience. Some children, as explained in previous writings (Crenshaw, 2004; also see Crenshaw and Mordock, 2005a, 2005b; Crenshaw and Hardy, 2005, Crenshaw 2005) will lack sufficient psychological and coping resources to undertake this demanding and taxing level of therapy at any given point in the course of treatment; and the Play Therapy Decision Grid (see chapter 2 and Crenshaw and Mordock, 2005a) was developed to guide child therapists in making this difficult judgment call. Following the developmentally sequenced model of Beverly James in trauma treatment (1989, 1994), it is important to take children as far as they can go at any one point in time, knowing full well that they will have further work to do at some later point when their resources allow.

Session Twenty-seven: Direct Work on the Trauma

Therapist: Max, you have said that you don't think your mother or your grandfather ever got over the death of your grandmother. Why do you think that?

Max: Both my mom and my grandfather have been sad a long time. They are not usually happy people. Mom almost never laughs, and she is so serious and worried all the time.

Therapist: Your grandmother died when you were only four. Do you have any memories of her?

Max: Not many. I have seen a few pictures of her holding me as a baby, and I remember on a summer night she would sometimes hold me in a rocking chair when I was about three or four and sing to me when I couldn't sleep.

Therapist: Do you remember any of the songs she used to sing to you as she rocked you on the porch?

Max: Just lullaby and good night.

Therapist: Did your grandparents live with you at the time?

Max: No, Mom and I lived with them. Mom was working but she didn't make much money and she told me she couldn't afford to pay rent, so we lived with my grandparents.

Therapist: You told me earlier that you were close to your great-grandfather. How old were you when he died?

Max: I was in third grade, about eight, I guess. He used to take me fishing and then one day he was gone. He had a heart attack and died alone in his house. Grandpa found him the next day. We couldn't believe it.

Therapist: I bet; you have had a lot of loss for such a young kid. That must have been a shock and very sad for you. You never knew your dad?

Max: I wouldn't know him if he walked right into this room.

Therapist: What have you been told about the story of the romance between your mom and dad?

Max: Not much, she only knew him for a short time, a few weeks, or months, but not very long. When she got pregnant he was gonzo, and she hasn't heard from him since. Not one phone call, letter, or anything.

Therapist: How do you think your life would have been different if you had grown up with a dad?

Max: I don't know, how would I know [becoming irritated]? He was never around, I never had him, so I never missed him.

Therapist: That makes me very sad. You never had it so you never missed it, but I am sure you were aware that your friends' fathers would show up at baseball games and take them fishing. Did you ever feel sad that your father was never a part of your life?

Max: More angry than sad. If he walked in here right now I would punch him in the face.

Therapist: I wonder if the anger keeps you from feeling the sadness. Maybe you feel there has been enough sadness in your home, and you are going to be mad as hell so you don't have to feel your sadness. I am not saying that you don't have the right to be angry. I probably would be pretty angry too if I were in your place. All I am saying is that I don't believe that is all you are feeling. Usually, kids don't just feel one thing but a whole range of feelings, including mixed and even opposite feelings. Sometimes kids hate and love the same person at the same time.

Note to Clinicians

In this therapeutic exchange, Max engages in the all too common denial of the significance of father-absence among males in our culture (Hardy, 2003). The typical macho stance taken by boys is "I didn't need him, he was never around, who cares?"

Underneath the bravado, however, is the hurt boy who does care, or at least once cared. The grief is not acknowledged, nor does it receive much support or facilitation from the other adults in the child's life, who may have dismissed the father a long time ago as irresponsible and unworthy of the boy's love. Neither he nor his family recognizes the buried grief of a boy who grew up without a father. When therapists pursue this sensitive area they are usually greeted with anger and denial that the father ever meant anything to the child, and the family supports this view. If the therapist persists, however, and explores how the boy felt when fathers showed up at their friends' ball games and other school functions, they begin to express in small steps the buried grief, rage, and sense of desertion/abandonment that has left them with a deep longing and unmet hunger for connection with a dad they may have never known.

The therapist in the above exchange is attempting to normalize the range and mix of emotions that is typical of grief. Bonime (1988) explains that feelings are like chords in music, not single notes. Children will not tell about, or even be aware of, the feeling mix unless the therapist takes an active role—normalizing, universalizing, educating, modeling, encouraging, and sometimes gently pushing. Our feeling life is where we truly live, it gives color and richness to our life, and it is the wellspring of deep sadness and sorrow—but also of joy and zest for life. If a child or adult is cut off from their feeling life, they are robbed of the very sources of reward, pleasure, and satisfaction that make life worth living. In order to have full access to the range of feelings that humans are capable of, however, children must also be able to embrace the deep and often profound sorrow that victims of multiple losses suffer, along with rage that accompanies these wounds. Children will often avoid going there due to the fear of being engulfed in pain that will be unbearable.

The goals of emotionally focused work with profound loss, and often trauma, is multifold and consists of efforts to:

- Integrate split-off and detached emotions that deprive the child of major portions of their affective life due to blocking, numbing, splitting, and dissociation
- Reduce the sense of isolation in the child who has struggled inwardly and alone with these powerful affects, which are threatening to break through
- Reduce and ultimately eliminate the unpredictable triggering of these powerful suppressed, often repressed emotions, when reminders of loss and/or trauma brings them forcibly and intrusively into awareness

- In the case of traumatic memories, to promote neural integration of these memories to reduce triggering, flashbacks, and intrusive memories
- Share the untold experiences and memories so they can be witnessed by another (Alice Miller [1997] has suggested that if we have been traumatized we have a great need to have our pain witnessed by someone)
- Promote healing by the active declaration of trust

To expound on the last goal, Bonime (1989) argues that it's not abreaction or catharsis that is primarily the healing ingredient but rather the active declaration of trust. When someone is able to take the risk that they can share their deepest hurt, trust that the other will understand and accompany them through their deep sorrow and rage, this more than any other factor provides for healing. For those who have been betrayed, whose trust has been shattered repeatedly, this is a risk beyond belief, but in Bonime's view it represents a major breakthrough in resolution of trauma.

It needs to be stated that some traumatic experiences do not have a resolution. Some events are so horrifying to children or even adults that going back to confront them would be overwhelming and unhelpful. In those cases, the efforts should be directed at increasing mastery and focusing on the things that are important enough to the child that it will take them forward in life, since there is no turning back to the past.

Max: The only thing I feel is that I would like to get even with the bastard someday.

Therapist: What is your fantasy about that? Do you have in mind a scenario of taking revenge against your father?

Max: Yeah, I would show up at his door when I am twenty-two, and when he opens the door, I would say, "I am your son, Max, you lousy bastard." Then I would punch him in the face as hard as I could!

Therapist: You would like to hurt him as badly as he has hurt you!

Max: I hate him. He never cared about me. He means nothing.

Therapist: Your own dad never took an interest in your life, in you, never took the time to seek you out or get to know you. I think that has hurt you very badly. I think there is both a lot of sadness and anger in you about the fact that he could never make the time and effort to get to know you. If he had done so, he would have discovered that he had a son more than worthy of his love, time, and attention.

Max (pauses for a long time and begins to tear up): Do you think if my dad had ever come back that he would have been proud of me?

Therapist: You know my answer to that question. What is your answer?

Max: I really don't know the answer [Max begins to sob]. I wish the hell I knew.

Therapist: The answer is within you. You don't have to keep searching, you have all the data you need to know about whether you are a boy worthy of the love of a dad. In my opinion, there is no such thing as a "bad baby." Parents who are capable of love offer love to babies. Babies are cherished and loved almost irrationally by their parents unless the parent is unable to love, to give, to commit to the well-being of the child. If a parent because of problems within him or herself is unable to love, it does not make the baby unlovable. You ask your question in the form of pride: would your dad be proud of you? But I think the real hurt is that he was unable to love a loveable kid. If he had been capable of love, yes, he would have taken great pride in his son, but something more basic has been missing—you missed out on the love that every boy hungers for from his dad.

Max: I guess there really isn't a "bad baby." How bad could a baby be?

Therapist: You are exactly right. How bad could a baby be?

Therapist: How did your grandmother die?

Max: I don't know. Mom would never talk about it. Neither does grandpa.

Therapist: Do you remember anything from the time when your grandmother died?

Max: I remember Mom picking me up from nursery school and she was crying and everyone was hugging her and she couldn't stop crying.

Therapist: Do you remember anything else?

Max: I remember Mom taking me to the mother of a friend, and she said that I was going to stay with my friend for a few days, and then I would be going to visit my Aunt Maud.

Therapist: When you returned home, did your mom or grandpa talk with you about what happened?

Max: I remember they said that Grandma was in heaven now and then they both started to cry. I didn't ask any questions because they were already sad enough.

Therapist: Had your grandmother been sick for a long time?

Max: I don't remember that.

Therapist: When you got older did you ask your mom or grandpa any questions about what happened to grandma?

Max: There were times when I really wanted to but I could tell that just mentioning grandma made them so sad, I just couldn't do it.

Therapist: Max, do you have your own ideas about what happened to your grandma?

Max: I am pretty sure she killed herself.

Therapist: Why do you think so?

Max: What else could make it so hard for this long to be able to talk about it? Besides, I remembered not too long ago something an older kid once said to me after my grandmother died. I didn't know what he meant at the time and then I forgot about it. But I remembered it one day when Mom was crying and the sadness in the house was too much for me. He said, "I hear your grandmother killed herself." Then as I remembered what he said and realized that this sadness has been in the house ever since, I realized what happened.

Therapist: Does your mom or grandpa know that you have figured it out?

Max: No, I don't think they have any idea.

Note to Clinicians

Max was correct. When we met with his mother and grandfather they were shocked that Max knew how his grandmother had died. They looked at each other and then at Max with a stunned expression and asked him, "How did you know?" Max simply said, "I figured it out." Family secrets can be very destructive and rob children of the ability to test reality. Secrets abandon children to their fantasies that are often worse than the realities that the family, in a misguided way, seeks to protect them from. The goal in the family sessions was to open up the communication within the family not only between Max and his mother and grandfather but between the mother and her father, who both had suffered enormously from tremendous guilt and self-recriminations, as well as blame of the other, for the tragic death of Max's grandmother.

All these years Max had had no one to talk to about his unattended sorrow (Levine, 2005), because the overwhelming and unresolved grief of his mother and grandfather made the subject taboo and kept it shrouded in devastating secrecy. The secrecy turned out to have deep roots in trauma related not only to Max's grandmother's tragic suicide but also to another experience in the mother's early life, one that she had never been able to talk about with her father or anyone else. When she was five years old a janitor had molested her in the parochial school where she attended kindergarten. She had told her mother and they had called the police. When the police arrived at the home, they found the man in his car dead from a self-inflicted gunshot to his head. Although her parents never talked to her directly about this shocking development, she had overheard the police telling her parents when they came back to the house to let the family know what had happened. She was shocked, stunned, and thereafter would always feel that she had been responsible for this man killing himself. She lived in fear that the man's family might hurt her in a desire to get revenge, since the man had told her she better not ever tell anyone.

During a portion of the family sessions we met all together, and at other times the mother and grandfather met with me; it was during these sessions that the mother and grandfather were able to talk for the first time about the devastating experience of the grandmother's suicide. Family sessions were also conducted in various dyads—mother and grandfather, mother and Max, and grandfather and Max—with the goal of opening up the communication within the family and addressing the invisible wounds of all members of the family. When this goal was achieved, Max's symptoms cleared, and he resumed his developmental progression after having been blocked for many years as a result of carrying such a heavy emotional burden. His burden replicated the huge emotional load and surrounding secrecy that had been carried all of those years by his mother and grandfather. When their load was finally lightened, the child in Max was awakened, and he no longer looked or acted like the kid who carried the weight of the world on his shoulder.

Jeremy: The Story of Courageous Triumph over Terror and Violence

INTRODUCTION

*J*eremy is constantly in trouble. He has spent a record amount of time in the principal's office during his fourth-grade year. Only ten years old, Jeremy loses his temper frequently on the playground, in gym class, during lunch, and he especially causes trouble during transitions between class periods, when going down the hall to gym or art.

A reputation that he has earned with great gusto and enthusiasm is that of the class bully. Jeremy teases and torments other kids, especially vulnerable ones, like Lucy, who has a reading problem and wears thick glasses. He pushes kids down on the playground with no provocation and laughs heartily when they are hurt. Jeremy picks his moments, attacking his classmates when he thinks no one is watching. His teacher complains that he talks back to her, trips other kids when they walk past him, and even swears at the principal on occasion.

The aggression that Jeremy acts out at school mirrors his home life, which is marked with scary and unpredictable violence. His dad, Gene, a big man who drinks heavily, is quite a bully also. He demeans and insults his wife in front of the kids. Jeremy has two younger brothers, Johnny (six years old) and Donny (eight years). Both are extremely active boys, and the three together were known in their home community as the "terror trio." Their overwhelmed mother, Ruth, did her best to control them, but taking them into the local grocery store often caused major-league mayhem. Ruth would be mortified as the two younger boys would pull items off the shelf as fast as she could put them back. In the meantime, Jeremy would be off with the grocery cart crashing into people; when the adults in the store would chastise him, he would swear at them. The store managers dreaded the next appearance of "the terror trio" but had considerable sympathy for their mother, because the three boys showed no more respect toward their mother than to adult authorities.

When Gene came home drunk, as he often did, it was a scary scene. He would sometimes start arguments with their mother by yelling, "Where is my g——d d——n dinner?" Then he might throw something or turn the table over or hit Ruth repeatedly. At times Jeremy would come to his mom's defense, and he would get belted too. When I first learned of these incidents, I reported it to Child Protective Services (CPS), only to find out that this family had a long history with CPS and that on two occasions the children had been removed temporarily from the home to foster families, with directives to the father to go to rehab and join AA to address his drinking problem. He had also been ordered to attend an anger-management program that was offered by a nonprofit agency for court-mandated treatment of violent offenders. In each of these prior incidents Gene had complied to the minimal degree required to get the kids returned and no more.

CPS had no objections to Ruth's parenting, although they viewed her as more or less helpless in the face of Gene's violence and drinking and as overwhelmed attempting to manage the three extremely active and impulsive boys. Ruth was depressed but caring and was doing the best she could for the boys under extraordinarily difficult conditions. CPS could not understand why she continued to stay with her abusive husband, but in fact she was frightened to leave, because she did not feel that she would be able to survive economically raising the three boys without Gene.

Gene was enraged with me for making the report to CPS and said he would not allow Jeremy to continue to see me. He had been unwilling from the beginning to meet with me and had strongly objected to my seeing his son from the start. The courts intervened through the boys' law guardian, however, and Ruth, to her credit, also took a firm stand that Jeremy should continue his work with me. Once again Gene was ordered to go to AA and attend another round of anger-management group sessions, and the whole family was ordered to participate in weekly family therapy sessions with another therapist.

JEREMY'S "FAWN IN GORILLA SUIT" STORY

"The fawn went crazy in the gorilla suit and scared the crap out of the other animals. She laughed so hard she pissed in her gorilla suit," Jeremy laughs. "She even scared the bears because they don't expect to see no d——n stupid gorilla around these parts. She said, "No stupid g——d d——n animals are ever going to scare me again. Not unless they want this mean b——h gorilla to kick the s——t out of 'em.

Therapist: Your story puts a lot of emphasis on how scared the little fawn was before she put on the gorilla suit.

Jeremy: She used to be scared s——t l——s!

Therapist: The little fawn must have been terrified enough never to want to be a fawn again.

Jeremy: She is no dumb f——k. She figured out a way to get back at 'em.

Therapist: Do you think she will ever scare the other animals enough times that she will feel that she got even?

Jeremy: No way she will never quit.

Therapist: What if the other animals are truly sorry for what they did to the little fawn. Would she be willing to give it up?

Jeremy: That would be just a g——d d——n lie. A big f——ing lie, a trick. They ain't sorry. They are a lying sack of s——t. You don't trust nobody!

Therapist: Sounds like the fawn believes she lives in a dangerous world and she better look out for herself.

Jeremy: That's the way it is.

Therapist: How would the fawn like it to be?

Jeremy: Ain't no use wishin', that's how it is.

Therapist: Its every animal for itself. You can't trust anyone.

Jeremy: Nope, that's it.

Therapist: How about when the fawn sees her family, her mother and father, does she take off the gorilla suit then?

Jeremy: No, they don't give a crap about her. F——k them!

Therapist: Was it always that way? Was there a time when the little fawn could trust her family?

Jeremy: For as long as she can remember, they don't care about her and she don't give a s——t about them.

Therapist: What signs would the fawn look for that would tell her that maybe things have changed? Maybe she could learn to trust her family again.

Jeremy: It ain't gonna happen.

Therapist: But how would she know if they did change, just in case?

Jeremy: She ain't looking for no signs. She don't care about 'em anymore.

Therapist: Does she feel this way about both of her parents?

Jeremy: The father is a no-good son of a b——h. Her mom tries but she can't get her s——t together. It ain't no use anymore.

Therapist: So she believes her mom tries even though her mom has problems, she believes her mom cares?

Jeremy: I don't know. I guess a little bit but she is no use because the mean old son of a b——h papa pushes her around.

Therapist: That must be awful for the mama and the little fawn.

Jeremy: Someone ought to shoot the bastard!

Therapist: Do you think somebody ever would shoot him?

Jeremy: Probably not, he is too mean to die, what's the use?

Therapist: What do you think is going to happen to the fawn's mama?

Jeremy: I think she ought to get as far away as possible from that mean bastard. One day he'll kill her. I know it.

Therapist: What do you know, Jeremy?

Jeremy: He has a mean, wicked temper that's scary as hell, one day she'll be dead.

Therapist: That must be an awful worry to the little fawn.

Jeremy: That's why the fawn sticks around otherwise she'd be long gone.

Therapist: By putting on the gorilla suit the fawn thinks she can protect the mama?

Jeremy: She keeps an eye on things.

Therapist: I guess the fawn cares about what happens to her mama?

Jeremy: She does, she worries a lot, a hell of a lot.

Note to Clinicians

In this dialogue stimulated by the stories of the "fawn in a gorilla suit" Jeremy expresses through the metaphor and symbolization of the story his shattered sense of trust, his disillusionment and rage at adults who have not provided the nurturance, secure base, and protection he has longed for. He shares his worldview, "It is every fawn [person] for herself and trust no one." The fawn, with which he so closely identifies, relishes her role as the aggressor and terrorizer, because she can't bear to be vulnerable and frightened again. It is clear that the fawn will find it extremely difficult to give up its aggressor role, not only because it is gratifying to be the powerful one instead of the helpless one but also because the fawn believes her very survival depends on never letting her guard down. "She never takes the gorilla suit off, she will never stop scaring the others."

The fawn lives by the credo of those who live in a daily violent world, "I'd rather die than be dissed," or "If I let my guard down, I will die." The fawn is enraged at the whole world but especially at her father, who she views as a "mean bastard" who brutalizes her and her mother. While initially holding firm to the position that the fawn hates her family and will never trust them and that they don't care about her, in the latter part of the dialogue a small but significant chink begins to appear in Jeremy's defensive armor. He admits that the little fawn's mother, although ineffectual, cares about the fawn; perhaps a bigger chink was the reluctant admission that the fawn cares about her. In fact, she cares enough to stay around "to keep an eye" on things, because of a wish to protect her mother. In addition, the fawn also worries a lot about the mother and is convinced that the violent father will one day kill her.

What a load this kid was carrying. No wonder he relished his aggressor role at school. To let any soft, scared, or vulnerable parts of self show equated in his mind to violent death. His biggest worry, however, was for his mother. He believed that if he could be "mean and aggressive enough" he could protect his mother from his father's unpredictable, drunken, and violent rages. The fawn "keeping an eye on things" was interesting in light of his disclosure to me that he could never go to sleep until both of his parents were asleep. Only then could he be sure that there was going to be no more trouble, at least for that night.

Jeremy described the typical physiological hyperarousal experienced by children traumatized by domestic violence when, as he lay in bed wide awake, his father would come home drunk, yelling in the next room at his mother: heart pounding in his chest, palms sweating, breaking out in a cold sweat, sometimes literally shaking and trembling in fear.

The frequency of these episodes didn't diminish as a result of the parent and family counseling, so I communicated to CPS that the children were being exposed to repeated witnessing of violence. The "final straw" came when Jeremy shoved a classmate into his locker at school and held the door shut while the panicked child screamed and pounded on the other side. That incident led to his disclosure of the unrelenting horror and terror that his home life had become. The mother and children were then hastily moved to a "safe home" for battered women and their children while the parents continued their joint counseling. In the meantime the mother gained enough strength in the battered women's shelter to pursue an order of protection against her husband and a court order to evict the father from the home with only supervised visits by the father allowed with the children when they were emotionally ready to have such contact. I provided the court with documentation of the psychological trauma that Jeremy was suffering including repeated nightmares, startle reactions, sleep disturbance, physiological hyperarousal, intrusive memories, and vivid reliving of violent incidents. I also documented the trauma re-enactment, entailing the incident at school.

Although Jeremy was not conscious of any such link at the time, I was worried from the description of the incident from school officials that this might be a re-enactment of a traumatic event that he had experienced himself. The school principal told me that when he arrived on the scene Jeremy had seemed oblivious to his presence and also to the screams and pounding of his classmate inside the locker. The principal told me it had been as if Jeremy's mind was somewhere else, as if he couldn't hear. It was impossible for the principal to make contact with him; the principal described a glazed, faraway look in his eyes: "It was very weird, almost eerie." I had a strong enough relationship with Jeremy at that point to feel that it would be safe and helpful to explore the underpinnings of this serious incident with him.

EXPLORATION OF A TRAUMA RE-ENACTMENT

Therapist: Jeremy, tell me what happened at school today.

Jeremy: I remember what happened at first, and then I just kind of blanked out, I guess.

Therapist: Tell me what you remember.

Jeremy: I was just fooling around. I thought it would be funny to put this kid Kenny in the locker. I was just going to put him in and close the door then let him out.

Therapist: What is the next thing you remember, Jeremy?

Jeremy: I remember Mr. Adams [a teacher] grabbing me and pulling me away from the locker and then Mr. Vander [principal] came along and also tried to pull me away. I fought like crazy.

Therapist: What were you thinking and feeling at that moment?

Jeremy: I didn't know what I was doing or what the f——k was going on. It took me a long time to realize that Kenny was still in the locker when they grabbed me.

Therapist: Do you remember Kenny screaming and pounding on the door from the inside?

Jeremy: I did at first, but then it was like my mind went blank.

Therapist: Jeremy, it sounds like Kenny was terrified, in a major-league panic when you forced him into the locker and closed the door on him. What happened in your mind when he panicked, screamed, and banged on the door?

Jeremy: What do you mean?

Therapist: I don't have anything specific in mind, Jeremy. I just wonder what happened in your mind that you weren't able to realize that Kenny was still in the locker and you could no longer hear his screams or pounding on the door. You said your mind went blank. Your mind was somewhere else. I am just wondering where your mind was. Was there something about Kenny's screaming, panic, and pounding on the door that took your mind far away to a different time, a different place? Suddenly, Jeremy turned white as a sheet. He started to talk, but his voice cracked, and he couldn't get the words out. In a soft, barely audible, quivering voice Jeremy said, "My dad locked me in a closet." He paused for more than a minute before he could continue. He was trembling. I told him to take his time. I asked him if he would like a drink of cold water or to take a little walk before he continued, but he said he was okay. For the first time since I had started working with Jeremy, ten months before, I saw a single tear roll down his cheek (a rare glimpse of the "fawn" that up to now had been well hidden inside "the gorilla suit"). I dared not call attention to it for fear it would cause a reflexive retreat back into his camouflage. He tried to resume, but his voice cracked again. Then another tear flowed down his check, and yet another down the other cheek. For a child accustomed to wearing a "gorilla suit" this was equivalent to a river of tears in another child.

I said, "Take your time Jeremy; we have all the time you need." When he was able to talk, he said, with frequent halts and a quivering voice, "Mom had taken Johnny and Donny [younger brothers] to visit our grandparents. I didn't wanna go; Mom tried hard to get me to go but I didn't want to. I made a bad mistake. I figured Mom would be back before the lousy bastard came home. But he came home from Mac's Tavern around 9 PM drunker than a skunk. He started screaming, 'Where the f——k is your mom?' When he realized Mom wasn't home he got crazy, real crazy. He started yelling, 'You little pr——k, I am going to teach you never to mess with me.'"

Jeremy explained that three nights before he had jumped into a fight to try to protect his mom. His father had been furious, pushed him across the room, and then stormed out of the house. Jeremy had been left lying on the floor on one end of the room and as he struggled to get up he had seen his mother on the other side of the room, her head buried in her hands, sobbing uncontrollably. Jeremy now recalled, "Seeing mom huddled in a corner crying so hard bothered me far more than my flying trip across the room even though my shoulder really hurt."

The story continued, with long pauses and intermittent tears. On the occasion three days later, Jeremy stated, "He grabbed me, put my arm behind my back and threw me into a tiny closet where mom kept the broom and mop. He held the door shut. It was a tiny closet, it was dark, it was hot, I thought I was going to suffocate, I thought I was going to die! I was screaming, yelling to let me out and I was pounding on the door. My Dad yelled, 'F——k you. You are going to rot in there, you little s——t.' I was scared, I was afraid I would suffocate. It was hot, I was sweating, I really thought I was going to die." Now, for the first time, Jeremy cried in a wholehearted way. The "fawn" had completely come out into the open. I said, "Jeremy I am glad you can let some of those tears out, what a scary, awful experience." I gently reached out and put my arm on his shoulder. He was able to cry with even more heart-felt intensity—a cry that was way overdue. I didn't need to make the link to what he had done to Kenny. I knew that it registered consciously when he turned white and a shocked look appeared in his face, and in the midst of his sobs he exclaimed brokenly, "I did to Kenny what that son of a b——h did to me. I can't believe it!"

Therapist: If you had known what was being triggered at the time, I am sure you would not have wanted to put Kenny through what you went through.

Jeremy: Hell no, no animal should be treated that way, let alone a human being.

Therapist: I am glad you were able to tell me the story, Jeremy. What happened at school today is a result of your reliving that experience as if it were happening at that very moment. You did to Kenny without realizing fully what you were doing, what had been done to you. [I canceled my remaining schedule that afternoon in order to give more time to Jeremy.]

Therapist: How long were you locked in the closet, yelling, pounding on the door, scared to death and thinking you were going to die?

Jeremy: I don't know, but it seemed like it when on forever. He let me out when Mom drove up the driveway. He yanked open the door, grabbed me by the neck, and said, "You little p——s ant, if you ever tell I'll kill you and anybody you tell. You read me, boy?"

At this point, Jeremy suddenly looked panicked as he realized the implications of what he had just said—that both he and I were going to die, as if it were an absolute certainty. I said, "Jeremy, your father is not going to hurt you anymore. You are safe now. We are going to take steps to make sure you, your mom, and your little brothers are protected. I am going to recommend that you will only see him under supervised conditions. I am going to recommend that your mom seek an order of protection so if your dad comes anywhere near you or your mom or little brothers, he will be arrested. If he makes any direct threats toward me, I will get an order of protection as well." Jeremy hesitated and then said, "He has said many times he is going to kill that 'f——king shrink.'"

Therapist: I appreciate your concern, Jeremy. But you don't have to protect me, you have carried a heavy load, and I am not going to let you add your worry about my safety as another burden that you carry on your back. It is up to me to take care of my safety. Your dad says a lot of things in anger and rage, especially when he is drunk. If he ever makes a direct threat to me I will take steps to protect myself, I will take responsibility for that. Now tell me what happened when your mom arrived home.

Jeremy: He let me go and I ran to my room. I jumped into bed and tried to go to sleep but I was afraid to. I thought if I fell asleep he might come into my room and kill me. I didn't sleep a wink all night.

Therapist: When did this happen, Jeremy?

Jeremy: At the end of last summer, the day before Labor Day. I waited until dad left the house. I told Mom I didn't feel well and went back to bed, and I slept and slept.

Therapist: Now it is June, so you have lived in constant fear for the past nine months?

Jeremy: I haven't slept much since. At night, I think this is the night he is going to kill Mom and me. When I do finally sleep, I have bad dreams. I wake up sweating, in the dream the mean, son of a b——h has his hands around my neck, trying to choke me. I try to scream but I can't make a sound and I can't breathe.

Therapist: You have lived as if you were part of a horror flick. How have you managed to get through this?

Jeremy: Many times I didn't think I was going to survive.

Therapist: But you did, you have a fighting spirit that I admire and respect Jeremy, and that's how you survived this nightmare.

Jeremy: I guess I am pretty darn tough.

Therapist: I am going to tell you something else that I hope you appreciate about yourself, Jeremy. You are tough as nails and as hardy as they come, but you also have a big heart. You have cared deeply and worried about your mom and little brothers, and you have put yourself in grave danger to try and protect them even though this is too big a job for any kid, no matter how tough that kid is. You even wanted to worry about me and protect me, but I won't allow that. You have a really big heart in addition to being very tough.

Jeremy: I guess I do.

Therapist: Damn straight you do! [Both of us laugh.] How about your mom and little brothers, do they live in constant fear?

Jeremy: They are scared of him especially when he yells, but Mom and I get the worst. I think Mom is scared he will kill us all.

Therapist: No one should have to live in this kind of terror. Jeremy, I think enough is enough. I think we need to ask your mom to come in. We need to make a plan, a plan for the safety of you, your mom, and your brothers. We will need to notify the child protective authorities again and probably the police, but we have to take some steps to change this dangerous situation.

Jeremy: I am afraid he will kill all of us when he finds out that I told.

Therapist: Of course you think that, because that's exactly what he threatened to do. Your father is sick in the head, Jeremy, from all the drinking and also because he is a very angry and bitter man. Probably his life has been very hard, and perhaps he was treated the way he treats you when he was a kid, I don't know. But what I know is that this can't go on. The adults have to get together as a team and take all of this into account to make sure that everyone is safe. Now I want you to just relax, choose a *Car and Driver* magazine [he loves cars], and make yourself comfortable in the waiting room while I talk this over with your mom.

Note to Clinicians

Clearly intervention into violence in a family requires a team approach. In this instance, the combined efforts of a Battered Women's Program and Safe House, and planning and collaboration with CPS, the police, the law guardian for the children, the courts, social service agencies, and the various clinicians involved with the family were required to ensure the safety of this family. The law guardian for the children obtained an order of protection for them against the father, and a nonprofit legal services agency obtained an order of protection for the mother against the father. The boys stayed with the grandmother while the mother, accompanied by the police and a CPS worker, went to the house to get some clothing and essentials before going that evening to the safe house for battered women and their children.

When the police served the orders of protection against the father, he became combative and had to be subdued by a group of police officers, who had anticipated trouble, especially since the father was once again drunk. He was arrested and put in jail for disorderly conduct, assault, and resisting arrest.

When the family members were informed that the father had been arrested, both Jeremy and his mom affirmed that it was the first time in months that they had been able to close their eyes in peace and not worry that they would be killed in the night by this exceptionally violent, deeply tormented man.

It is interesting to note that, as can be seen in the foregoing therapy dialogue with Jeremy, as therapy proceeded not only did he gradually reveal more of the vulnerable "fawn" within (expressing fear, sadness, caring, and worry about his mom, and, during the trauma narrative, a heartfelt cry) but less of the "gorilla." His language, with the notable exception of references to his dad, became less "street-wise," and he expressed genuine remorse for what he had done to Kenny ("not even animals should be treated that way, let alone a person," "I can't believe I did that"). From the shelter he called Kenny and apologized to both Kenny and his parents. He broke down and cried on the phone. He told Kenny's parents, "I have lots of problems but I am working on them, and I hope someday Kenny and I can be friends."

Jeremy made that call on his own, with no prompting from his mother. He was starting to truly believe that "he was not only tough, but that he also had a big heart." He was showing more of the fawn and even less of the gorilla.

POSTSCRIPT

Jeremy is eighteen at the time of this writing. He is finishing his senior year and living with his mom and his brothers. His parents were legally divorced six years ago. Because the father refused to comply with any of the court mandates, his rights to even supervised visits were curtailed, and neither Jeremy nor his brothers have expressed any desire to see him. Jeremy told me that he heard that his father remarried, lives in an adjoining county, and has two more children.

I still see Jeremy from time to time, when he has typical adolescent issues—girlfriend problems or worries about his future. He has not been viewed for a very long time as a school bully. He is planning to attend a four-year college in the fall. He is interested in becoming a therapist or a substance abuse counselor. He gave me permission to tell his story in detail in the hope that it will be useful to child and family therapists and others who work with kids traumatized by domestic violence.

Jeremy was pleased to be accepted at the same college as had another boy, who had been a good friend throughout high school. His friend had been picked on a lot during elementary school years but never once during high school. Jeremy had made sure of that. They have put in a request at the college to be roommates—Jeremy and his good friend, Kenny.

References

Achenbach, T. M. 2004. Cross-cultural perspectives on developmental psychopathology. In U. Gielen and J. Roopnarine, eds., *Childhood and adolescence: Cross-cultural perspectives and applications: Advances in applied developmental psychology,* 411–29. Westport, CT: Praeger/Greenwood.

Allan, J. 1988. *Inscapes of the child's world: Jungian counseling in schools and clinics.* Dallas, TX: Spring.

Andershed, H., M. Kerr, and H. Stattin. 2001. Bullying in school and violence on the streets: Are the same people involved? *Journal of Scandinavian Studies in Criminology and Crime Prevention* 2:31–49.

Appelbaum, S. A. 1966. Speaking with the second voice: Evocativeness. *Journal of the American Psychoanalytic Association* 14:462–77.

———. 2000. *Evocativeness: Moving and persuasive interventions in psychotherapy.* Northvale, NJ: Jason Aronson.

Arsenio, W. F., and E. A. Lemerise. 2001. Varieties of childhood bullying: Values, emotion processes, and social competence. *Social Development* 10:59–73.

Ashby, J. S., T. Kottman, and E. Schoen. 1998. Perfectionism and eating disorders reconsidered. *Journal of Mental Health Counseling* 20:261–71.

Aseltine, R. H., Jr., and J. Doucet. 2003. The impact of parental divorce on premarital pregnancy. *Adolescent and Family Health* 3:122–29.

Atkinson, L., and S. Goldberg. 2004. *Attachment issues in psychopathology and intervention.* Mahwah, NJ: Lawrence Erlbaum.

Barker, P. 1985. *Using metaphors in psychotherapy.* New York: Brunner/Mazel.

Benedict, H. E. 2003. Object-relations/thematic play therapy. In C. E. Schaefer, ed., *Foundations of play therapy.* New York: Wiley.

———. 2004. Using play themes in play assessment for understanding play therapy processes. Presentation at the Twenty-first Annual Association for Play Therapy International Conference. Denver, CO.

———. 2005. Attachment and trauma in young children: Play therapy theory and techniques. Presentation at the Twenty-second Annual Association for Play Therapy International Conference. Nashville, TN.

Benedict, H. E., and L. Hastings. 2002. Object-relations play therapy. In F. W. Kaslow and J. Magnavita, eds., *Comprehensive handbook of psychotherapy: Psychodynamic/object relations*, Vol. 1, 47–80. New York: Wiley.

Benedict, H. E., and L. B. Mongoven. 1997. Thematic play therapy: An approach to treatment of attachment disorders in young children. In H. G. Kaduson, D. and M. Cangelosi, eds., *The playing cure: Individualized play therapy for specific childhood problems*, 277–315. Lanham, MD: Rowman & Littlefield.

Benson, P. L. 1997. *All kids are our kids.* San Francisco: Jossey-Bass.

Berger, V., and D. R. Gehart-Brooks. 2000. "Feelings Jenga": Facilitating family communication through play. *Journal of Family Psychotherapy* 11:81–85.

Bettelheim, B. 1977. *The uses of enchantment.* New York: Vintage Books.

Boesky, D. 1976. Proverbs and psychoanalysis. *Psychoanalytic Quarterly* 45:539–64.

Bonime, W. 1962. *The clinical use of dreams.* New York: Basic Books.

———. 1982. Personal communication.

———. 1986. Personal communication

———. 1987. Personal communication

———. 1988. Personal communication.

———. 1989. *Collaborative psychoanalysis: Anxiety, depression, dreams, and personality change.* Rutherford, NJ: Fairleigh Dickinson University Press.

Boyd, J., and K. Ross. 1994. The courage tapes: A positive approach to life's challenges. *Journal of Systemic Therapies* 13:64–69.

Bronfenbrenner, U., and S. J. Ceci. 1994. Nature-nurture reconceptualized: A bio-ecological model. *Psychological Review* 101:568–86.

Brown, E. J., and R. F. Goodman. 2005. Childhood traumatic grief: An exploration of the construct in children bereaved on September 11. *Journal of Clinical Child and Adolescent Psychology* 34:248–59.

Bulik, C. M., F. Tozzi, C. Anderson, S. E. Mazzeo, S. Aggen, and F. Sullivan. 2003. The relation between eating disorders and components of perfectionism. *American Journal of Psychiatry* 160:366–68.

Burns, G. W. 2005. *101 healing stories for kids and teens: Using metaphors in therapy.* New York: Wiley.

Cairns, R. B. 1979. *Social development: The origins and plasticity of social interchanges.* San Francisco: Freeman.

Camp, W. D. 1990. *Camp's unfamiliar quotations from 2000 B.C. to the present.* Englewood Cliffs, NJ: Prentice Hall.

Cattanach, A. 1997. *Children's stories in play therapy.* London: Jessica Kingsley.

———, ed. 2002. *The story so far: Play therapy narratives.* London: Jessica Kingsley.

Chang, J. 1999. Collaborative therapies with young children and their families: Developmental, pragmatic, and procedural issues. *Journal of Systemic Therapies* 18:44–64.

Chorpita, B. F. 2002. Treatment manuals for the real world: Where do we build them? *Clinical Psychology: Science and Practice* 9:431–33.

Church, E. 1994. The role of autonomy in adolescent psychotherapy. *Psychotherapy: Theory, Research, Practice, and Training* 31:101–8.

Cohen, J. A. 2005. personal communication.

Cohen, J. A., and A. Mannarino. 2004. Treatment of childhood traumatic grief. *Journal of Clinical Child and Adolescent Psychology* 33:819–31.

Cohen, D. L., and T. A. Petrie. 2005. An examination of psychosocial correlates of disordered eating among undergraduate women. *Sex Roles* 52:29–42.

Commission on Adolescent Eating Disorders. 2005. Defining eating disorders. In D. L. Evans, E. B. Foa, R. E. Gur, H. Hendin, C. O'Brien, M. E. Seligman, and B. T. Walsh, eds., *Treating and preventing adolescent mental health disorders*, 258–81. New York: Oxford University Press.

Commission on Adolescent Substance and Alcohol Abuse. 2005. Prevention of substance abuse disorders. In D. L. Evans, E. B. Foa, R. E. Gur, H. Hendin, C. O'Brien, M. E. Seligman, and B. T. Walsh, eds., *Treating and preventing adolescent mental health disorders*, 412–26. New York: Oxford University Press.

Commission on Positive Youth Development. 2005. The positive perspective on youth development. In D. L. Evans, E. B. Foa, R. E. Gur, H. Hendin, C. O'Brien, M. E. Seligman, and B. T. Walsh, eds., *Treating and preventing adolescent mental health disorders*, 497–530. New York: Oxford University Press.

Cook, J. M., P. Schnurr, and E. B. Foa. 2004. Bridging the gap between posttraumatic stress disorder research and clinical practice: The example of exposure therapy. *Psychotherapy, Theory, Research, Practice, Training* 41:374–87.

Cooper, J. C. 1978. *An illustrated encyclopaedia of traditional symbols*. London: Thames and Hudson.

Cottino, A. 1995. "Wine is the blood of the Earth:" Popular drinking culture through proverbs. *Addiction Research* 2:251–57.

Crenshaw, D. A. 1990a. *Bereavement: Counseling the grieving throughout the life cycle*. New York: Continuum. Reprinted [1995] New York: Crossroads. Reprinted [2002] Eugene, OR: Wipf and Stock.

———. 1990b. An ego-supportive approach to children in residential treatment. *Perceptions* 26:5–7.

———. 2001. Party hats on monsters: Drawing strategies to enable children to master their fears. In H. Kaduson and C. E. Schaefer, eds., *101 more favorite play therapy techniques*, 124–27. Northvale, NJ: Jason Aronson.

———. 2004. *Engaging resistant children in therapy: Projective drawing and storytelling techniques*. Rhinebeck, NY: Rhinebeck Child and Family.

Crenshaw, D. A., and K. V. Hardy. 2005. Understanding and treating the aggression of traumatized youth in out-of-home care. In N. Boyd-Webb, ed., *Working with traumatized youths in child welfare*, 171–95. New York: Guilford.

Crenshaw, D. A., and J. B. Mordock. 2005a. *Handbook of play therapy with aggressive children*. Lanham, MD: Rowman & Littlefield.

———. 2005b. *Understanding and treating the aggression of children: Fawns in gorilla suits*. Lanham, MD: Rowman & Littlefield.

———. 2005c. Clinical tools to facilitate treatment of childhood traumatic grief. *Omega: Journal of Death and Dying* 51: 239–255.

Davis, N. 1985. *Therapeutic stories to heal abused children*. Oxon Hill, MD: Psychological.

———. 1996. *Once upon a time . . . Therapeutic stories that teach and heal*. Oxon Hill, MD: Psychological.

Dawson, G. 1994. Development of emotional expression and emotional regulation in infancy. Contributions of the frontal lobe. In G. Dawson and K. W. Fischer, eds., *Human behavior and the developing brain,* 346–79. New York: Guilford.

Douglas, J. D., and B. Peel. 1979. The development of metaphor and proverb translation in children grades 1 through 7. *Journal of Educational Research* 73:116–19.

Dundes, A. 2002. *Bloody Mary in the mirror: Essays in psychoanalytic folkloristics.* Jackson: University Press of Mississippi.

DuRant, R. H. 1995. Adolescent health research as we proceed into the twenty-first century. *Journal of Adolescent Health* 17:199–203.

DuRant, R. H., A. Getts, C. Cadenhead, S. J. Emans, and E. R. Woods. 1995. Exposure to violence and victimization and depression, hopelessness and purpose in life among adolescents living in and around public housing. *Journal of Developmental and Behavioral Pediatrics* 16:233–37.

Elliott, R., J. C. Watson, R. N. Goldman, and L. S. Greenberg. 2004. *Learning emotion-focused therapy: The process-experiential approach to change.* Washington, DC: American Psychological Association.

Eth, S., and R. S. Pynoos, eds. 1985. *Post-traumatic stress disorder in children.* Washington, DC: American Psychiatric.

Foa, E. B., T. M. Keane, and J. M. Friedman. 2000. *Effective treatments for PTSD: Practice guidelines from the International Society for Traumatic Stress Studies.* New York: Guilford.

Fortier, K. 2002. *Sled dogs of Denali National Park.* Anchorage: Alaska Natural History Association.

Fraiberg, S. E. 1959. *The magic years.* New York: Macmillan.

Frank, O. H., and Pressler, M. 1995. *The diary of Anne Frank.* New York: Doubleday.

Frankl, V. E. 1967. *Man's search for meaning: An introduction to Logotherapy.* 10th printing. New York: Washington Square.

Freeman, J., D. Epston, and D. Lobovits. 1997. *Playful approaches to serious problems.* New York: Norton.

Frost, R. O., R. G. Heimberg, C. S. Holt, J. L. Mattia, and A. Neubauer. 1993. A comparison of two measures of perfectionism. *Personality and Individual Differences* 14:119–26.

Furman, B., and T. Ahola. 1992. *Solution talk: Hosting therapeutic conversations.* New York: Norton.

Furth, G. M. 2002. *The secret world of drawings: A Jungian approach to healing through art.* Toronto: Inner City Books.

Fussner, A. 1986. *Family Training Seminar Series.* Astor Home for Children. Rhinebeck, NY.

———. 1986. *Family Training Seminar Series.* Astor Home for Children. Rhinebeck, NY.

———. 1998. *Family Training Seminar Series.* Astor Home for Children. Rhinebeck, NY.

———. 1999. *Family Training Seminar Series.* Astor Home for Children. Rhinebeck, NY.

———. 2001. *Family Training Seminar Series.* Astor Home for Children. Rhinebeck, NY.

Gabel, S. 1984. The Draw a Story Game: An aid in understanding and working with children. *Arts in Psychotherapy* 11:187–96.

Gandara, L. 2004. "They that sow the wind . . ." Proverbs and sayings in argumentation. *Discourse and Society* 15:345–59.

Garbarino, J. 1995. *Raising children in a socially toxic environment.* San Francisco: Jossey-Bass.

———. 1999. *Lost boys: Why our sons turn violent and how we can save them.* New York: Anchor Books.

Garbarino, J., and E. DeLara. 2002. *And words can hurt forever: How to protect adolescents from bulling, harassment, and emotional violence.* New York: Free Press.

Garbarino, J. (2006). *Words can hurt forever.* Daniel Kirk Memorial Lecture at Marist College, Poughkeepsie, NY. March 22, 2006.

Gardner, R. A. 1971. *Therapeutic communication with children: The mutual storytelling technique.* New York: Science House.

———. 1972. *Dr. Gardner's stories about the real world.* Englewood Cliffs, NJ: Prentice Hall.

———.1980. *Dorothy and the lizard of Oz.* Cresskill, NJ: Creative Therapeutics.

Ge, X., R. D. Conger, and G. H. Elder. 2001. The relationship between puberty and psychological distress in adolescent boys. *Journal of Research on Adolescence,* 11:49–70.

Gibbs, R. W., and D. Beitel. 1995. What proverb understanding reveals about how people think. *Psychological Bulletin* 118:133–54.

Gil, E. 1991. *The healing power of play.* New York: Guilford.

———. 1996. The healing power of play with abused children. Presentation at the Second Annual Play Therapy Conference, cosponsored by the Astor Home for Children and Dutchess Community College. Poughkeepsie, NY.

———. 2004. Play therapy with abused and traumatized children. Presentation at the Twenty-second Annual Association for Play Therapy International Conference. Denver, CO.

———. 2005. Family play therapy. Presentation at the Sixth Annual New York Association for Play Therapy Conference. Tarrytown, NY.

Gil, E., and A. A. Drewes, eds. 2005. *Cultural issues in play therapy.* New York: Guilford.

Gilligan, J. 1996. *Reflections on a national epidemic: Violence.* New York: Vintage Books.

Goldner, E. M., S. J. Cockell, and S. Srikameswaran. 2002. Perfectionism and eating disorders. In G. L. Flett and L. Hewitt, eds., *Perfectionism: Theory, research, and treatment,* 319–40. Washington, DC: American Psychological Association.

Gottlieb, G. 1998. Normally occurring environmental and behavioral influences on gene activity: From central dogma to probabilistic epigenesis. *Psychological Review* 105:792–802.

Graber, J. A., J. Brooks-Gunn, and A. B. Archibald. 2005. Links between girls' puberty and externalizing and internalizing behaviors: Moving from demonstrating effects to identifying pathways. In D. M. Stoff and E. J. Susman, eds., *Developmental psychobiology of aggression,* 87–116. New York: Cambridge University Press.

Graber, J. A., J. R. Seeley, J. Brooks-Gunn, and M. Lewinsohn. 2004. Pubertal timing and psychopathology: Are effects maintained in young adulthood? *Journal of the American Academy of Child and Adolescent Psychiatry* 43:718–26.

Granillo, T., G. Jones-Rodriquez, and S. C. Carvajal. 2005. Prevalence of eating disorders in Latina adolescents: Associations with substance use and other correlates. *Journal of Adolescent Health* 36:214–20.

Greenberg, L. S. 2002. *Emotion-focused therapy: Coaching clients to work through their feelings.* Washington, DC: American Psychological Association.

Greenberg, L. S., and R. Elliott. 1997. Varieties of empathic responding. In A. Bohart and L. Greenberg, eds., *Empathy reconsidered: New directions in psychotherapy,* 167–86. Washington, DC: American Psychological Association.

Greenberg, L. S., and S. C. Pavio. 1997. *Working with the emotions in psychotherapy.* New York: Guilford.

Greenberg, L. S., and J. D. Safran. 1987. *Emotion in psychotherapy: Affect, cognition, and the process of change.* New York: Guilford.

Greene, R. 1998. *The explosive child.* New York: HarperCollins.

Halifors, D. D., M. W. Waller, C. A. Ford, C. T. Halpern, H. Brodish, and B. Iritani. 2004. Adolescent depression and suicide risk: Association with sex and drug behavior. *American Journal of Preventive Medicine* 27:224–30.

Hanna, F. J., and W. Hunt. 1999. Techniques for psychotherapy with defiant, aggressive, adolescents. *Psychotherapy: Theory, Research, Practice, Training* 36:56–68.

Hanney, L. 2002. Healing traumatized children: Creating illustrated storybooks in family therapy. *Family Process* 41:37–65.

Hardy, K. V. 1998. Overcoming learned voicelessness. Presentation at the Psychotherapy Networker Symposium. Washington, DC.

———. 2003. Working with aggressive and violent youth. Presentation at the Psychotherapy Networker Symposium. Washington, DC.

———. 2004. Getting through to violent kids. Presentation at the Psychotherapy Networker Symposium. Washington, DC.

Hardy, K. V., and T. A. Laszloffy. 2005. *Teens who hurt: Clinical interventions to break the cycle of adolescent violence.* New York: Guilford.

Haynie, D. L., T. Nansel, A. D. Eitel, K. Crump, K. Saylor, K. Yu, and B. Simons-Morton. 2001. Bullies, victims, and bully/victims: Distinct groups of at-risk youth. *Journal of Early Adolescence* 21:29–49.

Havens, L. 1989. *A safe place.* Cambridge, MA: Harvard University Press.

Heffner, M., L. A. Greco, and G. H. Eifert. 2003. Pretend you are a turtle: Children's responses to metaphorical versus literal relaxation instructions. *Child and Family Behavior Therapy* 25:19–33.

Hewitt, L., and G. L. Flett. 1991. Dimensions of perfectionism in unipolar depression. *Journal of Abnormal Psychology* 100:89–101.

Hinde, R. A. 1987. *Individuals, relationships and culture: Links between ethnology and the social sciences.* New York: Cambridge University Press.

Hindman, J. 1999. *Just before dawn: From the shadows of tradition to new reflections in trauma assessment and treatment of sexual victimization.* Ontario, OR: Alexandria.

Holmberg, J. R., H. E. Benedict, and L. S. Hynan. 1998. Gender differences in children's play therapy themes: Comparisons of children with a history of attachment disturbance or exposure to violence. *International Journal of Play Therapy* 7:67–92.

Honeck, R. 1997. *A proverb in mind: The cognitive science of proverbial wit and wisdom*. Mahwah, NJ: Lawrence Erlbaum.

Horney, K. 1937. *The neurotic personality of our time*. New York: Norton.

Horvath, A. O., and R. Bedi. 2002. The alliance. In J. C. Norcross, ed., *Psychotherapy relationships that work: Therapist contributions and responsiveness to patients*, 37–69. New York: Oxford University Press.

Hoxter, S. 1983. Some feelings aroused in working with severely deprived children. In M. Boston and R. Szur, eds., *Psychotherapy with severely deprived children*. London: Routledge and Kegan Paul.

Hughes, D. 1998. *Building the bonds of attachment: Awakening love in deeply troubled children*. New York; Northvale, NJ: Jason Aronson.

Imber-Black, E. 2004. *The healing power of rituals*. Presentation at the Psychotherapy Networker Symposium. Washington, DC.

James, B. 1989. Treating traumatized children: New insights and creative interventions. Lexington, MA: Lexington Books.

———. 1993. Treating traumatized children in play therapy. Presentation at the First Annual Play Therapy Conference, cosponsored by the Astor Home for Children and Dutchess Community College. Poughkeepsie, NY.

———. 1994. *Handbook for treatment of attachment-trauma problems in children*. New York: Lexington Books.

Jessor, R. 1991. Risk behavior in adolescence: A psychosocial framework for understanding and action. *Journal of Adolescent Health* 12:597–605.

Jessor, R., and S. L. Jessor. 1977. *Problem behavior and psychological development: A longitudinal study of youth*. New York: Academic.

Johnson, D. R. 1987. The role of the creative art therapies in the diagnosis and treatment of psychological trauma. *Arts in Psychotherapy* 14:7–13.

Joiner, T. E., T. Heatherton, D. Rudd, and N. B. Schmidt. 1997. Perfectionism, perceived weight status, and bulimic symptoms: Two studies testing a diathesis-stress model. *Journal of Abnormal Psychology* 106:145–53.

Joiner, T. E., and N. B. Schmidt. 1995. Dimensions of perfectionism, life stress, and depressed and anxious symptoms: Prospective support for diathesis-stress but not specific vulnerability among male undergraduates. *Journal of Social and Clinical Psychology* 14:165–83.

Jordan, J. 2003. The courage to connect. Presentation at the Psychotherapy Networker Symposium, Washington, DC.

Jung, C. G. 1960. *Man and his symbols*. New York: Dell.

Kagan, J. 1998. *Three seductive ideas*. Cambridge, MA: Harvard University Press.

Kahn, C. 1983. Proverbs of love and marriage: A psychological perspective. *Psychoanalytic Review* 70:359–71.

Kaltiala-Heino, R. Riittakerttu, R. Matti, and A. Rimpela. 2000. Bullying at school: An indicator of adolescents at risk for mental disorders. *Journal of Adolescence* 23:661–74.

Kandel, E. 2005. *Psychiatry, Psychoanalysis, and the New Biology of Mind*. Washington, DC: American Psychiatry Association.

Kazdin, A. E. 2005a. Treatment outcomes, common factors, and continued neglect of mechanisms of change. *Clinical Psychology: Science and Practice* 12:184–88.

———. 2005b. Personal communication.

Kennedy-Moore, E., and J. C. Watson. 1999. *Expressing emotion: Myths, realities and therapeutic strategies.* New York: Guilford.

Kenney-Noziska, S. 2005a. From hurt to healing: Play therapy techniques for sexually abused children. Presentation at the Twenty-second Annual Association for Play Therapy International Conference. Nashville, TN.

———. 2005b. Personal communication.

Klorer, G. 2000. Expressive therapy with troubled children. Northvale, NJ: Jason Aronson.

Kozlowska, K., and L. Hanney. 2001. An art therapy group for children traumatized by parental violence and separation. *Clinical Child Psychology and Psychiatry* 6:49–78.

Lankton, C. H., and S. R. Lankton. 1989. *Tales of enchantment: Goal-oriented metaphors for adults and children in therapy.* New York: Bruner/Mazel.

Larner, G. 1995. Narrative child family therapy. *Family Process* 35:423–40.

Lawrence, M., K. Condon, and E. Nicholson. 2005. The playfulness of storytelling: The dance of archetypes and neurons. Presentation at the Twenty-second Annual Association for Play Therapy International Conference. Nashville, TN.

Leigland, L. A., L. E. Schulz, and J. S. Janowsky. 2004. Age related changes in memory. *Neurobiology of Aging* 25:1117–24.

Lerner, R. M. 2002. *Concepts and theories of human development.* Mahwah, NJ: Lawrence Erlbaum.

Levine, M. 2002. *A mind at a time.* New York: Simon and Schuster.

Levine, S. 2005. *Unattended sorrow: Reviving the heart.* New York: Rodale.

Liddle, H. A. 1995. Conceptual and clinical dimensions of multidimensional, multisystems engagement strategy in family-based adolescent treatment. *Psychotherapy: Theory, Research, Practice, Training* 32:39–58.

Loar, L. 2001. Eliciting cooperation from teenagers and their parents. *Journal of Systemic Therapies* 20:59–77.

Loring, D. W., and K. J. Meador. 2001. The evocative nature of emotional content for sensory and motor systems. *Neurology* 56:146–47.

Lundqvist, D., and A. Ohman. 2005. Emotion regulates attention: The relation between facial configurations, facial emotion, and visual attention. *Visual Cognition* 12:51–54.

MacDonald, F. F. 2005. Searching for the key: The power of story in the healing process. *Annals of the American Psychotherapy Association* 8:41–42.

Magnusson, D. 1999. Holistic interactionism: A perspective for research on personality development. In L. A. Pervin and O. John, eds., *Handbook of personality theory and research,* 219–47. New York: Guilford.

Magnusson, D., and H. Stattin. 1998. Person-context interaction theories. In W. Damon, and R. M. Lerner, eds., *Handbook of child psychology:* Vol. 1, *Theoretical models of human development,* 685–759. New York: Wiley.

Malchiodi, C. 1997. *Breaking the silence: Art therapy with children from violent homes.* 2nd rev. ed. New York: Brunner/Mazel.

———. 1998. *Understanding children's drawings.* New York: Guilford.

———, ed. 2003. *Handbook of art therapy.* New York: Guilford.

Markowitz, S., Chatterji, and R. Kaestner. 2003. Estimating the impact of alcohol policies on youth suicides. *Journal of Mental Health Policy and Economics* 6:37–46.

McAdoo, H., and L. A. McWright. 1994. The role of grandparents: The use of proverbs in value transmission. *Activities, Adaptation and Aging* 19:27–38.

McCreary, B. T., T. E. Joiner, N. B. Schmidt, and N. S. Ialongo. 2004. The structure and correlates of perfectionism in African American Children. *Journal of Clinical Child and Adolescent Psychology* 33:313–24.

McGee, B. J., L. Hewitt, S. B. Sherry, M. Parkin, and G. L. Flett. 2005. Perfectionistic self-presentation, body image, and eating disorder symptoms. *Body Image* 2:29–40.

Meyers, S. 2000. Empathic listening: Reports on the experience of being heard. *Journal of Humanistic Psychology* 40:148–73.

Miller, A. 1997. *The drama of the gifted child: The search for the true self.* Rev. ed. New York: Basic Books.

Mills, J. 2005. *Treating attachment pathology.* Lanham, MD: Jason Aronson/Rowman & Littlefield.

Mills, J. C. 1994. Ericksonian Play Therapy. Presented at the Sixth International Congress on Ericksonian Approaches to Hypnosis and Psychotherapy. Los Angeles.

———. 2001. Ericksonian Play Therapy: The Spirit of Healing with Children and Adolescents. In B. B. Geary and K. Zeig, eds., *The Handbook of Ericksonian Psychotherapy*, 506–11. Pheonix: The Milton H. Erikson Foundation Press.

Mills, J. C., and R. J. Crowley. 1986. *Therapeutic metaphors for children and the child within.* New York: Brunner/Mazel.

Mordock, J. B. 2004. Personal communication.

Moore, M. S. 1994a. Reflections of self: The use of drawings in evaluating and treating physically ill children. In A. Erskine and D. Judd, eds., *The imaginative body: Psychodynamic therapy in health care*, 113–44. London: Whurr.

———. 1994b. Common characteristics in the drawings of ritually abused children and adults. In V. Sinason, ed., *Treating survivors of satanic abuse*, 113–41. London: Routledge.

Nagel, L. 2004. Telling stories in therapy. Presentation at the Psychotherapy Networker Symposium. Washington, DC.

Newman, C. J. 1976. *Breaking the silence: Art therapy with children from violent homes.* New York: Brunner/Mazel.

Nippold, M. A., M. M. Allen, and D. I. Kirsch. 2001. Proverb comprehension as a function of reading proficiency in preadolescents. *Language, Speech, and Hearing Services in Schools* 32:90–100.

Nippold, M. A., S. A. Martin, and B. J. Erskine. 1988. Proverb comprehension in context: A developmental study with children and adolescents. *Journal of Speech and Hearing Research* 31:19–28.

Norris, C. J., E. E. Chen, D. C. Zhu, S. L. Small, and. J. T. Cacioppo. 2004. The interaction of social and emotional processes in the brain. *Journal of Cognitive Neuroscience* 16:1818–29.

Oaklander, V. 1988. *Windows to our children.* Highland, NY: Center for Gestalt Development.

O'Connor, K. 1995. Ecosystemic play therapy for victims of child abuse. Presentation at the Fairleigh Dickinson Play Therapy Institute. Teaneck, NJ.

O'Donohue, J. 2004a. *Anam Cara: A book of Celtic wisdom*. New York: Perennial.

———. 2004b. *Beauty: The invisible embrace*. New York: HarperCollins.

Oetzel, K. B., and D. G. Scherer. 2003. Therapeutic engagement with adolescents in psychotherapy, *Psychotherapy, Theory, Research, Training* 40:215–25.

O'Toole, D. 1995. Using story to help children coping with dying, death and bereavement issues: An annotated resource. In D. W. Adams and E. J. Deveau, eds., *Beyond the innocence of childhood*, Vol. 2, 335–46. Amityville, NY: Baywood.

Papp, P. 1983. *The process of change*. New York: Guilford.

Pardes, J. 2004. Mary Joyce's extraordinary adventure. In J. Shepherd, ed., *The Last Frontier: Incredible tales of survival, exploration and adventure from Alaska Magazine*, 303–8. Guilford, CT: Lyons.

Park, N. 2004. Character strengths and positive youth development. *The Annals of the American Academy of Political and Social Science* 591:25–39.

Pasamanick, J. 1983. Talk does cook rice: Proverb abstraction through social interaction. *International Journal of the Sociology of Language* 44:5–25.

Paul, N. L. 1967. The use of empathy in the resolution of grief. *Perspectives in Biology and Medicine* 11:153–68.

Pelcovitz, D. 1999. Child witnesses to domestic violence. Presentation sponsored by Four Winds Hospital, Astor Home for Children, and Ulster County Mental Health. Kingston, NY.

Perry, B. D. 1997. Incubated in terror: Neurodevelopmental factors in the "cycle of violence." In J. D. Osofsky, ed., *Children in a violent society*, 124–49. New York: Guilford.

Phares, V. 2003. *Understanding abnormal child psychology*. New York: Wiley.

Pompili, M., I. Mancinelli, P. Girardi, and R. Tatarelli. 2004. Making sense of alcohol policies on youth self-destructive behavior as part of suicide. *Journal of Mental Health Policy and Economics* 7:37.

Power, T. G., C. D. Stewart, S. O. Hughes, and C. Arbona. 2005. Predicting patterns of adolescent alcohol use: A longitudinal study. *Journal of Studies on Alcohol* 66:74–81.

Power, R., C. L. Taylor, and M. A. Nippold. 2001. Comprehending literally-true versus literally-false proverbs. *Child Language Teaching and Therapy* 17:1–18.

Preston-Dillon, D. 2005a. Fairy tales and narrative techniques in play therapy. Presentation at the Twenty-second Annual Association for Play Therapy International Conference. Nashville, TN.

———. 2005b. Personal communication.

Rodgers, K. B., and W. M. Fleming. 2003. Individual, family, and community factors related to alcohol use among Native American adolescents. *Adolescent and Family Health* 3:140–47.

Rubenstein, A. K. 1996. Interventions for a scattered generation: Treating adolescents in the nineties. *Psychotherapy: Theory, Research, Practice, Training* 33:353–60.

Rubin, L., and E. Gil. 2005. Countertransference play: Informing and enhancing therapist self-awareness through play. Presentation at the Twenty-second Annual Association for Play Therapy International Conference. Nashville, TN.

Rutherford, K. 1994. Humor in psychotherapy. *Individual Psychology: Journal of Adlerian Theory, Research, and Practice* 50:207–22.

Rutter, M. 1990. Psychosocial resilience and protective mechanisms. In J. Rolf, A. S. Masten, D. Cicchetti, K. H. Nuechterlein, and S. Weintraub, eds., *Risk and Protective factors in the development of psychopathology*, Vol. 3, 181–224. New York: Cambridge University.

Schavarian, J. 1992. *The revealing image.* London: Routledge.

Seligman, M. E. 2002. *Authentic happiness.* New York: Free Press.

Shelby, J. 2000. Developmentally sensitive play therapy. In H. Kaduson and C. Schaefer, eds., *Short-term play therapy,* 169–211. New York: Guilford.

———. 2004. Best 100 techniques: 10 years and 20 nations. Presentation at the Twenty-first Annual Association for Play Therapy International Conference. Denver, CO.

Siegel, D. 1999. *The developing mind.* New York: Guilford.

———. 2005. *Psychotherapy and the integration of consciousness.* Keynote address at the Psychotherapy Networker Symposium. Washington, DC.

Silver, R. 1966. *Silver Drawing Test of cognition and emotion.* Sarasota, FL: Ablin.

Silverstein, O. 1995. Inclusion/Exclusion. Presentation at the Ackerman Institute for the Family. New York, NY.

Smith, C., and D. Nylund.1997. *Narrative therapies with children and adolescents.* New York: Guilford.

Stacey, K., and C. Lopston. 1995. Children should be seen and not heard? Questioning the unquestioned. *Journal of Systemic Therapies* 14:16–31.

Sroufe, A. L., B. Egeland, E. A. Carlson, and W. A. Collins. 2005. *The development of the person: The Minnesota study of risk and adaptation from birth to adulthood.* New York: Guilford.

Steele, B. 1997. *Trauma response kit: Short term intervention model.* Grosse Pointe Woods, MI: Institute for Trauma and Loss in Children.

Steele, W. 1998. *Children of trauma: Tools to help the helper* [video]. Grosse Pointe Woods, MI: Institute for Trauma and Loss in Children.

Stern, D. N. 1985. *The interpersonal world of the infant.* New York: Basic Books.

———. 2004. The present moment in therapy. Keynote presentation at the Psychotherapy Networker Symposium. Washington, DC.

Steinberg, A. R., V. Phares, and J. K. Thompson. 2004. Gender differences in peer and parental influences: Body image disturbance, self-worth, and psychological functioning in preadolescent children. *Journal of Youth and Adolescence* 33:421–29.

Stoff, D. M., and E. J. Susman, eds. 2005. *Developmental psychobiology of aggression.* New York: Cambridge University Press.

Stronach-Buschel, B. 1990. Trauma, children, and art. *American Journal of Art Therapy* 29:48–52.

Susman, E. J., L. D. Dorn, and V. Schiefelbein. 2003. Puberty, sexuality, and health. In R. M. Lerner, M. A. Easterbrooks, and J. Mistry, eds., *The comprehensive handbook of psychology:* Vol. 6, *Developmental psychology,* 295–324. New York: Wiley.

Susman, E. J., and A. Rogol. 2004. Puberty and psychological development. In R. M. Lerner and L. Steinberg, eds., *Aggression, antisocial behavior and violence among girls: A developmental perspective,* 23–47. New York: Wiley.

Tangney, J., and R. L. Dearing. 2002. *Shame and guilt.* New York: Guilford.

Terr, L. 1990. *Too scared to cry: Psychic trauma in childhood.* New York: Harper and Row.

————. 2003. Play therapy with victims of trauma: What has been learned from 9/11 and Columbine? Presentation at the New York Association of Play Therapy Annual Conference. Melville, Long Island, NY.

Thoreau, H. D. 1970. *Walden and other writings.* Garden City, NY: Nelson Doubleday.

Tolkien, J. R. R. 1966. *The Tolkien reader.* New York: Ballantine Books.

Tracy, R. J., N. Greco, E. Felix, and D. F. Kilburg III. 2002–2003. Reframing and wisdom within proverbs. *Imagination, Cognition and Personality* 22:117–62.

Tylka, T. L., and M. S. Hill. 2004. Objectification theory as it relates to disordered eating among college women. *Sex Roles* 51:719–30.

Udwin, O. 1993. Annotation: Children's reaction to traumatic events. *Journal of Child Psychology, Psychiatry and Allied Disciplines* 34:115–27.

van den Bree, M. B., and W. B. Pickworth. 2005. Risk factors predicting changes in marijuana involvement in teenagers. *Archives of General Psychiatry* 62:311–19.

van der Kolk, B. 1999. *Neurobiology of trauma.* Presentation at the Sage/Parsons Fall Conference. Albany, NY.

————. 2003. The frontiers of trauma treatment. Presentation at the Psychotherapy Networker Symposium. Washington, DC.

Van Lancker, D. 1990. The neurology of proverbs. *Behavioral Neurology* 3:169–87.

Van Ornum, W., and J. B. Mordock. 1988. *Crisis counseling with children and adolescents.* New York: Continuum.

Waller, D. 1993. *Group interactive art therapy: Its use in training and treatment.* London: Routledge.

Webb, N. B. 2002. *Helping bereaved children: A handbook for practitioners.* New York: Guilford.

Werner, E. 1995. Resilience in development. *Current Directions in Psychological Science* 4:81–95.

Whaley, B. B. 1993. When "try, try again" turns to "you're beating a dead horse": The rhetorical characteristics of proverbs and their potential for influencing therapeutic change. *Metaphor and Symbolic Activity* 8:127–39.

White, M., and D. Epston. 1990. *Narrative means to therapeutic ends.* New York: Norton.

Wichstrom, L. 2001. The impact of pubertal timing on adolescents' alcohol use. *Journal of Research on Adolescence* 11:131–50.

Wieder, S., and S. I. Greenspan. 2005. Developmental pathways to mental health: The DIR-super™ model for comprehensive approaches to assessment and intervention. In K. M. Finello, ed., *The handbook of training and practice in infant and preschool mental health,* 377–401. San Francisco: Jossey-Bass.

Winnicott, D. W. 1971. *Playing and reality.* London: Tavistock/Routledge.

Wilder, T. 1927. *The bridge of San Luis Rey.* New York: Albert and Charles Boni. Reprinted [1955] New York: Harper and Row.

Index

About the Author

David A. Crenshaw, Ph.D., ABPP, RPT-S, is the founding director of Rhinebeck Child and Family Center, LLC, in Rhinebeck, New York. He is a Board-Certified Clinical Psychologist and a Registered Play Therapist-Supervisor, author of *Bereavement* (now in its third printing) and coauthor of *Understanding and Treating the Aggression of Children* and *A Handbook of Play Therapy with Aggressive Children*. He is co-founder and current president of the New York Association for Play Therapy.